# HOW

# TO SELL YOUR

# SCREENPLAY

The Real

Rules

of Film

and Television

# HOW

# TO SELL

new chapter press

*new york*

CARL SAUTTER

# YOUR

# SCREENPLAY

THE REAL

RULES

OF FILM

AND TELEVISION

Library of Congress Card Catalog Number: 90-91943

ISBN: 0-942257-24-3

*Jacket and interior design by Jacek Przybyszewski*
*Jacket photograph by Carl Fischer*
*Special section on formats by Courtney Flavin*

9    8    7    6    5    4    3    2

Manufactured in the United States of America

Dedicated to Paul Waigner
who once suggested I stop thinking of reasons I couldn't
be a screenwriter and concentrate instead on *being* one.

# ACKNOWLEDGMENTS

My deepest appreciation to all the writers, producers, and agents who have so generously offered their thoughts, suggestions, and support, both in my career and in the preparation of this book. If you think Academy Award thank-yous go on endlessly, try writing a second edition! I am particularly indebted to:

Betty Reardon, Susan Freedman, Bruce Cayard, Carolyn Hodges, Joyce Davis, and Barbara Rottman for their research assistance; William Blaylock, Frank Cardea, Phyllis Geller, Anne Gibbs, Darlene Hayes, Shelley Herman, Maddie Horne, David Lee, Robb Rothman, Lonin Smith, Ken Wheat, and Russ Woody for their critique;

Chuck Slocum and the Writers Guild of America for their cooperation;

Wendy Reid Crisp for the chance to write all this down;

Courtney Flavin for her special section on formats;

Steve L. Hayes for his insights and computer skills;

John LeMasters for making the second edition so much fun to work on;

Gayle Kusatsu for keeping me organized as best she could;

Deborah Zoe Dawson for that first chance;

Susan Baskin for that first encouragement;

Debra Frank for helping me to write better;

Glenn Gordon Caron for teaching me to take risks;

and special thanks to Emily Laskin and the American Film Institute, to Writers Connection, and to David Peterson and the Scriptwriters' Network, for their continuing support and, through their seminar programs, the opportunity to meet so many new writers.

# CONTENTS

# PREFACE

My God, a lot can happen in four years. That's how long it has been since the first edition of *How To Sell Your Screenplay: The Real Rules of Film and Television* hit the bookstores.

That edition advised prospective screenwriters to avoid screenwriting books that were more than ten years old — they were too outdated to be useful. New advice: make that five years . . . or even less.

In just the last four years, massive changes have occurred in the entertainment industry that have dramatically altered not only how new writers break into the business, but what kind of life they'll find once they get there.

Three years ago, for example, film companies such as Carolco, Weintraub, and Orion were riding the independent film crest of *Robocop*, *Rambo*, and *Teenage Mutant Ninja Turtles*. Now, all three companies have filed for bankruptcy. The "breakthrough" television season of *Twin Peaks*, *China Beach*, and *Thirtysomething*, gave way to the "season of the bland" in which those shows were cancelled and CBS pulled six of its seven new series off the air before Christmas. The big-budget blockbuster film summer of 1990 was a bust. The beleaguered television movie market suddenly became a bonanza, offering studios tremendous overseas sales potential. And the impossible happened: the studio film — that most American of all exports — went foreign as half of the major film studios came under non-U.S. ownership (and more revenue was earned from overseas rentals than from domestic rentals). Fox emerged as a legitimate fourth network; two of the networks pulled out of the once-lucrative Saturday morning cartoon business because of competition from cable and syndication; an animated film (*Beauty and the Beast*) had a real shot at Best Picture; and million-dollar-spec-script madness came and went. Like I said, a lot can happen in four years.

Many of those changes are good news for writers. The increase in foreign markets, for example, has spawned new opportunities for Americans to work overseas. The record number of television movies meant that companies such as HBO and Turner now eagerly read spec scripts from new writers. The growth of the animation, reality, and industrial markets fueled a boom in writing opportunities in which, for once, new writers compete on equal footing with established ones.

But the changes have also made a screenwriter's life tougher. A blizzard of lawsuits over stolen ideas makes it harder to get a script read. Cutbacks throughout the industry result in greater difficulty in getting an agent — representing untested writers is more of a gamble than ever. And many of the new markets aren't represented by agencies, so writers have to learn to make contacts and generate employment on their own.

Three issues are the driving forces behind these changes:

1. Cost: Our film and television product costs too much. Revenues from advertising and ticket sales have not kept pace with production costs.
2. Quantity: There is not enough product for all the new cable and foreign outlets. We can only watch so many reruns of *Murder, She Wrote.*
3. Quality: Today's product competes with everything an audience has seen before — it's harder to keep the viewer's attention and tougher than ever to have an original idea.

Both new and established writers can anticipate that these issues will become even more dominant in the future. The new Hollywood wants everything cheaper, faster, better. The result is alternative forms, such as reality-based programming (*Rescue 911, Unsolved Mysteries*); significant cutbacks in the development slates for both studio films and network pilots; reduction in the number and duration of development deals; cutbacks in staff positions; and the creation of new technologies such as computer animation, laser discs, and interactive television.

All of which make the opportunity to do a revised edition of *How to Sell Your Screenplay* a pleasure and a challenge. A pleasure because my own ups and downs the last four years provide plenty of new experiences to draw from: four television pilots, three feature films, an animated feature rewrite (*The Jetsons: The Movie*), two television movies, and a successful series for European television (*Lucky Luke*). On book and seminar travels, I've also had the chance to meet an extraordinary number of aspiring screenwriters who generously supplied their insights, anecdotes, hints, war stories, and feedback on what worked for them — and what didn't. I am grateful for their valuable contributions to this edition, and hope that with our combined experiences, this book will be a useful supplement to your expanding screenwriting knowledge — a resource for analyzing markets, improving the quality and commercial potential of your writing, guiding you through the maze of selling a script, and sharing tips on how to survive and enjoy this business.

Writing a revised edition is also a challenge. There are dozens of new markets that barely existed four years ago. Some offer promising options for writers, yet few people understand them. In the traditional markets, the rules are changing about pitching, outlining, and submitting scripts. The challenge, therefore, is to both update the reader on the realities of a screenwriter's life, and also give guidance about how these realities will change in the years to come. Above all, one rule is clearer than ever: this business is in transition and smart writers learn how to adapt quickly.

Despite the changes, one enduring frustration continues for new screenwriters: There is still no door marked "New Writers Enter Here" — no one, surefire way into this business. Instead, the changes are creating new *unmarked* doors — different ones for each writer. These days, a first break may come through industrial films (now under the jurisdiction of the Writer's Guild), animation, video games, or "how-to" videos. The door may not be the fantasy break of an assignment on *Murphy Brown* or selling the next *Dances With Wolves*, but it's a door nonetheless. A new way for writers to be paid to write. And that's good news.

Carl Sautter
*Hollywood*
*April 1992*

# CHAPTER ONE

# AN INTRODUCTION

I remember the night it happened — the night I lost control. An exceptionally mindless episode of *Three's Company* was playing on television.

"I can write that junk!" I screamed at the Sony. "Why is somebody else making all that money when it could be me?" I leaped to the typewriter; I had succumbed.

It's a scene that plays itself out every night in living rooms and movie theaters across America. Restless viewers, fed up with inane television shows and bad movies, decide they, too, can be screenwriters. But is it really so easy to write that badly?

Screenwriting certainly looked easy to me. I watched lots of television, had seen all the landmark films, had even scored in the ninety-eighth percentile of the S.A.T. verbal. God knows, I could come up with those same dumb ideas that surfaced on television week after week.

For days, I stayed up until the wee hours penning the definitive episode of *Three's Company*; silly beyond belief, suitably offensive, and rife with one-liners. The premise was vintage bad television: Chrissy was boarding pets without telling Jack; Janet thought Chrissy had become a prostitute; escaped hamsters frolicked around the apartment. It was easy. I wrote the entire script without even doing an outline and knocked off a first draft in a week. No matter that I had no clue about the format of the show or about building three jokes off one. My overriding concern was that my name would appear on television in time to make one hell of an impression at my upcoming high school reunion.

In the weeks that followed, I shared the script with my co-workers in city government on the pretense of asking for comments, but mostly to garner compliments. Yes, they thought the script was stupid, but then, the show was stupid, so the script was probably fine. The hamster jokes didn't get the guffaws I'd expected, but everyone said the premise was "cute." (See Glossary for "cute.") I was a bit distressed when one friend, who fancied herself a writer, questioned everything from holes in the plot to whether twenty hamsters running loose on a television stage was practical. She even suggested I read some books on screenwriting. I dismissed her attitude as professional jealousy. No matter; she thought the part where Jack ate the hamster food hidden in the Wheaties box was "cute."

I learned to talk some television: act breaks, story beats, foreshadowing, voice-over, physical comedy. After nearly failing four years of Spanish, I was suddenly bilingual. In a moment of particular headiness at a West Covina dinner party, I mentioned I was working on a script. It brought down the house.

I was somewhat embarrassed when I couldn't answer the dinner guests' questions with authority. "How long *is* a sitcom script?" I remembered hearing on *Entertainment Tonight* that a film is a page a minute. "Uh . . . thirty pages." (The real answer: forty-five pages. The format is different for a sitcom.)

"Can you get me into the audience for *M\*A\*S\*H?*" I'd seen *Wheel of Fortune* often enough to know. "Call the studio for tickets." (Only problem with that answer: there was no audience for *M\*A\*S\*H*; it was filmed, not taped before an audience.)

"Don't you think that my great-grandmother's journal about crossing the frontier from Indiana would be a fabulous television movie?" I let my astute literary instincts guide me on that one. "What a clever idea!" (Actually, it's one of the most over-pitched stories around.)

So what if my facts were a little off — I still savored the instant celebrity status. I knew I was a natural. I had a knack for the language, a talent to amuse at dinner parties, and a certain self-effacing humility that would serve me well on awards shows. All I needed now was to sell a script.

As an afterthought, I went to a bookstore. If I was this good with no knowledge, imagine how brilliant I would be if I knew how long a script was. I emerged with a library of books on film and television: books on formats, treatises on character development, anthologies of basic plot ideas. Maybe the whole business was more complicated than I realized, but surely a little reading would vault me right to major motion pictures.

I didn't understand most of the books. Why prepare a three-page background on a character when at best only a line or two of history will ever appear in the script? Why have a "big moment" ten minutes in? Why is "mango" funnier than "apple"? None of the books told me how to *sell* anything; I figured that part must take care of itself. Cream rises to the top, right? I skipped the other advice, read the sections on format, and speedily typed up my masterpiece. By now, I'd even found a contact on *Three's Company*. The lawyer of a friend of mine played tennis with one of the producers. I'd probably be asked to make the toast at my reunion.

Then, nothing. To this day, I don't know if anyone on the show ever saw that script. Perhaps the lawyer read it and decided not to risk losing a tennis partner. My meteoric rise as a screenwriter stalled abruptly.

After three months of waiting, I began to consider that I had underestimated screenwriting. For the first time in the whole process, I was right about something. My high school reunion came and went. I did not make my first sale for another five years.

In the fallow years, waiting to sell my first script, I dissected screenplays, took writing seminars, went to conferences, and watched television and films with a new perspective: how the hell do you sell something? I asked lots of questions of writers, producers, actors, and agents. I kept hearing that screenwriting is formula writing, but I never found anyone who could explain the formula. What I did find was formal and informal rules that came out in story meetings, at dinner parties, and on the racquetball court. By themselves, such rules probably won't help any writer to create the definitive American drama, but they will help writers find work and keep working.

This book is a compendium of those rules — observations, theories, and tidbits of advice gathered over the last twelve years from personal experience, working relationships, and friendships within the entertainment industry. The names of most of the writers quoted here won't be familiar except from their screen credits. They are the working writers of the industry — story editors of shows, "freelancers," writers on the way up the hierarchy. Many are only a few years removed from being outside the system which makes their hints and observations timely for writers trying to break in now. Those hints, ranging from how to make a script better to why new writers shouldn't give up, make up the real rules of film and television.

The rules contradict some cherished myths, most of them perpetuated by writers themselves.

**Myth #1: The ability to write for the screen is innate, a divine gift.** This is the elusive commodity called talent. True, some writers seem to start their careers with certain instincts that give them an advantage. For most of us, however, screenwriting is a learned skill that we've worked very hard to develop. The skills improve with each script.

**Myth #2: Screenwriting is the perfect career for illiterates.** Yes, film and television use a lot of slang, but the best writers know when they're breaking the rules of proper grammar. Slang is limited to the dialogue and used sparingly to define character. Much of the writing in scripts is stage direction, and that has to be written in clear, understandable English. The story editor who reads "Murphy and Frank ain't gittin' along today," ain't gonna read no further.

**Myth #3: The only way to get a break is to be related to a studio executive.** It helps if Uncle Harry owns a studio, but the truth is that few of us are related to anybody who's even been on a sound stage, let alone owns one. While Uncle Harry may get a writer in the door, no bloodline can keep a writer inside if he or she can't deliver.

**Myth #4: One script and I'm in.** One sale does not a career make. The Writers Guild of America (WGA) is filled with members and associate members who sold one project — and haven't sold anything since. Writers have to work just as hard on the tenth sale as they did on the first one.

**Myth #5: I'll sell my first script.** Sorry, it's not going to happen, even if you've worked on that script for ten years. In fact, if you've worked on any script that long, you've probably lost all perspective and it's brain-dead. The cold truth is, most first scripts read like first scripts. The only way to get better is to start on the next one.

The key to screenwriting isn't memorizing a specific formula: it's learning how to be a better writer than everybody else.

## HOW TO USE THIS BOOK

Begin this book by resisting the temptation to turn immediately to the section on television movies because you know Aunt Evie's life story will be the best movie ever. Instead, read about all the markets available to screenwriters. You may be surprised to discover that your skills and interests are better suited to daytime soaps or children's programming. Or not. But as any experienced gambler will tell you, playing the percentages means first looking at all the possibilities.

# THE MARKETS

There are three major markets for screenwriters: feature films, network primetime television, and alternative markets (everything else). Although certain writing skills apply to all three, the rules for each market are distinct and it is often difficult for a writer in one market to move to another.

Screenwriters soon realize "you are what you write." If a writer sells a situation comedy idea, he or she is a sitcom writer. A theatrical sale makes the writer a feature writer. A script for *Knot's Landing* creates a soap writer. Credits in one market are not necessarily transferable to the others. This is important to understand because a writer who hopes to work in a variety of markets has to learn to adjust his or her writing style to each.

**Feature films:** These are films that first receive theatrical release in movie theaters, then go to pay cable and cassettes, and finally to network television. About twenty percent of Writers Guild income is from features. The frustrations of feature writers are legion. Less than one in twenty scripts bought or commissioned is ever made into a movie; some observers believe the ratio is more like one in forty. Only a handful of the thousands of feature scripts read by studios each year are bought or optioned. Still, most feature film producers have readers who will look at new writers' scripts even if they don't buy many.

**Network primetime television:** This market refers to programs that air in the evening on the three major networks — ABC, CBS, NBC — and the rapidly rising fourth network, Fox Television. These include situation comedies, one-hour dramatic series, television movies, pilots for new series, and variety specials. Television represents the largest source of income for screenwriting: sixty percent of the income generated by members of the Writers Guild. This includes syndication, daytime soaps, and other screenwriting forms discussed here as "alternative markets." The disadvantages of network television are that competition is intense and, with the move to more staff writers, the market for freelance writers is diminishing. As a result, it's hard to even get a script read, let alone sell it. Ongoing series are considered most open to new writers; pilots are a lost cause without produced credits. Television movies at the network level are still generally closed to new writers, although there are new opportunities from such cable companies as USA Network, Lifetime, Turner, and Home Box Office.

**Alternative markets:** These include daytime soap operas, public television (PBS), children's programming, animation, first-run syndication, "reality programs," regional and local programs, game shows, news programs, magazine shows, industrials, commercials, foreign markets, and the increasingly important cable and home video markets. These are called alternatives by the Writers Guild only because the markets often are specialized and because they don't employ writers in the same numbers as networks or features. Many of these markets are not covered by the Writers Guild, and often agents do not represent these fields.

Alternative markets provide some of the best opportunities for new writers and are the places where much of the growth of the entertainment industry is projected. As a result, fields such as home video and pay cable were the central issues of strikes by writers, directors, and actors over the last several years.

The discussion of these markets throughout this book distinguishes between those that are under WGA jurisdiction and those that are not. The Writers Guild is critical in the life of any screenwriter (for more information on the WGA, see Appendix B, p. 269). Regardless of market, salaries are usually higher under WGA contract, and those contracts provide guarantees of minimum salaries, limits on the amount of rewriting a member may be asked to do, arbitration of disputes over writing credits, the handling of residual payments, and the registration of scripts. Writers Guild members may work only for the "signatory companies" and authorized agents.

Keep in mind that this book does not tell you everything you need to know. The Bibliography (see Appendix D, p. 283) recommends additional reading for topics not covered in depth. These include formats, the details of dramatic structure, history of the entertainment industry, politics of studios, and current trends. Read these books, subscribe to the recommended publications, and supplement what is written here with any information you can find. This is an industry where knowledge is power — or at least the *illusion* of knowledge is power.

To strengthen your basic writing skills, explore local screenwriting classes at colleges, adult extension programs, and seminars given by the American Film Institute, and private workshops. These classes help writers hone and polish specific skills for dialogue and storytelling and provide deadlines — one of the basic food groups of a writer's life.

But a word of caution: Many books and seminars promise a quick fix to your writing and selling problems — "Five Steps to Writing a Blockbuster," "The 19 Elements of a Perfect Script," "The Seven Facets of a Whole Character." Although all of these approaches may have useful elements, no 5-19-7 formula will suddenly make anyone the Great American Screenwriter. Learn what you can from each source of information and decide what works for you.

Many of the principles in this book are not new or earthshaking insights. A number of books and teachers preach the ideas that a script should have a "big moment" in the first ten minutes, or that the first and second act breaks should be major twists in the direction of a story, or that a "spec script" is the best way in the door. What I have tried to do is fill in the details, such as: It's good advice to tell writers to read scripts before they "spec" a show, but how do you get scripts in the first place? It's fine to tell writers to look at alternative markets, but how do you know what kind of writing samples you're supposed to have? For most of us, finding out the details is one of the most frustrating aspects of breaking in.

Finally, like all good subcultures, the entertainment industry has created a language of its own that is often bewildering. ''Going to the table,'' ''turnaround,'' ''beat,'' ''deal-breaker,'' and ''giving notes'' are part of the shorthand that has developed to facilitate (some would say obscure) communication in this fast-paced business. Throughout the book, words that are part of ''filmspeak'' appear in quotation marks, and are defined in the Glossary (p. 275).

CHAPTER TWO

# HOW TO MAKE YOUR OWN FIRST BREAK

For a new writer, selling that first script is the hardest step in building a career, although most writers will say that every step is hard. There's no question that one sale under the belt does wonders for self-confidence. You are not just another of the 200,000 people in Los Angeles peddling unsold material; suddenly, you are a contender.

The truth is, the hardest step in becoming a screenwriter is writing a script that's good. Most of those 200,000 would-be writers are peddling bad material. And the percentages for selling a bad script are much lower than the chances of selling a good one. Not that everyone who gets paid for writing is good. But they got lucky — and it's a lot easier to get lucky if you're good.

## HOW DO YOU GET GOOD?

**1. Research the market in which you're competing.** Where is there the least competition for your writing style? Learn to avoid mistakes such as the wrong length, wrong format, duplication of stories, or competing in a market where new writers are not welcome.
**2. Learn your strengths and weaknesses.** Find out the style of project that you write best. If you are an actor, you should have an advantage with dialogue — an instinct for the rhythms in which characters speak. If your background is journalism, you're no doubt

9

a good narrative writer; stage directions may come relatively easily.

**3. Write what you watch.** If you are addicted to sitcoms or soaps, those are the markets you should consider. If you're a movie fanatic, that's the market where you have the advantage. If you are a short story buff, look at the anthology shows.

**4. Write what you know.** Ask yourself which stories you can tell that no one else can. Don't pick a story because you think it's what they want, or because it's like the film you saw last week. Concentrate instead on stories only you can tell. For example, if you have teenage children, you should have a reservoir of irritating stories to bring to one of the network family shows.

**5. Don't mistake commercial for sloppy.** Never write down to the level of what you perceive film or television to be. There will be plenty of opportunities later in your career to be mediocre; for now, write the best you possibly can.

**6. Write a lot of projects.** Think of each script as a step in the learning process. Learn what you can, then move on to the next one. Becoming employable is a matter of taking basic strengths and skills, studying, and getting better with every script and rewrite. Particularly in the early stages, learn to rewrite what you write, then rewrite that.

One of the biggest mistakes a new writer can make is to finish the first project and wait for the offers to roll in. Russ Woody (*St. Elsewhere, Murphy Brown*) says: ''The day I finish a script, I force myself to start on the next one, even if it's only a matter of jotting down a few ideas or lines of dialogue. It helps me let go of what I've written.''

**7. Read a lot of scripts.** Scripts read differently than they play. A writer isn't just selling the finished project complete with dazzling performances and intricate camera angles. A writer is selling what is on the page. One of the best ways to write better is to understand what makes a script read well. Writers should read as many different scripts as they can — good, bad, indifferent. This is the specific value of writers' support groups — the critiques you give each other will help you understand the problems in your own work.

Duplicating scripts is technically illegal without written permission from the show, the writer, or the producer. Nonetheless, almost everyone Xeroxes and trades screenplays all the time. There are even script houses that sell copies of both film and television scripts — at up to $100 apiece for some movies. Given the copyright laws, it is best to be discreet about this practice. And it's far cheaper to start your own script library so you can trade it with other writers for scripts you'd like to read.

**8. Try to stay logical in an illogical business.** Deborah Dawson, producer (*Trapper John, M.D.*), describes show business as "show versus business." The various levels of the industry have different priorities and players. In one camp is the so-called creative talent (actors, writers, producers), and in the other, the money people (corporate vice-presidents, publicists, and accountants). These groups operate in parallel universes — working on the same projects with different goals. Directors want their projects to have artistic integrity; studio executives hope artistic integrity doesn't hurt box office. Writers want their words protected; producers want their budgets met.

And all the rumors about nuttiness and instability are probably true. The reasons, depending on whom you ask, range from "someone who goes into the entertainment business is irrational to begin with" to "only the off-center survive." Still, here is a certain order to it all if you keep in mind three factors that are unique to this industry.

• **The TV/film business constantly changes.** Smart writers get into the information flow, subscribe to industry publications, attend conferences and seminars, and meet people. They know which shows are on the way up, what movies are hot, where the new opportunities are. A writer does not have to know Steven Spielberg to learn this information. It's readily available through the dozens of daily and weekly entertainment industry publications, ranging from *The Hollywood Reporter*, *Daily* and *Weekly Variety*, to *TV Guide* and the entertainment section of your local newspaper, to specialized publications such as *Electronic Media*. It's also available from anyone who works in the industry, directly or indirectly. From location managers to assistants at film boards to advertising firms and caterers, everyone is part of a vast grapevine that churns out gossip, hot leads, trends, and rumors at a pace that no fax machine could rival. If a writer is not tied into that system in one way or another, it's much harder to compete effectively.

As fast as the industry changes, the marketplace changes even faster. For example, some years ago a *TV Guide* cover story lamented the demise of the half-hour situation comedy. A year later, *The Cosby Show* surged to the top of the ratings, a producer pitching anything other than situation comedies was in trouble. More recently, the TV movie market all but hit bottom; then a surge of buying by HBO, Lifetime, USA, and other cable services launched a new bonanza.

A 1991 headline was "The Hour Show is Dead." Yet hour shows, especially action-adventure, are strong overseas — so now the hour format is enjoying a revival. A smart screenwriter knows the flavor of the month, but always tries to write at least a year or more ahead of the market. What's hot now is probably not what will be hot two years from now.

• **Geography plays a key role.** The entertainment industry is centered in two cities — Los Angeles and, to a much lesser degree, New York. Although there are increasing opportunities in other regions of the country (see p. 235), the big guns (major studios, networks) are based on the coasts. This creates an industry that is insular: it has a certain in-group, out-group mentality. Agent Nancy Nigrosh of the Gersh Agency, takes this notion a step further. She describes the industry as xenophobic: "No one wants to hear about anyone they haven't heard of."

As a result, show business is an industry that promotes from within. The Peter Principle holds that employees are promoted to one level above their level of competence. Film and television have raised that principle to an art form. Despite failed series, unmade movies, or poorly written scripts, some established writers keep getting hired. In a town that is title happy, the lucky ones fail their way up to executive producers. The unlucky ones find themselves stuck outside the same door as new writers. Their only hope of getting back in is to prove they're good again. When you're hot, everyone wants to meet with you. When you're not, phone calls aren't returned.

The operative word is "contender" — at every film festival, story meeting, screenwriting group, and dinner party, attendees are evaluating each other to see who's a contender. Who's on the way up? Who's on the way out? Who's not even close yet? The reason is simple. The entire industry is small enough to work on recommendation. Writers recommend writers to agents and story editors, producers recommend art directors, actors recommend costumers. Recommendations are how everyone gets work. From production assistants to studio execs, Hollywood is one big referral system. Agents are in the center of it all, referring their clients to studios and producers and networks. The system has evolved to designate responsibility. If a writer or lighting designer or script supervisor doesn't cut it, the credibility of the person who referred them is on the line. Consequently, the referral process is never done lightly.

• **Finally, show business is an industry where a writer has to get lucky.** The right place, the right people, the right idea, the right timing. Some writers get lucky too soon and can't turn a break into a career. Others stumble into opportunities over and over, but because their writing isn't good enough, they can't take advantage of their luck. Still others with the skills won't put themselves into the business mainstream, and therefore never allow themselves the chance to get lucky. Perhaps in an ideal world, a writer would pen the definitive first script, give it to Uncle Harry (the one who runs a studio) and go on to film and television fame. Most of us, however, don't have an Uncle Harry and aren't going to win an Oscar on the first round. Therefore, we have to look at other options.

## GETTING LUCKY

• **It isn't enough to have good ideas.** Good ideas don't mean much if a writer can't prove he or she can write a full script. Spending time writing treatments and outlines or submitting ideas to anyone who will listen may be good practice, but it's a waste of ideas. Even if a producer buys one of those stories, he'll almost certainly hire someone else to write the script. Stephen Kandel (*McGyver*) says ''The only thing that will still catch attention is a written script.'' He's frustrated by writers who aren't willing to do the work. ''They come up with wild, funny ideas, but won't harness them into actual teleplays.''

• **First and foremost is a good writing sample.** A writer has to start writing. The writing tool of necessity is the spec script. This is a full script, written on speculation with no guarantee that it will sell or even be read. It is the tool by which every writer, regardless of the market, has managed to get an agent or a first break. The mechanics of a spec script vary depending on the genre: a spec feature to break into feature films; for television, spec episodes for existing shows; for the daytime soap operas, sample scenes.

• **Who is going to read it?** This is not as simple as it seems. Getting a script read by someone who can boost a career can be harder than writing the script in the first place. The most often heard clichè in Hollywood is "I'm working on a screenplay;" the second is "I'd love to read it." The truth is, nobody wants to read another script — unless it's good. Lots of people say they will read it, but few ever do. Some will skim a few pages and send it back. More often, they won't do anything. They won't read it, won't call, won't acknowledge the experience — except perhaps to joke about it five years later when they're trying to get a job from you. All of which means that at the same time a writer is contemplating what to write, he or she must also think about who's going to read it.

High on the list of goals for potential readers should be agents. (For a complete discussion, see page 185.) In most cases a writer needs an agent to even submit a script. Most shows and studios send unrepresented work back without opening the envelope. A legitimate reason for this practice is that it provides a measure of protection from lawsuits that claim ideas were stolen. This possibility has become even more of an issue since the highly publicized, successful lawsuit of Art Buchwald vs. Paramount, in which the columnist claimed the Eddie Murphy film *Coming to America* was his idea. Buchwald's victory has spawned dozens of other suits by writers claiming theft of material, some legitimate, many not. While the attendant publicity has probably discouraged producers and studios from obviously lifting a writer's ideas, the case has had the unfortunate side effect of making it harder than ever to get a script read without an agent or referral.

Equally important, however, submission by an agent attests that somebody (besides the writer) thinks the work is good. The need for an agent is a catch-22 for the new writer. It's hard to get a script read without an agent, and it's hard to get an agent without having sold something. Smart writers, new and established, learn to develop job opportunities on their own.

You don't have to have an Uncle Harry to do this. It isn't so much who you know as it is who knows you. If Harry has heard good things from someone he knows, that can be as important as any bloodline. Of if he knows you from a theater group, film festival, or even racquetball, the odds are improved that he'll actually read something you or your agent give him. (*Read*, not buy. Referrals get scripts read, but the quality of the script determines what happens from there.)

Some writers make the mistake of giving work that's not ready to be read to reliable contacts on the assumption "I don't have anything to lose." The truth is, they have a lot to lose. Most people are good for reading *one* script. If it's amateurish, or even mediocre, don't expect them to read another one. So unless Harry is especially smitten with your backhand, the script you give him had better be the one that proves you're a contender. Otherwise be patient and give Harry the one two years from now that's really good.

## DO I HAVE A CHANCE?

Enough bad news. If you didn't know before — now you do. Screenwriting is a tough field: competitive, difficult to break into, frustrating to make contacts and to find an agent. You have to be good, and you have to be lucky. And even the lucky ones complain most of the time about how miserable they are.

But each year, a lot of new writers make it. Vicki Patik, Emmy winner for the teleplay *Do You Remember Love?* was a secretary at Lorimar when she got her first chance to write. David Lee and Peter Casey, writer/producers of *Cheers* and *Wings* sold sandwiches on studio lots while they worked evenings on situation comedy scripts — the duo wrote nine spec scripts — before they finally sold one to *The Jeffersons.* Larry Hertzog (*Hardcastle & McCormick*) sent five spec *Hart to Hart*'s to that show over many months. He was finally hired with script number five.

For others, screenwriting has been a second career. Roger Director, producer of *Moonlighting*, was a magazine writer when he got the chance at *Hill Street Blues*. Gene Rodenberry (*Star Trek*), was a policeman. Terry Louise Fisher was a deputy district attorney who eventually went on staff at *Cagney and Lacey*. Subsequently, using her legal background, she co-created *L.A. Law.* And I threw away a sensible career in government (it's been observed that if a former urban planner can make it as a screenwriter, anything's possible).

The irony of all this is that everyone claims to be looking for new writers. The prevailing wisdom is that good scripts may not always get produced, but good writers always get noticed. Steven Bochco (*Hill Street Blues, L.A. Law, Doogie Howser, M.D.*) confirms that ''the gifted people will find their way.'' And an agent from Intertalent says, ''We are all out there hunting. If you're good, someone is going to find you.''

# CHAPTER THREE

# THE BASICS
# OF SCREENWRITING

There are some key principles that govern all of screenwriting, whether for feature films, television or the alternative markets. Primary among these is *the rule of dramatic structure*. Every story, every plot, every subplot has to have a beginning, a middle and an end. This is classic Aristotelian dramatic structure and it is still what makes a story a story. As simple as it seems, the lack of a complete story is one of the most common mistakes that new writers make.

## THE THREE-ACT STRUCTURE

The structure is most familiar from English Literature 1-A, where we learned there are three dramatic acts in a play:

1. **Act I. The Beginning.** Introduces the characters and the problem.
2. **Act II. The Middle.** Complicates the problem.
3. **Act III. The End.** Resolves the problem.

Act II is usually the longest act; Acts I and III are often equal in length. On television, dramatic acts are not necessarily related to the breaks for commercials.

The three-act format is followed in feature films on the very rough guideline of 30/60/30: a twenty-five to thirty-five page first act, a fifty-five to sixty-five page second act, and a twenty-five to thirty-five page third act. Movies take approximately a minute per page. The end of each act is a major twist or complication in the story. These complications are the key factor in generating momentum, literally creating the next act. Well done surprises and twists hold the viewer's interest by raising tension and expectations.

Act break twists are also called "reverses" because the direction of the story reverses itself. These reverses are not gimmicks, but rather believable turns in the plot that create momentum and propel the characters (and the audience) through the next section of the story. The best measure of a first act twist is "Does it carry the middle of the movie?"

The Oscar-winning script for *Witness* is a simple and classic example of the three-act structure in film. The end of the first act is a major twist — the surprise realization that the police department is involved in the murder. This surprise moves the entire second act of the script, including Harrison Ford's character hiding in the Amish community, his attempts to expose the department, and his developing relationship with Kelly McGillis. A story that was going in one direction in Act I (we expect Ford to solve the murder) surprises us by suddenly spinning off into a new set of complications.

The second act twist is Ford decking one of the non-Amish townspeople because "It's his way." This moves the story into the final act — the discovery by the police of where he is hiding, the chase sequence, the resolution between characters, and Ford's return to the city. The structure is simple and very effective, with strong twists and detailed exploration of the relationships between characters.

A good twist grows out of the characters and story points already established. For example, "Okay, I'll make her the killer" is a bad twist if it's only being done because you don't know what else to do as a surprise. It might be a good twist (although not very original) if it explains the character's erratic behavior or otherwise grows out of the information the audience already has.

The three-act structure is as close to the Ten Commandments as screenwriting has. And Syd Field is Moses. His book *Screenplay*, first published in 1979, is the entertainment industry version of the stone tablets.

Recently, it's become chic to propose alternative structures — one enterprising screenwriting instructor runs ads proclaiming "The three-act structure is dead!" Some teachers and writers espouse a five-act structure, or Joseph Campbell's "the hero's journey." I use four acts in plotting feature films; otherwise, I seem to run out of anything to do between pages 60 and 90. These are cosmetic changes: they're all variations on beginning, middle and end.

## COMMERCIAL ACTS

Even though television poses artificial interruptions in the form of commercials every fifteen minutes or so, dramatic structure still holds true. There are still three dramatic acts, but they have been adjusted to reflect the "commercial acts." In most half-hour comedies, for example, the first commercial act introduces the characters and the problem and the major complications of the problem usually happens just before the commercial break. Commercial Act II is devoted to exploring the complications and resolving the problem.

*The Golden Girls* is a show that follows this structure consistently. The first major complication in the story is before the first commercial break: on this show the dramatic first act and the commercial first act are the same. There is a second complication (end of dramatic Act II) about five minutes from the end of a typical episode. The last few minutes are the resolve or dramatic Act III. As an example, Dorothy's old friend comes for a visit and we find out she's a lesbian. At the Act I break (dramatic and commercial) she's fallen in love with Rose. The problem is complicated in Act II because Rose doesn't know, Blanche is upset someone picked Rose over her, and Rose and the friend stay in the same room. The Act II dramatic break is Rose's realization. In a short Act III the women come to terms with each other and that's the end of the final commercial act.

Recently, some producers with enough clout have adjusted the commercial breaks on their shows to reflect the dramatic breaks. Series such as *The Wonder Years*, *Murphy Brown*, and *The Simpsons* have two commercial breaks in each episode to coincide with the dramatic act breaks. This has the particular advantage of speeding up the storytelling in Act I to allow more time for a satisfactory resolution in Act III.

Hour shows have four commercial acts. Commercial Act I introduces the characters and the Act I break is the first complication of the problem. Again the commercial and dramatic acts coincide. Acts II and III further complicate the problem. In a story well-structured for television, the Act III break is the most dramatic complication of all, so it's also the end of dramatic Act II. In *Moonlighting*, this was the point Maddie and David would find out the killer is not who they think it is, or they realize they've been trying to solve the wrong crime. And then commercial Act IV is the resolve (dramatic Act III). For example, in *Shootout at the So-So Corral*, Blue Moon is hired to reunite a dying father with his long-lost son. The two twists are clear: first the son turns out to be a hit man, then the father turns out to be a hit man, too, and not the father at all. A nice surprise at the end of the episode is that the older man wasn't looking to kill the young man, but to talk him out of his career.

All of which means that in both film and television *the story has to fit the form*. A story with too many complications and twists runs out of time in a half-hour comedy. A story with only one major complication is too dull for an hour show. Other stories are simply not big enough or compelling enough to be a feature movie, but might make a dandy episode. And some of the cleverest ideas are better as sketches on a variety show because the notion is too limited to sustain even a thirty-minute story. The same is true of the segments of the so-called "reality shows" like *Unsolved Mysteries*, *Rescue 911*, or *Cops*. Whether re-enactments or footage of actual events, the material is structured in such as way as to tell a story — beginning, middle, end. Three acts.

Most classes in screenwriting story structure also preach that the first ten pages (roughly ten minutes) of a feature script are critically important. In episodic television, it's the first five pages. Audiences tend to make a decision about whether they like or don't like a movie or TV show within that span. Producers, agents, and others who read scripts do exactly the same. According to agent David Dworski, "Generally I can tell after five pages if I'm dealing with a professional or not, and if I'm not, I stop reading." Somewhere in the early pages a script should hook the reader. Some call it an inciting incident, others a grabber. I like the notion of a big event in the early pages — something that surprises, whether by comedy or dramatic impact or sheer excitement such as the opening of *Raiders of the Lost Ark*, the teaser of a dramatic moment on *Thirtysomething*, the child witnessing a murder in *Witness*. Producer David Lee of *Cheers* says it can be as simple as a great joke in a sitcom. He advises writers to watch how hard situation comedies look for a very funny line or moment in the first minute of an episode. All of these surprise and hook an audience — or a reader.

This emphasis on complications and surprises is important because a second key principle of any form of screenwriting is that *a script is not linear*. An interesting screenplay does not move from one obvious step to the next. Instead, a good script surprises us by skipping the steps we don't need to see and letting information come out where it is most interesting, not necessarily where it is the most logical. In discussing his success with the final rewrite of the last of the *Raiders* films, Jeffrey Boam said his secret was simple: ''I cut out the boring parts.''

This is a direct contradiction to the fundamentals of expository writing: The lead paragraph introduces the most important information; each paragraph starts with a topic sentence, etc. Not in a screenplay. If the most important information is in the first scene of a movie, the movie has no plot. If each scene begins with a lead sentence, there's no reason to see the rest of the scene. The emphasis in expository writing is on making a point clearly. The emphasis in screenwriting is on making the point in the most interesting way possible.

## ELIMINATE THE OBVIOUS

All of which leads to a third important basic of the screenwriting craft — *avoid anything that is ''OTN'' (on the nose)*. This pejorative acronym is used widely (and excessively) by story editors, producers and critics. OTN means that the writer has made an obvious choice. A plot twist may be OTN because it's exactly the twist the reader expected, which means that it wasn't a twist at all. A character may be OTN because he or she is a clichè: the prostitute with the heart of gold, an evil villain with a missing finger, the smart-aleck maid. Dialogue may be OTN when characters say exactly what they are feeling or what they have learned. When a character facing a gun says ''I've got to get out of here,'' that's OTN. When the crisis is resolved and the hero kisses the heroine and proclaims, ''I'm so happy,'' that's OTN. The audience should realize these feelings and lessons from the story they're seeing, not from what the characters say about themselves.

To avoid being OTN, the writer has to find subtle and surprising ways to advance the story and the characters. This is much easier if *the writer starts with a good idea*. As story editor on *Moonlighting*, one of my primary duties was to listen day in, day out to writers pitching stories. I was astonished that almost every writer pitched variations of exactly the same plots. The most popular: Maddie and David are trapped together in a mountain cabin, elevator shaft, duplicating room, haunted house, skiploader, deserted island, etc. The middle of the story was always the same — Maddie and David fight, band together to escape, fight some more, give up hope, and in the big final twist, they escape and feel closer to each other than ever before. Each writer pitched this isolation idea with fervor. But *Moonlighting*'s creator and executive producer, Glenn Gordon Caron pointed out over and over that there were no surprises in the story. We knew they would fight, then escape. Simply changing the location didn't make it an interesting story.

The process taught me a valuable lesson. Writers have to work hard to make sure their ideas are original. Most new writers are so anxious to write dialogue that they race through the story process and tell stories that are ordinary. They forget that the basic idea is a blueprint from which the whole script unfolds. If the story is obvious and uninspired, no amount of brilliant writing is going to overcome the lethargy of the plot.

Writers soon realize that the stronger the initial idea, the easier the script is to write. The writer does not have to go back to keep fixing the story. The black-and-white episode of *Moonlighting*, written by Debra Frank and me, called *The Dream Sequence Always Rings Twice,* is a case in point. The original idea was simple and clear: Maddie and David become preoccupied with an unsolved murder from the 1940s and in separate dreams imagine themselves the participants, reaching different conclusions about the identity of the murderer. With such a clear story base, we were able to emulate two different styles of 1940s movies, experiment with voice-overs, dabble in the conventions of film noir, and have fun. Debra Frank had previously pitched the idea to other series, but Glenn Gordon Caron recognized the possibilities of this simple premise. (One of my contributions was to set the episode in an abandoned theater.

The opening credits were exactly a scene I remembered from walking into the old Pasadena Playhouse years before.)

Similarly, executive story consultants Jeff Reno and Ron Osborne came up with the clever and simple idea to cast Maddie and David as characters in a Shakespearean play. They began writing an episode based on *King Lear,* but had a difficult time until they realized they had chosen the wrong play. By substituting *Taming of the Shrew,* they found a structure and characters that meshed perfectly with the characters in *Moonlighting.* With the story taken care of, the team created *Atomic Shakespeare,* an episode some critics called "the single most inventive hour on television." The lesson of these two scripts is that the stronger the story idea, the easier the script writing will be.

As these examples illustrate, *the best ideas are usually the simplest.* An engaging premise with lots of implied conflict and some inventive plot twists is the structure that characterizes the best scripts of both film and television. A clear conflict is critical to any script, since conflict is the very definition of drama.

> "Drama: a state, situation or series of events involving interesting or intense conflict of forces."
> — *(Webster's New Collegiate Dictionary)*

The central conflict of the story should be apparent in even the simplest explanation of the premise. As a result, much of the industry talks in *TV Guide* "log lines" — those one-sentence blurbs that describe each program. It's done for both feature films and television episodes and it is a good way to test an idea for a spec script. Describe a potential story in one sentence emphasizing the conflict and possible complications. If it provokes what I have come to call the "ooooh" response, it's probably a good idea. The "ooooh" indicates that the reader is intrigued, which means that it could be a story someone wants to buy. Yawns, confused looks, or "I just saw that movie" are not good signs.

The best guarantee for an "ooooh" response are stories that have substance. A story is a blend of two elements: the plot and the theme. The plot is what happens in your movie; the theme answers the age-old question, "Why do we care?" The theme is the emotion in what you write. So, for example, the plot of *Moonstruck* is very familiar — a woman falls in love with the brother of her fiancè. It could be a *Love Boat* episode, for heaven's sake. What makes *Moonstruck* a compelling story is Cher's character — a woman who has given up on love. Put the plot and the theme together, and now we've got some substance: a woman who has given up hope agrees to marry a man she doesn't love — until she meets his brother, a man who no matter how many times he's been hurt, will never give up on love. Now it's a movie.

Similarly, *Witness* was lifted above the run-of-the-mill mystery genre because it's about a man of violence trapped in a world of peace. Most often, the theme will be found in the personality of the main character. *Tootsie* shows an unemployed actor who treats women terribly, and then finds the only work he can get is *as* a woman. Theme plus plot equals story.

**SHOW, DON'T TELL**

Finally, *screenwriting is visual writing*. John Sayles (*Matewan, City of Hope*) describes screenwriting as "thinking in pictures." The writer has to paint visual images so that the reader literally sees each scene.

Writing visually isn't confined to stage directions. Dialogue should be visual, too, by being specific. "I'll really miss you" is bad screenplay dialogue, but in *Terms of Endearment*, the daughter bids her mother goodbye with "That's the first time I stopped hugging first." The line is loaded with insight and instantly evokes a vivid image.

Visual writing is critical even to the forms of television that rely heavily on dialogue, such as situation comedies. The less the characters talk about the plot, the better. The dialogue should be real, and the story should move through visuals as much as possible — reactions from the characters, physical action, anything the audience can see. Surprisingly, the rule even holds true for radio drama. We've never seen Lake Wobegon, but we all have an idea what it looks like.

## CRITICISM AND HOW TO TAKE IT

Probably the most underestimated skill required for any kind of writing is the ability to take criticism and suggestions about your work and give useful criticism to others about theirs. This is especially important in screenwriting, where the whole process is called "giving notes." It is inescapable: story editors, producers, other writers, actors, networks — everybody gives notes. Learning how to listen, what to listen for, whom to listen to, and what to say can benefit a writer more than any other screenwriting skill. Script consultant Linda Seger advises writers, "It's not the writing, it's the rewriting that counts."

It's important, therefore, to keep in mind that screenwriting is no place to be word proud. Every screenplay is rewritten, edited, polished, and rewritten again: scenes are restructured by directors; dialogue is changed by actors; whole sections of a script are eliminated in editing. Many scripts are given to other writers to be completely redone. If a writer can't take criticism or learn from this process, screenwriting will be a frustrating endeavor. The proof is in who has the power; it's never the writer. In television the combination of short deadlines, tight budgets, ongoing series with existing characters, overworked actors, and network meddling combine to give power to whoever can get a show on the air. That's the producer, and so television is known as a producer's medium. Actors and writers quickly learn this. Almost every successful TV writer is a writer-producer, and actors Angela Lansbury, Lindsay Wagner, Tom Selleck, and Bill Cosby have all gotten producer credit on their respective shows.

Feature films, on the other hand, are considered a director's medium. Because shooting schedules are longer, much of the decision making happens on the set. The look and style of a film are for the most part the director's responsibility. In most cases the film is a "go" (for filming) only after a director is attached. From that point on, he or she is actively involved in making decisions about rewrites, casting, and production. Writers are expendable by comparison; the pattern for feature scripts is to use a series of writers (some receive screen credit, some do not) for various stages of the rewriting of the screenplay.

If the most important goal for you is to have your words presented exactly as written, consider playwriting. The Tony award for best play, after all, is given to the writer and the producer. Plays are considered the true writers' medium. Unlike screenwriting, the playwright owns his product and leases it for production. The screenwriter sells his product and has no rights after that.

\*     \*     \*

And on that uplifting note, it's time to look in more detail at the markets screenwriters sell to. These are the important questions to ask as you read the following chapters:

• What types of film and television do you watch the most? Write for the forms you like. If you have disdain for a particular series or type of movie, it will probably show in your writing.

• How competitive is this market? Do you have any special advantage competing here? Do you know people who can offer inside advice or get your script read?

• Which market plays into your strengths as a writer? Which type of writing do you most enjoy? Which market takes the best advantage of your background or special training?

• Where do you have the most (and best) ideas? Remember, one idea does not an entertainment mogul make (unless you're Sylvester Stallone).

CHAPTER FOUR

# FEATURE FILMS

To the purist, feature films are the only true screenwriting art. Television is dismissed as commercial, exploitative, and formulaic, it is criticized for appealing to the lowest common denominator. To an extent, all that is true. Even the *Los Angeles Times* calls its entertainment section "Television and the Arts."

But feature films are as prone to commercialism, exploitation, and formula as the worst of television. Artistic depth is not the motivating force for *Rambo, Nightmare On Elm Street,* or the Care Bears doing anything. Film historians have been surprisingly kind, mostly chronicling only the genre's high points while forgetting that from the earliest days the makers of motion pictures wanted to make money as much as they wanted to make movies. We tend to overlook, for example, that for every *Birth of a Nation* there were scores of long-lost clunker silents, and that the supposed heyday of the motion picture in the '30s and '40s was also the heyday of the "B" and "C" movie.

Why are features considered nirvana by so many new writers? To begin with, there is a powerful history of great films. The best of these, from *Citizen Kane* to *Casablanca* to the more recent *Chinatown* and *2001*, made film the dominant art form of this century. The collective film consciousness is as much a part of our culture as any social trend. Film has become a powerful bond that has shaped our perspective and chronicled our history. This dominance has given rise to a certain mystique about film, and that mystique is the source of much disillusionment when writers discover how the making of films actually works.

Perhaps the most startling realization is how few films are produced. On an average, there are less than three hundred English language films (excluding "pornographic" films) released into U.S.

theaters each year, totalling perhaps six hundred hours. This is roughly the equivalent of *one day* of television product.

The combination of a limited marketplace and high prestige means features are an extremely competitive field. The allure is that features offer more freedom than television. A writer has the opportunity to create a world peopled with original characters, and to tell a story that can unfold at its own pace without commercial breaks. A film can deal with explicit material that faint-hearted television censors would never allow. And movies have the potential for big-budget stunts, exotic locales, and feature-calibre stars. But, in addition to the competition, there are some characteristics of motion pictures that make them a tough market.

**THE REALITIES**

**1. A lot of feature scripts are bought; few are filmed.** Making a movie is incredibly expensive. The average feature film budget these days hovers near $20 million, and the industry rule of thumb is to at least double that for promotion and distribution — which raises the average cost to $40 million. By comparison, the average budget for a television movie of roughly the same length is $2.5 million.

When measured against other costs, the script in a feature is comparatively cheap. So scripts are bought, and writers are paid to rewrite, polish, rewrite. and polish some more, even though as few as one in forty is ever produced. It is quite possible to have a successful screenwriting career in films without ever having a single movie produced. A case in point is Leslie Dixon, author of *Outrageous Fortune*. Over a six-year period, she was paid to write ten feature film scripts, each leading to the next assignment. *Outrageous Fortune* was the first film of her scripts ever made. Similarly, Jeffrey Fiskin was a highly regarded and employed writer for ten years before his first film, *D. B. Cooper*, was shot.

**2. A completed script that gets a go-ahead still takes about two years to appear on the screen.** That's when everything is going well. Movie producers have to wait for the right director and stars to be available; release of the movie has to be timed with the season when it has the best chance of competing for audience and theater space;

promotional campaigns have to be developed, revised, approved, and put into place; post-production and special effects have to be completed. And the process is taking longer and longer. One development executive admits it takes five to seven years on average for a film to travel through the development maze at his studio.

Even the filming and editing are slow. A good day of television filming is seven pages of the script; a great day on a feature film is two pages. It is not unusual for a movie to take five months to film, compared to seven days for the average hour-long television show or eighteen days for a television movie.

This leisurely pace extends to the script process as well. The Writers Guild allows three weeks to write a first draft for an hour television show, and that deadline is important to the show. A contract for a first draft in features is normally ten to twelve weeks and it is assumed that the writer will more often than not miss this deadline. Why the cavalier attitude?

**3. The first draft of a feature is just the beginning of a very long process.** A typical contract will provide for: a First Draft, a Second Draft, and then the option for a Set of Revisions, a Second Set of Revisions, and a Polish. This does not include the very controversial Producer's Rewrite which is a revised draft of the script based on the producer's notes before the script goes to the studio. This version does not count as one of the five drafts listed in the contract. Although the Writers Guild forbids these off-the-record rewrites, they are a widespread practice. Producers persuade the writers to do the gratis work with the carrot that it will increase the chance of a film being made. And this process only deals with the first writer.

**4. Many features have multiple writers,** some credited, most not. The second feature Debra Frank and I did (*My Stepmother is an Alien*) had been worked over by seven writers before we came on the scene and three more followed us. Eventually, there were twenty-two versions of the script, including an early one described by the story analyst Harrison Reiner of RKO Pictures as ''one of the ten best scripts'' he read all year.

Nonetheless, for seven years *Stepmother* was passed around by four studios, and each commissioned its own version of the script.

The Writers Guild arbitrated the on-screen credit for this epic by reading every draft and deciding who contributed most to the final product.

Studios do not set out deliberately to use so many writers on a film. The intent from the beginning is to find the writer who is right for a particular film. But the temptation is strong to bring in one more writer to polish the script. In a plea for unity at a Writers Guild meeting in the '80s, Hal Kanter (*You Can't Take It With You*) reminded the membership to be civil to each other since "every one of us will be rewritten by everybody else in this room."

After this long history, *Stepmother* was finally made and released. Why? The movie had a director.

**5. Directors are often the reason a movie gets made.** Once the director is hired, he or she is involved in the rewrites and revisions of the script and is the dominant force in story choices, casting, and pre-production. This is in marked contrast to television directors, whom producer Paul Waigner of *Beverly Hills 90210* likens to traffic directors. They inherit shows where the characters are already established, the scripts are done before they arrive, and the same crew stays with the show week after week. "Their job is to move the actors around, get the job done on time and under budget, and — if a director is particularly talented and clever — leave their signatures on a couple of scenes."

### THE PROCESS

The script development process in movies is also the opposite of television. Television stories are talked to death before the actual writing of the script begins — in meetings among the freelancers, story editors, and producers of the show. During my feature from hell experience at Warner Brothers with *Tough Cookies* (a film about meter maids), the first story meetings consisted of enthusiastic producers saying "brilliant, we love it, wonderful." Little did I know that this is what every film producer has said to every writer in every first meeting since the invention of film. Once the script is finished, the "brilliant" ideas of two months ago have suddenly become problems. In features writers tend to get notes after the script is done.

*Tough Cookies* went from a comedy to a hard-edged action film, from a vehicle for Barbra Streisand to one for Roseanne Arnold, from a female buddy film to one about a male cop who gets demoted to meter maid . . . you get the idea. After six drafts and two production companies, *Tough Cookies* languishes in turnaround oblivion somewhere on the shelves at Warner. Well it should. After two years of such severe changes, none of us, myself included, can remember exactly why we wanted to do this project in the first place.

Those first meetings were about how much the producers trusted the writer, not about the story. The pattern is common because most feature producers don't know what they want. First and foremost, they tend to be deal-makers. The priority isn't the movie they want to make as much of the movie they *can* make — the movie that will sell a studio, sell a director, sell a major star. Most producers are trained to recognize that script when they see it, but not before. More than in television, non-writers tend to be the note-givers for feature films. The freedom a writer has in the early stages of a feature is just a promissory note for the critique to come.

That's not all bad. At least the writer has a chance to do one version of the script without a lot of interference. It may not be the movie that is filmed, but there is an undeniable satisfaction in being paid to write a script that is entirely yours. And that script will probably get the writer his or her next job.

Much of this pattern has been blamed on the new ownership of the entertainment industry: the invasion of the multinational corporations, such as Sony (Columbia) and General Electric (NBC). Leaders of Hollywood's unions and guilds periodically vilify these "intruders." They lament the demise of the small-town atmosphere in which heads of studios *were* the heads and not middle management in sprawling organizations that manufacture luggage, light bulbs, and petroleum by-products.

The fickleness of the movie industry is the stuff of legends. It took Oliver Stone ten years to make *Platoon*, after he was turned down all over Hollywood, and it took John Huston twenty-five years to make *The Man Who Would Be King*. In such cases, projects that one studio may hate, another studio will come to love. Rejected scripts that are paid for go into turnaround. Other studios can buy them for the costs already invested. According to agent Nancy Nigrosh, those costs can be substantial. "Meeting time, Xeroxing, accounting costs, and even monthly interest are charged to turnaround scripts. In most cases, if another studio wants it, they'd better *really* want it." Some well-known scripts that spent time in turnaround and eventually moved to a new studio are *Stand By Me*, *Splash*, *The Big Chill*, and *Risky Business*. Some of the biggest hits have been developed at one studio and later produced by another, including the biggest money-maker of all time, *E.T.*

In 1989, the major Oscar contenders illustrated this point. The one common characteristic all six movies had was the long, frustrating battle to get them made. Oliver Stone reports that *Born on the Fourth of July* was in development for a decade before it was finally green-lighted. The script for *Dead Poet's Society* was turned down by every major studio; in some cases, twice. *Field of Dreams* similarly languished on the desks of various studios for years. *My Left Foot* and *Henry V* had trouble getting American distribution. Best Picture winner *Driving Miss Daisy* was only given go-ahead for production after budget cuts of 50% and a major infusion of British financing. The moral: don't get discouraged. Tenacity for good projects can still win out.

## PAY AND OPTIONS

Despite these problems, a feature writer has some distinct advantages over other screenwriters. Features generally pay more than the commensurate assignment in television; a TV movie, for example, pays roughly half of the rate of a comparable feature. And the credited writer gets a bonus if the movie is made. Often this bonus is larger than the original fees paid, and the writer may even get "points" in the film (a percentage of the profits). Still, agent Beth Uffner wryly observes, "Don't count on it." The money would have to come in so fast and in such volume that the studios wouldn't have time to hide it in their expenses.

Finally, the "option" can be a source of income to feature writers. Anything can be "optioned" — an idea, a true story, or a script. An option is a payment by a producer, director, actor, writer, or studio granting the right to sell that idea, story, or script to somebody else, usually a studio. Options always have a time frame, most often six months to a year. The payment the writer receives may be small (anything from nothing on up), but option money can mean a lot to a struggling screenwriter. Usually the deal is structured so that the writer receives a small initial payment ($500 to $3,000 is the typical range) for twelve months, a second small payment if the option is extended beyond the twelve months, a bonus if the idea sells, and yet another if the film is made. The Writers Guild has a schedule of option minimums, but few option agreements seem to be based on these, since producers consider them too expensive and restrictive.

## THE MARKETPLACE PLAYERS

It is difficult to explain the complicated system for deals, options, and players in feature films without oversimplifying, but here goes.

• **Major studios.** Called the "majors," they have long dominated the feature film market, although there is competition from the "independents." The majors are considered to be: Paramount, Universal, 20th Century-Fox, Columbia (now Sony), Warner Brothers, and Disney. A key element of the dominance of these studios is that they have their own distribution systems which place completed films into movie theaters. This distribution system is enormously important for a film because the competition for theater space is intense. Most majors also maintain strong divisions for foreign sales, pay cable, and home video. The finances of movies have changed with the growth of these new alternatives. A film that is not a big box office success can still be a financial success in ancillary markets.

Each of the players has development deals with established writers and producers, hears pitches from outside writers, commissions material, buys completed scripts, and acquires completed films from smaller suppliers.

• **Independents/mini-majors.** The leading independents are a force in both film and television, but their future is always speculative. The peak of the independents' ascendancy was probably 1987, when independently produced films collected forty percent of the Oscar nominations, including *Platoon* and *A Room with a View.* Usually, they do not have their own production facilities; they rent studio space and co-finance films. Some have their own distribution systems and are an important release outlet for smaller, non-studio films.

The independents have either strong affiliations with a particular major to minimize their financial risk or strong foreign financing. Glen Shipley of Management Company Entertainment says, "There's no such thing as an independent any more. You've got to have an affiliation to survive." That is the case for Imagine (*Parenthood*), Castle Rock (*When Harry Met Sally*), and Morgan Creek (*Young Guns, Dead Ringers*). Imagine is affiliated with Universal; Castle Rock with Columbia (Sony) Pictures; and Morgan Creek, primarily with 20th Century-Fox.

• **Independent producers.** Independent producers or partnerships maintain a small staff and develop deals with the majors and mini-majors. They find writers, oversee development of the scripts, and supervise productions. Sometimes their deals allow them to undertake these with the studio's money. It's a high stakes game, and aggressive producers often have twenty or more projects in process at one time at a variety of studios.

To do this, independent producers will attach themselves to a product and sell it to a studio on behalf of the writer. This makes independent producers, especially smaller ones on the way up, the single most important entrè for new writers into the feature film business. Since independent producers often cannot afford the salary scales of A-list screenwriters, they specialize in finding promising new writers and scripts.

The principals of these production companies may be producers such as Simpson and Bruckheimer (*Top Gun*), directors (Joel Silver's Silver Screen Productions), or actors (Bette Midler's All Girl Productions). Many independent producers have a particular fondness for projects that can be made as low budget features (under $6 million by most studio definitions, under $2.5 million by WGA definition) because there is less financial risk involved.

• **Independent filmmakers.** In the feature film business, the term "independent" is applied to many different entities: independent studios, independent producers and independent filmmakers. The word is more an indication of everyone's yearning to be independent rather than evidence that any of them actually are. The independents are large production companies trying to be studios; independent producers are successful producers trying to become successful independents. The only true independents are so-called independent filmmakers who exist on the fringes of the industry, and even they are not independent. They are dependent on grants, on donations from friends and family, and on either volunteer or cheap services.

Independent films are films made by an individual or by a group of friends who may do everything from raising the money to producing to directing to acting in the production. Independent film is the heart of the film industry in much of regional America — the strong-willed writer or director determined to see his or her work on the screen who risks life savings, cajoles friends, and struggles to nurture the project to its end, convinced that the final result will sell itself. Independent filmmakers are best known for documentaries and small movies with strong social or political themes. But by no means are these projects all documentaries or treatises; most are designed to be highly commercial. So why don't we hear more about them? Because the majority of small independent films are financial and/or artistic disasters: the romantic mystique of filmmaking runs head-on into the problems of production and distribution.

As usual, there are exceptions. Successes like *Hollywood Shuffle*, completed on credit card financing; *She's Gotta Have It*; or *Return of the Secaucus Seven*, can launch careers. But overnight stardom is not the norm.

Writers/directors Jim and Ken Wheat (*Ewoks: The Battle for Endor*) had a typically frustrating experience in producing their own feature script, *Lies*. Underfinancing jinxed their project. "We took the plunge even though we had only raised seventy percent of the budget," explains Ken, "figuring that we could at least get it in the can." Getting the completed film from the can to the screen proved to be the real battle. In order to obtain completion financing, the Wheats were forced to sell off all of the ancillary rights (home video, foreign distribution, etc.) at fire sale prices. Jim likens the arrangement to a pact with the devil since few distributors are disposed to spend money on theatrical release if they don't hold the ancillary rights as an insurance policy. Eventually *Lies* found a small-time distributor, and in spite of favorable reviews, was dumped into double bills and independent film oblivion. Not all the news was bad. The film was noticed by George Lucas and other mainstream types. It served as a writing and directing sample to get the Wheats steady work ever since — which is fortuitous since they are still paying off the bills from *Lies*.

If a writer/producer is adamant about doing his or her own film, one approach is to prepare a demo tape and market that tape to raise financing rather than completing the whole film. The Wheat's ten-minute demo cost $100,000 and got them into a number of studios. The producers of *Blood Simple* and *This Is Spinal Tap* used a similar strategy, showing a trailer of sample scenes for their as-yet unproduced films. *Fatal Attraction* started out as a short film. Writer/director James Dearden was eventually hired to write a feature script based on it.

Despite the risks and difficulties inherent to independent film, Geoffrey Gilmore of Sundance Institute says, ''A number of independent films are getting made by hook, by crook, by mom and dad, by Aunt Sally, by corporations and grants.'' But distribution has become tougher as a result of what's become known as the *sex, lies and videotape* phenomenon. The success of that independent effort raised expectations so that independent distribution companies now look for a couple of films that might make $10 million, rather than many films that might make only $2 million.

• **Producers.** Anybody can call himself or herself a producer, and nearly everyone in Los Angeles does. A real producer, one who might actually get a script made, has the three Cs: credits, contacts, cash: *credits* on previous movies as a producer, *contacts* with studios and independents to whom he or she can sell the project, and *cash* to pay for the rights to peddle the script. There is also a fourth C — a *contract*. Everything should be in writing.

The producer or executive producer credit in movies is sometimes given to a person who financially backed the film and is not necessarily a reflection of knowledge of the filmmaking process. The associate producer credit is often given to a boyfriend, wife, best friend or even a writer trying to gain some measure of control over the project. In recent years the Academy of Motion Picture Arts and Sciences has drastically changed the definition of producer under its membership rules to eliminate the proliferation of so-called producers flooding the Academy ranks.

• **Directors.** Since established directors have so much clout in determining which scripts are made, a director attached to a script may be the reason it gets a production order. (Conversely, a director who is not a known commodity is a liability. So writers should drop any illusions that they will write the script and hold out for their best friend to direct.) These days, even well-known directors can't always get the projects made that they want. Martha Coolidge (*Valley Girls*), waited for seven years to get *Ramblin' Rose* done.

• **Actors.** Actors with feature clout who are attached to a project can also be a catalyst for a script being bought or made. As a result, actors' names are bandied about constantly in discussions of any project. During the last few years I've been in meetings about half a dozen scripts "for" Bette Midler. The Divine One as a meter maid? Of course . . . *everybody's* name came up at some point for that one. The truth is Ms. Midler has never heard of *Tough Cookies* or any of the other projects; using the hook of a well-known actor is a way producers and studios get writers enthusiastic about a project — the chance to write for Bette Midler, Meryl Streep, Kevin Costner, Mel Gibson, Eddie Murphy.

## WHO WILL READ YOUR SCRIPT?

One of the surprising advantages of features is that it is easier to get a script read than it is in television.

Every studio and independent and many stars, directors, and producers have people employed to read new submissions: story analysts or readers, sometimes known as story editors (although most do not really edit as television story editors do). As with everything in Hollywood, there is a hierarchy for readers. At the top are the over one hundred-and-sixty members of the Story Analysts Union who serve as staff readers for the larger studios. The union is an affiliate of International Alliance of Theatrical Stage

Employees and has no formal relationship with the Writers Guild except for occasional denigrating remarks about analysts in the Writers Guild newsletter.

Next in line are non-union readers who are full-time staff. They are expected to read an average of ten to fifteen scripts and/or novels per week. Lowest in the hierarchy are freelance readers who are paid by the script at rates from $15 to $75 each.

The function of readers is the same in any company:

• **Read the material** (in its entirety, one hopes) and prepare a summary of the basic plot. This is known as coverage. Often there are two parts — the concept or short summary and the more detailed one- or two-page version. These summaries are done for submitted scripts, novels, and the galleys of novels soon to be published. If a script goes into turnaround, this coverage is the document passed back and forth between studios.

• **Dissect the material** and rate it according to elements such as basic idea, story development, characters, dialogue, and stage directions. If the story rates high, but dialogue low, the studio might decide to buy the story and hire a new writer for revisions. If dialogue and stage directions receive glowing notices, the studio may pass on the script but keep an eye open for the writer's next work.

• **Make a recommendation** — should the studio buy the project? A yes recommendation is not an automatic buy, but rather a signal that other story analysts at the company should review the script and offer their own coverage. If the opinions are consistently positive, higher executives in the studio will read the script. Competition is tough: one in fifty scripts reaches this level.

Readers are usually asked: Do you recommend this script? Do you recommend this writer? Recommending the writer has more long-term importance than recommending the script because it means that writer will be considered for other projects. Good writers are much more in demand than good ideas.

Most of the non-union or freelance readers are young and hope to parlay the opportunity into an executive job or a writing career. A number of prominent executives began as story analysts, including Paramount's David Kirkpatrick and Dave Madden. Ket Lamb, assistant to the writers of *Moonlighting*, freelanced as a script reader for a variety of small production companies at $50 per script. She estimates that this averages out to $10 an hour; she had to continue in a full-time job at the same time. The investment paid off. She became director of creative affairs for one of those companies, Agincourt Ventures.

Other story analysts have gone on to successful careers as writers and producers, including Marcy Carsey (Carsey/Warner Productions: *The Cosby Show*) and Edward Neumeier (*Robocop*). A good writing sample in the form of a script is sometimes one of the interview requirements to be a reader. The reasoning is that writing skills and the ability to analyze a story step-by-step (the skills necessary to be a writer) are also the criteria for a good reader.

The following is a reader's report that has had wide circulation among writers' groups as a sample of what upper echelon executives see in lieu of full scripts.

TYPE OF MATERIAL: Screenplay    TITLE: Good Morning, Vietnam
NUMBER OF PAGES: 120    AUTHOR:
NUMBER OF SCENES:
PUBLISHER/DATE: 5/14/86
SUBMITTED BY: Anonymous   CIRCA: 1965   LOCATION: Saigon; Crete
SUBMITTED TO:
ANALYST:    DRAMA CATEGORY: Comedic Drama
DATE:    ELEMENTS: Turnaround from Paramount
    Robin Williams to star

-------------------------------------------------------------------------

THE FILM: A ne'er-do-well goof-off with a spontaneous gift for comedy becomes a popular Army disc jockey in Vietnam and develops a sense of commitment as his awareness of the war increases.

-------------------------------------------------------------------------

THEME: Army airman ADRIAN CRONAUER is serving his reluctant stint on Crete, partying his heart out as he acts as the disc jockey on Armed Forces Radio. But GEN. TAYLOR has other plans for Cronauer's talents, and soon he finds himself on a plane headed for an unfamiliar place — Saigon, where the General thinks he'll do worlds of good for the morale of the soldiers. Cronauer is greeted by PVT. ED GARLICK, who acts as his guide to his new surroundings. He meets LT. COL. DICKERSON, who takes an immediate dislike to Cronauer who has an obvious disregard for all Army regulations. But Cronauer's new audience loves him, and support from the service men pour into the radio offices, allowing Cronauer to get away with just about anything on the air, as long as he checks his news stories for clearance before he goes on mike. Cronauer settles into life in Vietnam, hanging out with Garlick and fellow dj DREIWITZ, a guy with a booming top 40 voice on and off air. He also befriends a young Viet, TUAN, and is intrigued enough by Tuan's sister TRIN to volunteer to teach an English class at the cultural center, where he becomes a popular favorite with his odd bunch of foreign students. But Trin makes Cronauer aware of the major cultural differences which makes a relationship with him impossible, no matter how strong his friendship with Tuan is. One night, Cronauer is badly shaken by the aftermath of an explosion that rocks a bar he's just left, and he goes on the air with a story that hasn't been approved by the censors. He's pulled from the air, and HUAK, the company commander replaces him unsuccessfully. The demand for Cronauer's return is so overwhelming that Dickerson can't ignore it, and reinstates him, but Cronauer's spirit isn't quite the same until Garlick convinces him he really does the servicemen good. After an adventure in the underbrush with Garlick, from which they're rescued by Tuan, Cronauer is told by his superiors that his Viet friend is actually a Cong operative. Their friendship gives Dickerson the reason he's been waiting for to get rid of Cronauer for good, and arranges for his transfer and discharge. Cronauer confronts Tuan before he goes, and the two friends come to blows in a heated argument about the nature of the war. Cronauer bids goodbye to his adoring students in a last-minute crazy game of baseball, and makes his way towards his plane. Tuan comes out from the shadows to address his friend, telling him that he does indeed care for the American, but that it's unfortunate that the two are caught on opposing sides of a senseless war. They reconcile, and Cronauer boards the plane. As it taxis down the runway, Garlick's voice is heard over the air, imitating his friend Cronauer's opening show line — Good Morning, Vietnam.

RECOMMENDATION: MAYBE

|  | EXCELLENT | GOOD | FAIR | POOR |
|---|---|---|---|---|
| PREMISE |  | XX |  |  |
| CHARACTERIZATION |  | XX |  |  |
| DIALOGUE |  | XX |  |  |
| STORY LINE |  |  | XXX |  |

CHAPTER FIVE

# WHAT DO
# FEATURES
# LOOK FOR?

Television looks for the hook that will get viewers to tune in. Movie people look for "heat." What is it about a particular project that will excite a potential audience to see it? After all, moviegoers are demanding. They go to a lot of trouble to be there — leaving the house, driving to a theater, and paying six dollars or more a seat. They expect more from a movie than from a comparable product on television: audiences go to movies for an experience. Part of that experience is a roomful of strangers watching celluloid images together and reacting as a group — a gasp when the plot takes a sudden turn (as in *Fatal Attraction*), uncontrollable laughter (the "I'm a great tomato" scene in *Tootsie*), the spontaneous applause that breaks out after a particularly well-done chase sequence (the opening for *Raiders of the Lost Ark*), or the shared emotions at a touching moment (*Terms of Endearment*). This affects our opinion of a movie and is the basis for the most important selling tool of the feature business — word of mouth.

The industry rush for heat has spawned an on-going rage in the entertainment industry — the high concept film. As with most showbiz lingo, exactly what high concept means is not all that clear. I define it as "one leap of logic away from the ordinary." *Splash* is a prototype high concept film. At heart, the plot is ordinary enough — boy meets girl, boy loses girl, boy swims off into the Atlantic. The big difference, the leap of logic, is that the girl is a mermaid. The leap in *E.T.* is that the wicked alien intruder we've come to expect in space movies is a mensch; in *Victor, Victoria*, it's a "woman playing a man playing a woman." Most of these ideas probably sounded weird to audiences when they first heard about them. That's high concept. But ad campaigns, trailers and word of mouth got the audience into the theaters and once there, they suspended that first step of logic and loved these films. Interestingly, the rule is that the audience will accept one leap in logic (Darryl Hannah is a mermaid), but not two (Darryl Hannah is a mermaid and Tom Hanks is an android). It's exactly the same rule as in television: silly plus silly is stupid. Silly plus *real* is interesting.

In an effort to indicate the heat, story ideas for features are sold or talked about by comparison to other movies that were big hits — a project may be a cross between *High Noon* and *Ghostbusters* or *Pretty Woman* meets *Beverly Hills Cop* or a youthful *Cocoon*. This makes complicated ideas easy for studio types to grasp and speaks to the underlying raison d'etre: big box office. A writer pitching stories for motion pictures is well advised to know which movies to cross-reference. This can also backfire and contribute to the rewriting chaos of features. When I began *Tough Cookies*, the comparison film was *Working Girl*. But then *Lethal Weapon II* was an enormous hit and midway through the process, the notes were to make it more action-adventure. Friends dubbed the new hybrid *Lethal Cookies*. Once it was turned in, the higher-ups at Warner were disappointed it wasn't more like *Police Academy*. Aaaaaghhhh!

Features are usually discussed as a particular genre, despite the fact that many films overlap genres. *Aliens* was both science fiction and horror, *Rain Man* was both comedy and a character study. As a way to analyze and compare various types of films, the following informal groupings are still used:

**Action adventure.** The hard-core action pictures: *Dirty Harry, Terminator 2, Rambo*, with plenty of chase scenes, bloodshed, explosions, and seemingly unconquerable villains. The best of the genre have interesting lead characters and chase sequences that aren't predictable. The worst have simple (often jingoistic) morals to the story, one-dimensional villains, and a loner good guy. The typical plot of this genre puts the hero into ever-more dangerous situations. The jeopardy builds from big problems to bigger problems to unbelievable life-threatening problems. Dialogue is usually secondary to strong visual images. The genre is promising for new writers. *Lethal Weapon* was a spec script for eventual million-dollar writer Shane Black. Think inventive chase sequences, big opening, and an even bigger finale.

**Character movies.** These are most often thought of as "quality" films. The emphasis is on a study of characters rather than big effects or intricate plots: *Terms of Endearment, Kiss of the Spider Woman,* any Woody Allen film. Sometimes referred to derisively as talking-heads films, the scripts mix comedy and drama in slice of life stories, and the "real" story in these movies is the complicated changes each character goes through. Personal little incidents such as the funeral of a friend in *The Big Chill*, Thanksgiving dinner in *Hannah and Her Sisters*, or the bus ride in *The Trip to Bountiful* become the key to the story. The "bigness" of these films is the attention to detail and the evolution of characters.

Many character-driven films also use a variation on the three-act structure. Rather than one main story driving the plot, there are individual stories of roughly equal balance for each of the key characters. These are known as ensemble films — *Diner, Dead Poets Society, The Big Chill*, are examples. Each separate story has three acts complete with dramatic act breaks. In a well-structured ensemble film the various stories intersect, parallel and propel each other.

There has been a fundamental change in the last few years in the standards that distinguish a motion picture from a television movie. Films like *The Accused* with Jodie Foster or *Reversal of Fortune* with Jeremy Irons historically would have been television movies, not features. The growing importance of the cassette market has allowed these smaller features to do well.

**Comedies.** Comedies are the backbone of the contemporary movie industry. Everyone is looking for a good comedy: *Tootsie, Ruthless People, Beverly Hills Cop*. Some comedies are buddy movies (*Butch Cassidy and the Sundance Kid, Outrageous Fortune*); others, ensemble pieces (*Animal House, Ghostbusters*).

There is a great demand for more adult comedies (e.g., *War of the Roses, City Slickers, When Harry Met Sally*) that can attract affluent over-thirty audiences back to theaters without losing the traditional young moviegoer. Good scripts in the adult comedy genre (*Pretty*

*Woman, Working Girl*) are widely respected. Now add a love story and a few chase scenes and you've got . . .

**Romantic adventure,** as in *Romancing the Stone* and *Raiders of the Lost Ark*. Although these movies may seem to be more adventure than romance, they are primarily love stories. The basic formula is odd couple pairing. When in doubt, a chase scene or confrontation with the bad guys is played for humor rather than real jeopardy.

**Satire** is a popular but narrow segment of contemporary comedy — *Airplane, Naked Gun*, the *Vacation* movies or most Mel Brooks projects. By definition, movie satire is broad comedy, most often lapsing into a series of loosely connected skits that range from hysterical to stupid. Satire is dependent on the sensibility of the director and it is no coincidence that most are written and directed by the same person. To be good, satires require enormous skill. As a result, satires are not regarded as representative writing samples for new writers.

**Epics and period pieces.** These are the high budget prestige films: *Out of Africa, The Mission, The Last Emperor*. Often dubbed "mainstream" films, they are the ones most likely to be released in the fall season or at the end of the year in order to qualify for the Academy Awards. Dramatic and visually spectacular, these are the movies written by the big guns of the industry such as Robert Towne (*Chinatown*) and Kurt Luedke (*Out of Africa*).

Complicated stories are the norm, but the real focus is the period in history and locales they capture. Certain historical periods are hot. Biblical epics topped in the '50s, westerns in the '60s. Mob films (*Good Fellas, Bugsy*) have enjoyed a resurgence, as apparently has anything pre-twentieth century, from *Amadeus* to *Robin Hood*.

**Family films.** These are the G- and PG-rated films, which producers hope will cross over to mainstream audiences: *Benji, Honey I Shrunk the Kids*. They often involve animals or animation, and in many cases both: *An American Tale, The Little Mermaid*. The market is specific, as are the studios that most often make these films: Disney, Universal, and smaller independents.

**Fantasy films.** These were the hottest properties in the film business for a while: *Cocoon, Splash, E.T., Big*. They are part science fiction and part human interest with liberal amounts of comedy mixed in. What happens if a human falls in love with a dummy (*Mannequin*), a mermaid (*Splash*), an alien (*Starman*)? A family finds an alien (*E.T.*) or a walking hedge-clipper (*Edward Scissorhands*). The audience is asked to accept a leap of logic in the premise, but after that the ploy plays out the logical consequences. In *Cocoon*, the leap of logic is that a group of senior citizens finds the fountain of youth. But after that the story is played for real — how this miracle affects the lives of each of the couples, the pandemonium the realization creates in a nursing home, the deadly effect on the aliens, and eventually, the choice each has about the opportunity for eternal youth.

Many of the films in this genre are fish-out-of-water stories — the outsider struggling to cope with the little things we take for granted (*Starman, Splash*). The best of the form comment on the incongruities of how we live, and prompt laughs or empathy in recognition. The heat of this genre, however, has dissipated in a flood of bad fantasy films, and so the word most heard at studios and in agency halls these days: more reality-based stories.

**Foreign films.** Often with subtitles, foreign films tend to play on the art circuit — a series of movie theaters in major cities that specialize in out-of-the-mainstream offerings. Foreign films are often distributed through the classics division of companies such as Samuel Goldwyn, Skouras, Miramax, or Hemdale. Although some cross over to be commercial successes — *My Left Foot, My Beautiful Laundrette, Cinema Paradiso* — most foreign films have a difficult time breaking into the American market. Foreign companies will claim that the reason their films don't do well in the U.S. is that American studios have a stranglehold on distribution. American producers counter that foreign product is not story-driven enough for American audiences. Both are right. As an example, the U.S. is the only market that will not accept subtitled or dubbed material on television. Also, American-style storytelling is different from European or Asian stories. Films like *Hope and Glory, My Beautiful Laundrette,* or the masterpieces of Japanese director Kurosawa are a collection of beautifully written cinematic scenes that have a minor central story. Even the character arcs are not as fully realized as they would be in an ensemble film structure. The result is that the American audiences often find foreign films slow-moving.

**Horror films.** Once the mainstay of the cheapie drive-in market, the horror film has gone mainstream. At the high end of the spectrum are top quality films such as *The Fly, Poltergeist, The Omen*. At the low end are *Friday the 13th, Halloween, Chainsaw* anything.

Well-plotted, suspenseful horror films are in big demand. A well-crafted script in this genre has launched many careers. The key to a good spec horror script is to make it different from previous films. Writers Charles Edward Pogue and David Cronenberg added a moving human element to the 1986 version of *The Fly*, a film which could easily have been a run-of-the-mill remake. New writers are well-advised to avoid the standard "who lives" premise (this is the opposite of the "whodunit"). There is not much suspense in trying to figure out which teenagers at camp will live to see the final credits. We already know: it won't be the leggy woman, the shy nerd who has a sexual awakening, or the loudmouths who are so obnoxious that the audience cheers when they go. The handsome guy and his hard-won new girlfriend survive. Not good spec script material.

**Issue dramas.** Examples are *El Salvador* or *JFK*. These films dramatize individual experiences in dealing with contemporary issues, such as drugs in *I'm Dancing As Fast As I Can*, or foreign imprisonment in *Midnight Express*. While often critically acclaimed, they are seldom big box office. As a result, budgets tend to be modest. These are terrific writing samples, because when well-done they showcase a writer's ability to handle difficult material. Such scripts are also strong on theme and substance — two commodities woefully lacking in most feature scripts.

**Musicals.** This form is among the most celebrated by film historians. In recent years *Fame, Cabaret*, and *Yentl* were notable. Plotless hybrids of MTV, such as *Purple Rain*, have done passable box office, but nothing to rival the dominance the musical film once enjoyed.

Most films aimed at the youth audience use music as an integral element, including at least a couple of stirring montages of Top Ten hits (*Flashdance, Top Gun, Dirty Dancing*). However, these are not musicals as much as films with music; the music doesn't tell the story, it adds texture. Most studio execs believe that the musical has not found an identity for the '90s, except on MTV.

**Science fiction.** Ironically, as some segments of the horror films genre have sunk to lower levels, science fiction has become increasingly sophisticated. The camp space films of the '50s, with aluminum foil sets and stilted dialogue, have given way to big budget extravaganzas: *Star Wars, Star Trek, Aliens*. The emphasis is on special effects, intergalactic wars, computer graphics, and Industrial Light and Magic (the George Lucas group that does so many of the sci-fi effects). While these films have gotten bigger and more expensive, the best are not just sound and fury, they tell good stories. The real drama is in the characters — the flawed Han Solo (*Star Wars*), the tough but devoted surrogate mother in *Aliens*, or mystified-by-the-'80s Captain Kirk in *Star Trek IV*. The best sci-fi mixes effects with humor and character: Luke Skywalker has a dark side; Hal, the computer in *2001*, has the soothing voice of a radio talk show host. The plots are borrowed by and large from *Flash Gordon, Buck Rogers*, Japanese samurai films, and especially old westerns. This market is facing its own aging process. The problem is cost: these are risky films to make, and it's difficult to out-do the special effects that have gone before. Most producers predict the emphasis will be less on effects and more on character.

**Thrillers.** These used to be the basic mystery: whodunit and why. The best thrillers these days are a study of characters under extreme pressure and tension: *Silence of the Lambs, Sea of Love*, and *Fatal Attraction*. This is an enduring form: *Dial M for Murder, Three Days of the Condor*, and *Witness*. The suspense is carefully drawn, the characters complicated and prone to sudden revelations. Especially popular are romantic thrillers such as *Fatal Attraction*, although no one has ever quite mastered this form as well as Alfred Hitchcock. A taut, well-written script in this genre is always a welcome writing sample. Many are transferable to television movies, where the woman-in-jeopardy premise is a mainstay of both network and cable telefilms.

**War movies.** The war movie reached its peak of popularity during the decade after World War II. The tenor of the genre gradually changed, however, from the support-our-boys-overseas war-is-glory theme to war-is-hell *Born on the Fourth of July* and *Apocalypse Now*. Recent war films are probably better categorized as issue dramas.

**Westerns.** Even though there have been plenty of B-movie westerns, the classics of this genre such as *High Noon* celebrate the triumph of man over adversity and provide riveting drama. Audiences admire the heroes of these films as much for their flaws as for their heroics. There may be a lesson in reviving the western in the success of *Young Guns*, *Dances with Wolves*, or the mini-series *Lonesome Dove*: forget the pyrotechnics and concentrate on characters and theme.

## WRITING NON-UNION

There is an ongoing parallel business in non-union screenwriting of features. The market is usually very low-budget projects: often horror/slasher/sex. Their nicknames include:

- "adult" films — the porno market;
- "slasher" films — the cheapie segment of the horror market;
- "bubble-gum" films — teen sex, teen violence, teen revenge — strictly drive-in or home video fare.

The companies that specialize in these films are rarely union. As a result, they are most often the companies that look for new writers. They are also the companies most likely to be accused of exploiting new talent.

The producers of non-union product may be individuals with no ties to the entertainment business whatsoever, independent filmmakers, or companies that specialize in the market. Interestingly, however, money does filter its way from studios into these non-union undertakings through distribution deals, supplemental rights agreements, and loans on investments. It is widely thought that most production companies have "gentlemen's agreements" for this purpose with non-union companies. Depending on the project and writer, scripts are shuffled into the appropriate production entity. The advantage is financial: no union minimums, no rules for hours or working conditions, no residuals, no health and welfare. A low-budget film may have union actors (for box office), but it's not unusual for the Screen Actors Guild (SAG) to be the only union contract on the project. That doesn't mean the production people aren't union members. Often they are, but they aren't working under union jurisdiction. The National Alliance of Broadcast and Engineering Technicians (NABET) members, for example, may do a few days of union work on one project, then a few days non-union on another. Without sanctioning the practice, NABET looks the other way rather than deprive its members of consistent employment.

Writers don't have the luxury of bouncing back and forth between union and non-union jobs. Once a writer is a member of the Guild, he or she is barred from working for non-signatory companies. The rule is enforced.

This can cause a writer problems because some writers find there is more non-union work available. Lonin Smith has supported himself for thirteen years writing non-union. During that time he's written seven spec scripts and three feature movies overall, of which two have been made (a somewhat better percentage than the one-in-forty average for union films). As Smith has worked his way up in the non-union market, he's grown increasingly concerned about making the eventual jump to WGA membership and projects. "I work low-budget, non-union on a regular basis as opposed to friends who can only land a WGA script every year or two." Suspended between union and non-union, Smith says he feels "like an adoptee on a search — who are my real parents?"

The problems of non-union work are many. WGA agents are not allowed to represent clients to non-signatory companies, so Smith finds his own jobs. "Mostly these come from word-of-mouth, I hear about them or they hear about me." For Smith, an agent becomes useful in negotiating the best deal. Over the years, Smith's price has edged closer to WGA minimums — $15,000 a script (up to $22,000) which buys a treatment (scene outline), a first draft and two rewrites. This compares to WGA minimums for a low budget feature ($2.5 million or less) or $25,000 for a treatment (scene outline) and two drafts. There are no residuals on non-union films. A writer may get "profit participation," but like most writers, union or not, Smith has yet to see any. Finally, non-union companies will often try to defer payment to the writer until the film is made.

Non-union films tend to be shorter — scripts average ninety pages for a running time of one-and-a-half hours as compared to one-hundred-twenty pages for a typical two-hour feature.

Many non-union writers find that they have to do a certain amount of this work free to get the job. Typically, a writer may be asked to do a treatment of twenty pages or so as part of the negotiating process. This practice is forbidden in films under WGA jurisdiction.

According to Smith, a non-union writer has to be very careful. "A lot of low-budget producers are fly-by-night — getting what they can from writers for free, then moving to the next writer. *Always* research a non-union company or producer before working for one. And remember that the check is *never* in the mail."

Like most writers, Smith laments the lack of quality films in the non-union market. "Most of these guys aren't even trying to make *Psycho*; everything has scream, horror, or some double entendre in the title." There is a booming market in made for home video, low-budget films of this ilk. Kids go out and rent the grossest, most disgusting movie they can find for a Saturday night: *Surf Nazis Must Die* or *Slime Zombies*."

But there may be hope for films without "bimbo," "slut," or "blood" in the title. The critical acclaim and box office success of Merchant Ivory's *Room With a View* (made for under $1 million) stirred new interest in the high quality, very low budget market. Ken Wheat confirms that the burgeoning home video market means that "little" dramas and offbeat independent product have more value than ever. Some independent filmmakers such as Robert Redford's Sundance Institute and writer/director John Sayles only do quality small budget pieces. Exposure for these films is often provided through film festivals that showcase the best of both domestic and foreign independent efforts. The biggest challenge is gaining a theatrical release.

Among the "don'ts" for non-union and independent films cited by Smith and the Wheat brothers are:

- Don't put your own money into it — unless you're willing to risk losing it all.
- Don't ask your friends for money unless they are incredibly wealthy.
- Don't do more than a treatment for free, unless you have a contract that guarantees your future participation.
- Don't assume the producers know what they're doing. Even if they have the money, they may have no experience. Know their track record.

- Don't assume your work will get noticed by mainstream film or TV. It happens, but by no means always. Non-union credits can sometimes even be a liability; you are characterized as a writer of schlock.

## HOW TO DO A SPEC FEATURE SCRIPT

Some writers break into union features by parlaying credits from television, stage plays, or novels into film opportunities. These credits need to be from well-regarded projects — successful television movies, critically acclaimed novels, or the most respected TV shows such as *Cheers*, *Northern Exposure*, or *L.A. Law*. Writers of less-prestigious television shows may be surprised that their credits mean nothing to the people in features. Even veteran television writers are told by their agents to "spec" a feature if they hope to write for motion pictures. The reasoning is that most TV scripts do not prove that the writer can do the following:

**Tell a good two-hour story**. TV scripts, of course, are generally hour or half-hour. To sustain story momentum and interest for two hours is the challenge of a theatrical feature.

**Develop fully-realized original characters** that can sustain a movie. Episodic TV scripts emphasize the regular characters of the show.

**Create strong visual images** whether in comedy sequences, dramatic moments or car chases. TV scripts, including TV movies, rely more heavily on dialogue than the visuals of a feature film.

At a recent writer's conference, one executive of a major studio vowed never again to give sitcom writers a first chance at features unless they have a good spec movie sample. "Most sitcom writers simply can't fill two hours. The jokes are fine for the first twenty-two minutes (the length of a sitcom), then there's no story to keep it going!"

For a new writer hoping to write for motion pictures a spec feature script is the only real option. The percentages for outcomes for a spec feature are as follows:

*Least likely:* A studio or independent will buy the script. Although spec features are bought more often than spec television scripts, the sheer volume of scripts that are read by each studio means the percentages are still low. Even if a spec feature is bought, it will most often be treated as a story idea and the writer contracted to do subsequent drafts and revisions. The idea may be bought outright and a more experienced screenwriter brought in to do the next drafts. On three of the studio films I've done, I was never even shown the initial spec scripts they bought — just told the basic idea and encouraged to write a new version. And given the pattern of most features, other writers may eventually be hired to do further drafts. The original writer who sold the script will usually share story credit if the film is ever made.

The best position to be in, by the way, is to be the last writer on a major feature that has its stars, its director and a shooting date. That writer is likely to get credit and the production bonus, and the chance to see something he's written actually on the screen. All agents report those are exactly the reasons those jobs go to the "A" list. Facing a $20 million production budget, the savings in hiring a newcomer instead of a veteran are negligible. Besides, the stars and director want assurances someone with major credits is being brought in.

*More likely*: The script will be optioned. If a producer, director or small independent thinks the project is promising, they will pay the writer option money for the rights to sell it to a studio or otherwise raise money to finance it. Although this is a source of income to new writers, it's important to remember two things: 1) options payments are usually small; and 2) most options don't result in a sale. Since the option process is not monitored by the unions, it is difficult to determine the exact percentages. Estimates are that less than one in twenty-five options ever result in the actual sale of a script, and having a script optioned means little in terms of future employment.

*Most likely*: The writer uses the script to get an agent and the opportunity to pitch ideas to a studio. A spec feature is a calling card that says the writer has talent and interesting ideas and can do long forms. Years later successful writers may dust off those early unsold spec scripts and finally get them made. Daniel Petrie's spec script led to a job rewriting *Beverly Hills Cop*. His original spec script *The Big Easy* was finally released four years later. Similarly, *Jacob's Ladder* was the writing sample that landed Bruce Joel Rubin *Ghost*. *Jacob's Ladder* finally went into production a year later. Much the same happened with Tom Schulman's spec script *Dead Poets Society*. It got him lots of other work before the film was finally made.

There is a fourth likely outcome: a writer may be invited to *hear a pitch* from a producer. Every studio and production company has a variety of projects in development. Warner Brothers, for example, has about two hundred at any point in time; Paramount, one-hundred-fifty; an independent such as Stonebridge, thirty or forty. Every company looks to match writers with those ideas. Executives will pitch their hearts out to writers they want in a sort of "man bites dog" scenario. The idea may be a pet project of someone within the company, a notion of an investor, a book they've optioned, or a script that's been kicking around for years that they want to hire yet another set of writers to tackle. Most often the writer is then sent off to come up with his or her version of the story in an audition process.

In any event, the company already has an emotional and/or financial investment in these projects, and executives will argue there is an increased likelihood the movie will get made. There is also the obvious advantage that the writer doesn't have to come up with the initial story idea.

There are disadvantages, too. Many writers simply don't want to work on somebody else's story. Secondly, even though most of these projects are rewrites, they turn out to be "page ones." Page one means that beginning with the first page, almost every word and story point ends up being changed. It's another way of saying you're writing a brand new script.

How much is this the life of a film writer? I have now worked on eight features — and seven were ideas or scripts that already existed at the studio.

**HOW TO BEGIN**

Pick the genre of the film that you most watch and enjoy. There's no point in writing a character piece (because you think that's what *they* want) if your real love is action-adventure.

Factor into your decision-making process *how hot the genre is* these days. Have there been movies of this style that were hits recently? Did those hits saturate the market for a while or create a new demand? Were there recent bombs in this genre? Did they kill the market or create one (because it will be so easy to do better)? Other genres have simply passed their peak: families crossing the frontier and Vietnam stories are not hot spec scripts these days. Writer Richard Graglia, who has sold five spec scripts, advises writers to concentrate on lower budget genres. "Avoid space epics or scripts that only Jack Nicholson could play." The four genres where spec feature writers have had particularly good luck are thrillers, action adventure (including cop stories), comedy, and horror films.

Add to this mix *who you know* — who's eventually going to read your work? Agents, other feature writers, friends of producers? Which genres do they specialize in? Which ones do they recommend?

In the meantime, read as many scripts from that genre as you possibly can. Supplement reading by renting videos of recent films in the genre, especially those that are referred to in pitch meetings as "it's a cross between x and x." The latter gives a spec writer an indication for better or for worse, or the directions in which the market is going.

And, finally, do a spec script in the genre where you have the best ideas. The test of a good spec feature idea is:

- Does the story have a beginning, middle and end?
- Is the story "big" enough to sustain two hours and ticket prices of $6 plus?
- Does the story have good twists at the first and second dramatic act breaks? Are the plots and subplots also full stories?
- Does the story provide clean, strong characters with complexities that can unfold over two hours? Does each character have an "arc" so he or she changes and develops over the course of the movie?
- Does the movie have a "point of view" — a character through whose eyes the story unfolds? Does your personal voice show through that character?
- Is the story set in a colorful area that will provide texture, visuals, and movement for the script?
- Can the plots be told visually?

- Does the story provide for a big moment during the first ten pages that will hook the reader?
- Does the story provide for a big finish — a dramatic final sequence, emotional jeopardy, or climactic twist?
- Is the story original or is it a cliche of its genre? Remember that a good feature idea is at least two years ahead of the market. Can it compete with other films of its genre? Will the idea still be original two years from now?
- Is there enough momentum to the story to drive it along?
- Can the hook for the movie be succinctly pitched in a sentence or two? Are there movies to which it can be compared; i.e., "a cross between *Pretty Woman* and *Terminator*?
- Is there a terrific starring role that might attract a major box office star?
- Is the movie potentially "low-budget" (under $6 million by studio definition), or is it likely to sell to a non-union or independent company (under $2.5 million)? Is it in reality a television movie without a major star attached?
- Is someone interested in the idea, even before you start writing? It can't hurt to pitch it a few times, even informally, to find out.

Ultimately, Patricia Resnick (*Nine to Five, Straight Talk*) advises, "Don't get wrapped up in trying to write things that you think will make money. Write a movie you'd go to."

# CHAPTER SIX

# PRIMETIME EPISODIC TELEVISION

Television is the ultimate mass media — more people see the lowest rated show on television each week than have seen the highest grossing movie of all time in theaters.

And despite what often seems like a thrown-together product, television is extraordinarily complicated. Even the worst programs are the outgrowth of an awesome amount of money, pressures, and people (not all untalented). From actors to network executives, hundreds of major and minor participants shape the product you finally see. If it's terrible (as is so often the case), it's not necessarily because you or Aunt Evie could have written the script. The writing might have been quite good in its early incarnations, but in the shaping and reshaping it's not unusual for a script to self-destruct. A bad performance can make even the most timeless lines sound dippy. A weak director can ruin both the script and the performance. Of course, the reverse is also true. A brilliant performance has saved many a mediocre piece of material. The important lesson is that the final product is deceptive.

Because so many people play a hand in every show, television and film are sometimes described as collaborative art forms. But collaborative suggests participants working in a room together to create a product. The process of television is more like the assembly line at an auto plant. Each participant works on one piece. Whether the pieces add up to a car or not is a crapshoot. Writers, particularly, tend to work in a vacuum. The story may begin with the writer, but unless he or she is on staff, the fate of the story quickly moves to others whom the writer may never meet, let alone collaborate with.

At any point in the process, the script can be rewritten by other staff writers or the producers of a show.

Television writing has a hierarchy that can be measured in terms of money and prestige. At the top of this hierarchy are "pilots" of new series that are ordered because the creator is a recognized entity. These creators become "the show runner" — the person most responsible for getting the show on each week. Also high in status, although not money, are "longforms" — made-for-television movies and miniseries. Networks and studios must approve writers to do pilots and longforms. As a result, new writers have a difficult time competing in these two network markets.

Next in the hierarchy is a staff job on an ongoing series, particularly a show that wins awards and is respected within the industry. Low person in the system is the freelance writer — moving from one show to the next, pitching ideas, and hoping for an assignment. This is the level at which most new television writers get their first break. They write sample episodes for an ongoing series on spec and use those scripts to generate work. In recent years, television shows have added more staff writers; there has been a corresponding rush to create job titles. Just being a staff writer doesn't carry the requisite prestige, so now there are story consultants, executive story consultants, and supervising producers. But they are all staff writers.

## WHAT THE TITLES MEAN

Of course, titles do convey a certain amount of status; a producer is higher than a story consultant which is higher than a story editor. And the higher the title, the more money associated with it. But some writers are so credit-happy that one studio executive suggests that television created all those fancy-sounding jobs so they could give away titles instead of money. A show on Fox network, for example, recently offered a "term writer" a chance for on-screen credit. The trade-off was a $500-per-week pay cut! Deciding that glory wasn't worth the price, the writer left for another show where he got both the title and a raise.

Starting with the most prestigious, the following are job titles in television usually occupied by a writer. The highest credits appear at the beginning of an episode, the others at the end.

**Executive producer.** Often the creator or co-creator of a series; frequently wrote the pilot episode. Responsible for the overall supervision of the show. Known as the show runner.

**Supervising producer.** May be either the head writer or a "line producer." Sometimes the title is given to a fix-it person brought in during a crisis to help fix or "punch up" the scripts of the staff.

**Producer.** Increasingly a writer's credit, though not many writer/producers can tell the difference between a key light and a klieg light. A few are truly writers and producers. A **Line producer** is usually the real production-oriented person on the show and is not a writer.

**Executive story consultant.** Most writers move up to this title when they've been with the show for a year or when they jump shows. Usually works with freelancers, rewrites scripts, and writes two or three episodes each season.

**Story consultant.** The same job as above for slightly less money. Both titles may also be part-time positions for people who come in weekly to help punch up situation comedy scripts.

**Story editor.** The same job as above for still less money.

**Term writer.** A staff writer on a regular weekly salary who does the same job as above, but does not receive screen credit except on the episodes he or she wrote. Most often this job is the writer's first staff position.

**Apprentice writer.** A staff writer on a regular weekly salary who was not a member of the Writer's Guild when hired, but now qualifies. Salaries average 75% of that of a term writer.

**Freelance writer.** Not on staff; moves from one series to another, doing one episode at a time. May sign for "multiples" which guarantees the writer two or three assignments on a particular show.

The following credits are shown at the beginning of an episode, just before the director's credit. The Director's Guild requires that the director either be the last credit before the "body" of the episode or the first credit after the episode ends. The Writers Guild requires that the writer's credit be next to the director's.

**Created by.** Appears on every episode of a series. Gives credit (and money) to whoever wrote the original episode or came up with the idea, whether that person continues with the show or not.

**Written by.** The staff or freelance writer(s) who did the most work on the episode, including the initial story idea. Although staff may have done a rewrite, the best-regarded shows do not ask the freelancers to share his or her credit unless the rewrite was extensive.

The Writers Guild arbitrates any on-screen credit disputes by reading each draft and assigning the credits. Credits are important not only to a writer's ego, but also to the pocketbook. Shared credits mean shared residuals when the episode is rerun. The arbitration system often results in split credits:

**Story by.** The credit given to the writer who came up with the initial idea for that particular episode, but for whatever reason either he or she did not write the full script or it was substantially rewritten.

**Teleplay by.** The person(s) who did the most work on the full script. Frequently this is a shared credit between the original writer and a staff writer who did a major rewrite.

The trend to more staff and fewer freelancers seems to have passed. A large highly-paid staff is a luxury few shows can afford. Universal Studios implemented a new rule that has come to be known as the three-typewriter policy. There can be no more than three staff writers on a Universal show. This is in contrast to shows which retain seven or eight staff writers (all disguised with other titles).

## WRITING TO TV'S LIMITS

Any form of television places arbitrary limits on a writer. The first is length. A half-hour show, for example, has to run twenty-two minutes — not twenty or twenty-five. It doesn't matter if a story is better served by more or fewer pages. The script has to translate to twenty-two minutes. If it's too long, whole scenes may be eliminated. If the episode is too short, the script will be padded with extra material. The "bumpers" at the beginning of *Moonlighting*, in which Maddie and David talked to the audience are an example. Lauded as a clever breakthrough for television, the short segments were actually created at the last minute to fill time on an episode that was too short.

A television script also has to conform to other artificial conventions of the form — act breaks for commercials and shorter scenes that move quickly to keep an audience's attention. Perhaps most frustrating to any writer are the limitations placed on story-telling — the kinds of stories that are appropriate for television movies versus situation comedies versus detective shows. There are also rules for how a story should unfold, censorship of language by networks, time slot of the show (8:00 p.m. shows are family-oriented; 10:00 p.m. shows, more adult) and budget constraints that mitigate against elaborate special effects, complicated action sequences, or multi-million dollar sets. Writing for television means writing within limits. The rule is, simpler is better.

## HOW EPISODIC TELEVISION WORKS

Ongoing series are the backbone of primetime television, occupying nearly eighty percent of available hours each week. "Primetime" is 8:00 p.m. to 11:00 p.m. Monday through Saturday (7:00 p.m. to 10:00 p.m., Central Time) and 7:00 p.m. to 11:00 p.m. Sunday (6:00 p.m. to 10:00 p.m., Central).

The season for new shows is September through May when audience levels are the highest. Summer months are devoted to re-runs or to limited series that are candidates for regular programming later in the year. Historically, the fall season has marked the debut of the networks' new shows. But the pattern is changing. There is now a widely acknowledged second season for new shows that runs January through April, during which debuting shows replace those with low ratings and are tested for possible inclusion on the fall schedule. Some shows such as *Moonlighting* and *The Days and Nights of Molly Dodd* successfully debuted in March and April. Many programmers believe that debuting during the second season gives off-beat shows a better chance of being sampled by viewers. Fox Network has declared a year-round season by successfully airing new episodes of *Beverly Hills 90210* during summer that boosted that teen angst drama into a phenomenon.

The typical order (the number of episodes ordered by a network) for a successful show is twenty-two to twenty-six episodes per season (down from thirty-nine in the '60s). Only recently have hit shows such as *Beverly Hills 90210* received larger orders — thirty episodes. These days, new series or shows that have marginal ratings usually receive an initial order of thirteen episodes, with the option for a "back nine" (nine more episodes). Mid-season shows and back-up series often receive short orders of six episodes.

The twenty-two shows in a successful season are produced back to back. While one show is filming, another is being edited, another is in pre-production, three others are being written, and five others are at story stage. And so television series operate on **a crushing schedule**. Deadlines are important. Late scripts can wreak havoc on a schedule.

This makes television immediate compared to other forms of screenwriting. A script can be on the air within months of completion or, in the case of a show such as *Moonlighting*, days. (*Moonlighting* would finish shooting on Friday episodes that were aired Tuesday.) The downside of the pace for any show is that scripts that could have used another polish or rewrite are rushed before the cameras. Sometimes the finished episode gives the misleading impression that television writers can get away with sloppy work.

Episode television operates on **strict budgets**. Every show is deficit financed which means the licensing fee (the budget provided by the network) does not cover the cost. The difference is made up by the studio or production company in hopes of gaining profits when the series goes into syndication reruns of foreign sales. These constraints limit the number of scripts a series is willing to buy. If the development process for a particular story is not going well, the show has the option of cutting off the writer at any point to save money and time. Most series commission only a few scripts beyond those which are filmed or taped. This is in contrast to television movies, pilots, or feature films where many more scripts are paid for than are ever made.

The ability to write for existing characters who have established patterns of dialogue and interaction is one of the most important skills for an episodic writer. A freelance writer must be able to capture this for each show; he or she has to avoid stories already done, structure scenes in a style and with a tone specific to a show, and please a staff of writers who are far more familiar with the quirks of a show than a freelancer could ever be. To a great extent, writing for episodic television is clever imitation. A writer must capture the style, stories, and characters of a series while still adding his or her own creative touches.

Part of this style is what's called **a franchise** — a set of circumstances and tone that determines what the stories will be each week and what the viewer can expect to see. One of the commandments of episodic television (to the dismay of most writers and producers) is that there be a certain sameness to a series each week so that the viewers will know what they will be watching. This doesn't meant that there are no surprises in the stories, but it does mean that the show will operate within the same established parameters each episode. And so Jessica Fletcher (*Murder, She Wrote*) determines the murderer each week from a group of suspects, *MacGyver* uses everyday items from safety pins to hair spray to stop terrorists, and *The Golden Girls'* schemes always backfire. These are the franchises for these shows. The powers-that-be believe that viewers find comfort in consistency and that consistency builds loyalty. That's why it's so important for a writer to pay attention to the nuances of each market, genre, and show.

The fact that **episodic opportunities for freelance writers are diminishing** is one inescapable reality of network television these days. Writers Guild records show that in 1978 seventy-two percent of episodes on television were written by non-staff writers. The average is currently hovering at forty percent. The explanations for this are varied. Some writers point to the rise of the serialized show (such as *Dallas* or *L.A. Law*) where storylines are developed by the staff. Also a factor are the reality shows, whether dramatic (*Rescue 911*) or comedic (*America's Funniest Home Videos*), since these shows work with existing material rather than new story ideas.

Some writers, particularly those trying to make a living in the freelance market, blame the shrinking market on greed among staff writers who take as many assignments as they can. The retort from producers is that they can't find freelancers who can write the show. David Lee (*Cheers, Wings*) believes that all television producers are desperate to find talented writers: "Good writers are a rarity; mediocre ones are not." Whatever the reasons, the marketplace is more competitive than ever.

One of the results of this declining marketplace is that **it's become harder and harder to get a television script read**. Most shows have a backlog of submissions. At one point *Moonlighting* had nearly four hundred scripts waiting to be read for no more than seven available episodes. No producer, not even one committed to open access for new writers, could possibly read all that material or meet all these writers. The situation has not been helped by lawsuits from free-lancers accusing shows of stealing their work. *Quantum Leap* has been a particular target; in its second year Universal forbade the staff from reading any spec *Quantum* scripts.

On most shows, the scripts that do get read are those recommended by friends, those submitted by agents with an especially good relationship with the staff or, on occasion, those scripts that arrived first and, quite simply, are at the top of the pile. Some story editors advise the best time to get a spec script read is during the hiatus period of a show when it stops shooting for one season and begins preparing for the next. Staff writers and producers tend to continue working during these breaks, and this is often when they catch up on unread material. Hiatus periods vary, but most shows take two or three months off between March and July.

Finally, television writers are particularly vulnerable to the syndrome of **"you are what you write."** Situation comedy writers, for example, have a notoriously difficult time breaking into hour episodic drama. An hour action-adventure script from *Hunter* is not a useful writing sample for a show that considers itself "character-based," such as *The Wonder Years*. As a result, even established writers in one genre end up doing spec scripts to move to another. Debra Frank did a spec *Remington Steele* to make the jump from sitcoms into hour dramatic. Susan Baskin (*Dynasty, Remington Steele*) did a spec movie to move from television into features.

## ANALYZING EPISODIC MARKETS

The Writers Guild groups primetime series into five markets:
**Episodic comedies.** Half-hour shows in which the emphasis is on comedy and dialogue. Most are done on videotape before a live audience (*The Cosby Show, Roseanne*), although there is an increasing number of film comedies (*Wonder Years, Cheers*).
**Episodic dramas.** Hour shows in which the emphasis is on the development of a dramatic story, some involving comedy elements. All are done on film. Examples are *In the Heat of the Night, Star Trek: The Next Generation*, and *Northern Exposure*. There are experiments

with half-hour episodic dramas each season, although so far not too successfully.

**Serials.** Hour shows with continuing stories each week — in effect, evening soap operas. All are done on film and are almost identical in structure to daytime soaps. Examples are *Dallas*, *L.A. Law*, and *Twin Peaks*. Some episodic dramas such as *Wiseguy* and *Beverly Hills 90210* have made effective use of "mini-arcs" — stories that cross over two or three episodes. But the majority of stories on these shows are not serialized.

**Anthologies.** Hour or half-hour shows that tell self-contained stories focusing on characters that are not regulars on the show. These are the television equivalent of the short story. Anthologies can be comedy (*Love Boat*) or drama (*Twilight Zone*).

**Variety shows.** Tape shows that feature skits and musical numbers with no particular story. They can be specials, half-hour, or hour shows. Examples are *The Carol Burnett Show*, *In Living Color*, and Bob Hope specials. Also proliferating in primetime these days are magazine shows, reality programs, and awards shows. The clever patter of hosts for these are sometimes written by WGA members. Animated programs, like *The Simpsons*, are not. Those writers are under jurisdiction of the Cartoonists local.

## EPISODIC COMEDY

Comedy on television, except for the occasional television movie or *Northern Exposure*, is confined almost entirely to the half-hour format. The reasoning of the networks is clear, if not necessarily logical. Network types believe it's not possible to be funny on television for more than thirty minutes. Few hour comedies have ever aired that were not in the variety format. Sitcoms take their name from the notion that placing amusing characters in an amusing situation is funny. Sometimes yes. Sometimes no.

There are two structures for comedies: those done on videotape and those done on film. The differences between film comedies and tape comedies are important for the comedy writer to understand. Can the characters go outside? On taped shows, they almost never do. Can the script incorporate a montage sequence? Film shows frequently do. Film allows mobility for location filming and an emphasis on visuals such as intercutting between scenes. Videotape shows are shot almost always in a studio, usually with an audience. Nearly all the scenes are interiors. The scenes are shot in order. As a result, tape sitcoms tend to function more like a play than other forms of television or film. The line between tape shows and film shows has blurred in recent years.

Multicamera film shows, such as *Cheers*, have an audience and shoot scenes in order. Other shows start in one form and move to the other (*Mr. President* went from film to tape). But it's important if a sitcom is film or tape because the script formats differ.

Most situation comedies employ two stories per episode: a main story (the A story) and a subplot (the B story). The two stories may or may not be related. The A story predominates, receiving the most scene time. If the episode has a moral, it usually evolves from the A story. The B story is designed to be especially humorous and allows the telling of the A story to be less linear. Some sitcoms, such as *Golden Girls*, employ three stories in each episode. The third one, the C story, is called a runner. This story is always very minor and is designed expressly to be funny.

A situation comedy has only three to five scenes per act, occasionally less as the story dictates, rarely more. Scenes tend to be full scenes with a beginning, middle, and end. Most have a button — a last line that ends the scene on a laugh from the audience. Those irritatingly loud guffaws at jokes that aren't funny are sometimes the writers regaling in their own words. More often giggles and belly laughs are the result of ''sweetening,'' the addition of a laugh track to supplement the response from the audience.

Just as important as understanding whether a comedy is film or videotape is understanding the style of a particular show. What kinds of stories does it do? How much time is spent on a complicated story and how much on developing characters? Sitcoms tend to fit specific forms that relate to their franchise.

• **Family comedies** focus on the trials and tribulations of families, emphasizing small stories and warm upbeat endings (*The Cosby Show*, *Roseanne*).

• **Ensemble shows.** Much situation comedy these days is ensemble-based, the interactions of a weird collection of characters with the lead acting as a stabilizing force, observing and reacting. This is the formula employed so effectively in the original *Mary Tyler Moore Show*, *Newhart*, and *Night Court*, among many others.

• **Sexual tension comedies**, such as *Cheers* and *Who's The Boss?* use the relationship between the two leads as the sparkplug. The plot of each episode is secondary to its impact on the relationship between the hero and heroine.

The other question sitcom writers have to ask is where does the show most often find its humor? Almost every situation comedy mixes different styles of humor to make the show funny, but each series relies on particular devices as the primary source of "funny."

• **Physical comedy** uses physical "bits" and visuals — pratfalls, pie fights, a character glued to a chair. Shows such as *Laverne and Shirley*, *Perfect Strangers*, and, of course, *I Love Lucy*, developed physical comedy as a trademark. A story idea for a sitcom that emphasizes this style of comedy should have plenty of opportunity for physical interplay and sight gags.

• **Character comedy** relies primarily on the quirks and problems of the regular series characters to move the story, instead of complicated plots, outside influences, or guest stars. The success of *The Cosby Show* brought about a resurgence of the "small" story, entire episodes that focus on seemingly small problems: the death of Rudy's goldfish, Vanessa using makeup, whether Denise should attend her parents' alma mater. The essence of character comedy is familiarity. We laugh in anticipation because we know how characters will react to a problem. On *Family Ties*, when Mallory brings home a refugee from a punk band as her new boyfriend, we start laughing because we know exactly how Alex will respond. The opposite is also true: we laugh in surprise when the character reacts in a different way than we expect. An example is a normally out-of-it character who suddenly says something inspired: Marianne on *Perfect Strangers*, Corkie Sherwood on *Murphy Brown*.

• **Issue comedies:** "light" stories are the norm for situation comedies. Most episodes don't have much of a message to communicate other than the basics — love is good, greed is bad. But *All in the Family* broke new ground and issue comedies such as *Maude* or *Murphy Brown* regularly take on controversial subjects from abortion and bigotry to cancer. The humor comes out of the character's pain. Because the issues themselves are complex, the best shows don't have a neat moral at the end of the episode that tells the audience what they've learned.

• **Insult comedy:** cracks about the other characters, name-calling, witty (and not so witty) repartee, put-downs, and one-liners have long been a staple of sitcoms. Shows that rely heavily on insult comedy include *Married With Children*. The franchise is that the regular characters already get on each other's nerves and the stories each week only aggravate those conflicts.

• **Shaggy dog humor** is the domain of particular characters on a show: Rose on *Golden Girls*, Urkel on *Family Matters*, Balki on *Perfect Strangers*. It is derivative of the "shaggy dog" story in which the *non sequiturs* and ramblings of a long story are funnier than the punchline.

A number of shows have experimented with a hybrid of comedy and drama, nicknamed "dramedies." Former NBC president Brandon Tartikoff cites *Molly Dodd* and *Wonder Years* as examples: "Take *Hill Street Blues* in one hand and *Cosby* in the other hand and whop them together." The reliance is less on joke setups, pratfalls, and laugh tracks and more on the ironic humor of dramatic situations.

### WHAT DO EPISODIC COMEDIES LOOK FOR?

Whichever forms of humor a particular show uses, the comedy writer has to demonstrate an ability to capture that style for that show. Funny is paramount. An informal rule of thumb for a sitcom spec script is three to five laughs per page. This may not seem that hard, but each page is only about forty-five seconds of screen time. Cramming five jokes into forty-five seconds and still telling a story makes sitcom screenwriting deceptively difficult. One of the first principles that comedy writers learn is the Rule of Three — try to make three jokes out of one. Ideally, the jokes build: funny, funnier, funniest. Four jokes become repetitive, two jokes don't have enough build.

As an example, the following two sequences are from the *Boys in the Bar* episode of *Cheers* written by Ken Levine and David Isaacs in which Carla is obviously pregnant.

CARLA
How do you like it? Maternity chic. [JOKE #1]

NORM
Who are you trying to sweep off his feet?

CARLA
Are you kidding? Tom Jackson, I've been in love with him ever since I first saw him get into a crouch. [JOKE #2]

SAM
I'll introduce you first thing.

CARLA
You think he'd mind signing my belly? [JOKE #3]

---

SAM
Right. Tom Jackson, this is Carla Tortelli.

CARLA
I love you, Tom Jackson. (RE: HER PREGNANT CONDITION) And don't worry about this. I'll be back in commission come July. [JOKE #1]
(HANDING HIM A PIECE OF PAPER)
Here's my number and a couple of quotes from past lovers. [JOKE #2]

TOM
Thank you, Carla.

CARLA
He breathed on me, Sam. I'm a whole woman. [JOKE #3]

Similarly, lists are funnier in threes. The following examples are from *Newhart* and *Cheers*.

*Newhart*: *The Snowman Cometh* by Arnie Kogen and Gary Jacobs

CHESTER
When the town hears about the cancellation tomorrow, there'll be rioting in the streets (#1), lynch mobs.(#2)

JIM
Take it easy, Chester. We're more of a tar-and-feather community. (#3)

*Cheers*: *The Boys in the Bar* by Ken Levine and David Isaacs

COACH
Y'know, I always loved that Tom Jackson. He was such a riot. He'd hide my toothbrush in my socks (#1), he'd leave dead animals in my locker (#2), one time he and another guy held me down and shaved my body. (#3)

Joke writing is so important to situation comedies that television comedy has evolved its own rituals to make a script funnier. One approach is "punch up" night. All the writers of a show sit around a table until the wee hours making the jokes funnier (or trying to).

The most frequent criticism of spec comedy scripts is that they're not funny enough. Inexperienced writers simply don't exploit the characters and situation to find all the humor. A close second on the complaint list of story editors is that there's no story. Comedy writers frequently abandon the principles of dramatic structure in a headlong rush toward hilarity. Unless the quips and cracks and one-liners are grounded in a story with conflict, tension, and twists, the script will read like a *Tonight Show* monologue rather than an episode of a sitcom.

## EPISODIC DRAMA

Drama on television, except for television movies or occasional anthology shows such as *Amazing Stories*, is one hour. But the demand for hour shows in domestic syndication is weak, and some series (such as *Knight Rider*) have been re-edited from their original hour length into half-hours, wiping out whole sections of the plot (which indicates that the original plots were probably not that strong to begin with). At last report, the "Reader's Digest" versions of these episodes had mixed sales.

Hour episodic scripts are fifty to sixty pages in film format. There are exceptions. *Moonlighting* scripts typically ran over ninety pages — the characters talked fast, much of the dialogue was overlapping, and there were more stage directions. *Hunter* filmed scripts of forty-five pages because chase sequences and stunts took more time on the screen than the written page.

As a rule, the main story (A story) in an episodic drama relies heavily on guest stars and does not extend beyond one episode. The subplot (B story) focuses on an issue of one or more of the regulars; often a B story is related to the A story. The C story is a humorous runner involving one of the supporting regulars. So in an episode of *Cagney and Lacey* entitled ''Stress'' written by Debra Frank and Scott Rubenstein, the A story was about a man stalking Cagney, the B story was a stress group at the police station where the pressure Cagney feels finally comes out, and the C story was a completely unrelated runner about the captain finding a lost dog.

Until recently, hour episodic shows were completely self-contained, allowing shows to run in reruns or syndication without regard to the order. But shows such as *Wiseguy* and *Thirtysomething* used multi-parters as a way to tell more complicated stories than one hour could accommodate. Writing multiple episodes is not a good writing sample for new writers. Often, new writers only have enough good material for an hour and want to do multiple episodes because they can't (or won't) edit themselves.

Also increasingly popular are mini-arcs. These are stories told over multiple episodes that gradually build. An interesting character may be introduced in Episode #1 as a C story. Then in Episode #2 we see the development of that character's story as a subplot. And in Episode #3 the escalations in that character's dilemma become the A story. Such was the case on *Beverly Hills 90210* where a seemingly innocuous new student gradually evolved over eight episodes into a *Fatal Attraction*-style romance with one of the leads, and then went off the show.

Episodic dramas can be loosely grouped into the following genres or styles:

• **Action/adventure shows.** Rely heavily on car chases, daring rescues, and shoot-outs. Examples are *Baywatch*, *Hunter*, and *Miami Vice*. There's not much humor, but there's lots of action and complicated plotting. Networks have been known to *require* that something be blown up or crashed four times an episode. The stories are short on social commentary and character development, but long on daring escapes and jeopardy. These shows have proven the strongest in foreign syndication.

- **Romantic comedies.** Emphasize humor, character development, and off-beat characters. While there may be action sequences, series such as *Moonlighting* or *Northern Exposure* will make the jeopardy funny instead of dangerous. The relationship between the lead characters is more important than the particular story of the episode.
- **Issue shows.** Shows such as *Cagney and Lacey* or *Quantum Leap* use the regular characters to explore various sides of a contemporary problem — black market babies, alcoholism — sometimes to great effect. An episode of *Quincy* about orphan drugs resulted in national legislation. An episode of *Lou Grant* about pit bulls brought that issue to the public consciousness in disturbing dramatic fashion. Issue-based shows often deal with headlines from last night's newspaper or segment of *20/20*. My first sale, to *Trapper John, M.D.*, for example, was about American men importing Asian brides, a segment on *Nightline* the evening before my pitch meeting. Issue-based shows use humor, but mostly as a relief from the intensity of the main story.
- **Warmedys** are hybrids of dramas and comedies — hence the name. Shows such as *The Waltons, Eight Is Enough,* and *Life Goes On* are family-oriented with small stories that communicate a warm message with an upbeat ending. The comedy is low-key and grows out of the characters. The stories may touch on controversial issues, but usually in non-controversial ways. *Thirtysomething* dramatically upgraded this form with its contemporary slice-of-life dramas.

## WHAT DO EPISODIC DRAMAS LOOK FOR?

An episodic drama writer has to demonstrate the ability to tell a good original story through the existing characters. If the franchise of the show is the conflict between the two leads, a spec script should bring new dimension and insight to that conflict. If the focus is action, the stunt sequences should be inventive and exciting. If a show emphasizes small stories, the spec script should show a knack for finding the interesting nuances in the characters. Staff writers look for the correct balance of humor, message, action, and character development for their particular show.

The key to writing for any episodic drama is the lead character or characters. The personality of the lead(s) determines the kind of stories the series will tell and how the stories evolve. On *Murder She Wrote*, for example, the producers are careful that Jessica

Fletcher not be a meddler, so she never initiates her involvement in a story. This is one of the reasons she has so many relatives and old college friends who bring her into the crime. The stories are always "whodunits" — five suspects, give or take a potential murderer or two. And in her methodical, low-key pursuit of the truth, Jessica rarely makes a mistake.

This is in marked contrast to *Magnum, P.I.*, where Thomas can be counted on to be wrong about something every week. He is the reluctant detective — his little voice always telling him that things are not what they seem. They never are. The franchise for the show is to lead the audience in one direction and then at the third commercial act, spin the story in the opposite direction of what the audience expects.

Much of the storytelling in shows with one lead is the relationship that develops between the lead and the guest stars. *McGyver*, for example, usually develops a heartwarming rapport with his downtrodden and sympathetic client.

Episodic dramas with dual leads are "odd couple" pairings: *Scarecrow and Mrs. King* (described by the creators as Erma Bombeck meets James Bond), *Hardcastle and McCormick* (James Dean meets Judge Wapner), and *Moonlighting* (the hustler and the princess). Often there is romantic tension; always there is a difference of opinion. *Cagney and Lacey* was a prime example. In most episodes, the main guest star was seen in only a handful of scenes, and the rest of the plot unfolded through the disagreements between Chris and Mary Beth in the car, at their desks, in the ladies' room. The relationships between the main characters on shows such as *Cagney and Lacey* and *In The Heat of The Night* show a progression from week to week.

Finally, there are episodic dramas which are "ensemble pieces" — a group of regular characters, roughly equal in significance to the show. Examples are *21 Jump Street*, *Thirtysomething*, and *Northern Exposure*. The stories are rotated among the regulars.

## SERIALS

A serial is a series of stories that (when done properly) progress from week to week. A staple of daytime television in the form of soap operas, serials took off in primetime with *Dallas* and *Dynasty*.

Daytime soaps come in both hour and half-hour forms; evening soaps are always hour shows. Daytime soaps are done on tape (with no audience); primetime serials are on film. The intent of a serial is to get the viewers hooked on heart-rending stories so they will tune in faithfully each week. As a result, shows such as *Dallas* and *Dynasty* tend to be melodramatic — characters operating at the extremes of good and evil. Little attention is paid to comedy in these shows, other than the campy joy of watching Diahann Carroll insult Joan Collins's caviar.

The form has not done well in reruns or syndication because of the serialized format. First, episodes have to be shown in order if the stories are to make sense. Second, audiences who miss a show or two quickly lose track of who's trying to do what to whom. An exception has been the half-hour parody *Soap*. Despite continuing storylines, the emphasis is humor, so it apparently doesn't matter to audiences if they understand the intricate plotting or not.

The evening serial was elevated to a new level with the advent of *Hill Street Blues*, *St. Elsewhere*, and *L.A. Law*, which emphasize both humor and reality-based drama. Although these shows are not thought of as soaps they have all the trademarks of the daytime formula: multiple stories that carry over from week to week, a large cast of ten to fifteen regular characters, and a mathematical structure to each episode that is almost identical to the soap opera form. In daytime this formula is specific: five stories per hour episode — two main stories, two developing stories, and a runner. Of these, one story ends in each episode and one begins. There is always a "cliffhanger" from one of the stories to end the hour.

Occasionally, evening serials depart from the traditional soap structure. *Falcon Crest* did as many as seven stories per episode and as few as three. In its second season, *Hill Street Blues* was told to add one story per episode that both began and ended within that episode. *St. Elsewhere* sometimes did self-contained episodes — Dr. Fiscus's brush with death, the hospital's experiment in dream research. And of course, *Twin Peaks* was an experiment in the gothic novel as serial, and who could predict from week to week what they would do!

The stories for a serial are charted for the entire year at the beginning of the season. The summary is called the "bible" of the show.

The bible lays out how the various characters will develop and the stories will intersect. This is in marked contrast to other forms of episodic television which make their story decisions episode by episode.

Once the bible is finished, the writing staff for a serial prepares "breakdowns" which detail the story points and scenes for each episode. Often these are twenty-five to thirty pages (for a fifty- to sixty-page script). The scene outlines provide the structure into which the writer inserts dialogue and stage directions. Since to a certain extent this is "fill in the blank" writing, the staff members rotate writing of the actual scripts. Serials rarely use freelancers on the dual principle that most of the work has been done and the staff knows the characters better.

Since reality-based shows such as *L.A. Law* deal with contemporary issues, they sometimes buy story ideas from outside writers. Actors Alan Toy and Darryl Ray, through their involvement in the Media Access Office on Disability, pitched and sold a story to *Hill Street Blues* that dealt realistically with the problems of a man in a wheelchair. The team got story credits; the actual script was written by the staff of the show.

## ANTHOLOGY SHOWS

In hour anthologies, such as *Love Boat* and *Hotel*, three separate stories (occasionally, four) are told. Although there is a regular cast each week, the emphasis is on guest stars, plots that are self-contained, and stories that can be told in fifteen minutes, roughly the time allotted per episode for each plot. According to Kathy Shelly, a former producer of *Love Boat*, "We didn't even try to look for new stories any more; we'd done them all. We started looking for old stories with a new twist."

Sometimes the stories in a particular episode of an anthology show are written by different writers. The staff of the show makes the decision as to which stories fit best together. A typical episode of an hour anthology tries to strike a balance — one story is particularly dramatic, another is designed for humor, and a third focuses on a problem of one of the regular characters.

The half-hour anthology format was much esteemed during the days of the original *Twilight Zone* and *Alfred Hitchcock Presents*. Many writers believe that some of these old episodes represent the finest writing ever to appear on television. The half-hour anthology is the television equivalent of the short story. There are no regular characters other than the host, and each episode tells one story.

The half-hour form resurfaced in recent years with *Amazing Stories* and new versions of both *Twilight Zone* and *Hitchcock*. None of these survived weak network ratings. Interestingly, the form has done better in syndication with shows such as *Tales From the Dark Side* and the *Ray Bradbury Theater*. The form is also alive and well on PBS in the form of *American Playhouse* and *Wonderworks*.

# CHAPTER SEVEN

# HOW TO DO A SPEC SCRIPT FOR EPISODIC TV

The spec television script is the tool most writers have used to get their early breaks in television — but that break does not come from selling the script to the show it was written for. A spec episodic script is most often a useful writing sample to get work on similar shows. Ironically, it does not even matter to those shows if the script was ever bought or even read by the first show. The percentages work as follows:

• **Least likely.** The show may buy the script. Of hundreds of writers I've met over the years, only a handful ever sold a spec script to the show it was written for. If the script did sell, it was regarded as little more than a story idea, or, at best, a treatment with two more drafts required.

• **More likely.** The show will have the writer in to pitch other ideas. The spec script proves that the writer knows the show and can write for that show's characters, so even though the staff does not buy the story, the script generates an opportunity to pitch other ideas to that show. Depending on the ideas that are pitched, the writer may get an assignment to write an episode. Some shows will give the writer the story idea. *Simon and Simon* had perhaps the best record in using freelancers of any recent show on television — nearly eighty percent of its episodes were done by non-staff writers. Producer George Geiger says, "The show didn't have cattle calls. We didn't invite people in, hoping we'd find a great idea. We usually had something in mind . . . just a one-line idea. And the writer, with our help, massaged that idea into a full-blown story."

• **Most likely.** The writer uses the script to get work on other shows of the same genre. In most cases, the original show not only doesn't buy the script, they don't even read it. Instead, the writer uses the material to get an agent and/or a chance to meet with other shows. This pattern is so consistent in television that many writers and producers tell freelancers not to bother submitting a spec script to the show it's written for. "It's simply too discouraging," executive producer Stephen Cannell observes, "and you may be hurting your chances to pitch to that show in the future."

Why? One would think that a show would be thrilled to receive a completed script they could buy, polish, and shoot. The system is more complicated than that. First, the staff members have no investment in a spec script from a writer they don't know. They did not choose the story or decide how it should be told, and it's safe to assume they would have guided the writer toward different choices. Often the story is too similar to another show they're writing or an idea they just turned down or has a climactic scene "just like" the one they're doing next week.

Second, it's harder to fix a story when the script is already written. The details of dialogue and scenes obscure plot problems, and most staff writers think too much time and trouble are required — it's easier to start fresh. Experience has also taught staff writers that the author of a full script is less likely to understand or accept notes than one whose script is still an outline.

Third, the most popular and prestigious shows are the ones that receive the most spec scripts. *Cheers* holds the record — three hundred to four hundred scripts per year. The show is so widely respected that the producers have their pick of freelance sitcom writers. Former producer David Lee explains that they tried to read everything that came in. "It may take a year or more. I can remember only one spec script where we bought the story idea." As a matter of policy, the staff returns scripts without agents unread. The same situation exists at other popular spec script shows such as *Golden Girls*, *Murphy Brown*, and *Northern Exposure*.

Additionally, outside writers are at a disadvantage because they tend to make too many little mistakes. Without benefit of guidance from the staff, the spec writer will more often than not break some of the taboos of the show. On *Scarecrow and Mrs. King*, for example, Amanda was never allowed to hold a gun; on *Remington Steele*, Laura said, "Mr. Steele," not "Remington." On *The Cosby Show*, Cliff was always given a block of time to do a Bill Cosby routine. These may seem to be minor points, but such mistakes in a spec script combine to give the impression that "this writer doesn't know our show." On *Moonlighting*, the classic mistake in spec scripts was the Maddie/David arguments. Although those scenes were a trademark of the show, they were used sparingly and the disagreements were always *about something*. Almost every spec script included pages of:

DAVID
Good.

MADDIE
Good!

DAVID
Fine.

MADDIE
Fine!

The problem with these exchanges is that they are arguments for the sake of argument. They had nothing to do with the story and told us nothing new about the characters.

But *other shows don't know that*. If the *Magnum P.I.* staff writers think the script reads like a good *Moonlighting*, they know all they need to know:

This writer can write our genre.

This writer can write established characters and has demonstrated a good ear for dialogue.

This writer can tell a story.

The television industry is full of writers whose spec script was snubbed by the original show, but admired by others. Doug Molitor's spec *Night Court* got him an assignment on *Sledge Hammer*; Scott Gordon's *Cheers* was never read by *Cheers* but he used it to get an agent and his first sale ever — at *Moonlighting*; Gene and Noreen O'Neill used their rejected *Moonlighting* to generate two feature movies . . . and John Gaspard and Michael Levin sold their spec *Moonlighting* story to an Italian series, *Lucky Luke*!

All of which results in an interesting dilemma for the spec writer — which show to write for? Is it better to write for a series that may buy the script or might at least see the writer, or to write for a show which probably won't read it, but which might be of interest to other shows? Here are the factors to consider:

• **Prestige.** The more acclaimed a show, the more spec scripts it probably receives, and the less likely the staff is to buy or read unsolicited material. But a writing sample for a prestige show is more likely to generate work elsewhere. If the story editors of *Northern Exposure* are fans of *Cheers*, they will tend to read a spec *Cheers* over a script for a less prestigious *Full House*. Assume that shows which receive lots of awards and critical acclaim are shows that staff writers from other shows watch and respect. These are also the shows that other new writers are specing. A spec *Murphy Brown* is in competition with the thousands of other spec *Murphy Brown*s.

• **Transferability.** A spec script for one genre is not a good writing sample for others. A *Coach* script is not a good sample for *Hunter* since one is half-hour comedy, the other hour drama. *Hunter* is not a good sample for *Thirtysomething* because one is action/adventure; the other, warmedy, even though both are hour shows.

There are exceptions. Prestigious shows from one genre can overlap into another. For example, *Murphy Brown* is so well regarded that a *Murphy Brown* script can be a good sample for hour shows with comedy such as *Northern Exposure* or even *Murder, She Wrote*. How does a writer know which shows transfer to which? By watching them — and then categorizing shows into markets based on style, story, and structure. It also can't hurt to find a connection to staff on a show and ask which sample scripts they are most likely to read.

• **Durability.** Much like cottage cheese, a spec script quickly becomes dated, especially when a show is canceled. So although a *Moonlighting* script was once a prime writing sample, that script would now be too old to be representative of the writer's current abilities. If the intent is to have a writing sample that can be used for a few years, it should be for a show that will be around for that long. A writer has to be aware of the ratings and future of shows by reading the trades and tapping into the gossip network wherever possible.

These three factors — prestige, transferability, and durability — are important if the writer's spec script strategy is to have a writing sample that can corral an agent and create pitch opportunities for other shows. There is also a second strategy that some writers have used successfully: targeting a specific show and setting out to write a script that show will buy. This strategy eliminates most of the long-running prestige shows and focuses on shows that are either new or overlooked. This was how I garnered my first sale to *Trapper John M.D.* In contrast to *Cheers*, *Trapper John* rarely received more than fifteen to twenty spec scripts per year. The staff read all of them and saw an average of three or four of the writers. Over seven years, the series bought five spec scripts outright. I picked *Trapper* because I knew people on the show. I watched it. And I had access to scripts, opportunities to discuss story ideas, and advice on the nuances and pitfalls of the series. As a result, a spec script got me in to pitch. In the short term, the strategy worked because I made a sale. But a *Trapper* script was not highly transferable to other shows, and so that script did not generate additional work for me except at *Trapper*. Other writers report similar experiences. Mike Coumatos sold an *Airwolf* script, but had to do other spec scripts for other shows. Ken Berg had sixteen produced shows including episodes for *Hart to Hart*, *Eight Is Enough*, and *Angie*, but he had to do a spec *Moonlighting* to get in to pitch for that show. While producers at *The Jeffersons*, David Lee and Peter Casey did a spec *Cheers*, out of frustrations that other producers didn't respect their show. They went on to produce *Cheers* for five seasons.

Despite this lack of transferability, there are some advantages in doing a script for a less regarded show: the script is competing in market where there is less material; the script is more likely to be read; and it's easier to get information from the staff.

Particularly good candidates for this strategy are new shows that other writers have not yet discovered. During the first few months of *Moonlighting*, for example, the staff accepted and read a number of unsolicited *Moonlighting* spec scripts. We provided sample scripts to the writers, offered suggestions over the phone, and even had a meeting with one of the writers to give him notes. (That particular writer never sold us his *Moonlighting*, but went on to receive Emmy and Writers Guild nominations for his work on *China Beach*). As the first season went on, that openness gradually disappeared under the pressures of so many writers clamoring to work on the show. Eventually, a policy was adopted to accept scripts only through agents; then came a directive to stop sending out sample scripts; finally, as the unread scripts piled up, the decision came to stop accepting submissions entirely.

The process at *Moonlighting* is typical of a new series — the initial openness to new writers gradually diminishes the longer the show is on the air. The first spec writers through the door had the best chance. This risk in this strategy, of course, is that the show may not stay on the air and your script will be obsolete before it's ever read. And if a script for a low-regarded show doesn't sell or generate work on that show, you don't have a useful writing sample for other shows.

A third strategy is to submit a feature script of the same general tone and style as the series. Some story editors will read features as a writing sample, but most will confess that a feature is simply too long. The competition for reading time is so intense that a one-hundred-twenty page script is at a serious disadvantage. This is particularly true with half-hour shows because the style of writing is so different from features. Additionally, a feature script does not prove that a writer can write for someone else's characters nor does it demonstrate that the writer can tell a good story in the allotted thirty or sixty minutes.

Among the worst possible strategies is to submit a spec pilot script as a writing sample, since the goals of a pilot episode differ markedly from those of an episode of an ongoing series (See p. 57). Similarly, most story editors discourage submitting a spec episode of a serial, since by definition the form does not tell whole stories in a single episode. The best writing sample for an evening serial is a non-serialized hour show, such as *Thirtysomething*, which emphasizes dialogue and the emotional conflicts of the characters.

Whichever strategy you choose in developing a spec script, here are some criteria to keep in mind:

• **Choose an episodic show you watch and know.** If you've only seen a show once or twice, it's unlikely you have enough information to be able to duplicate the style and characters. Don't ever write down to a show you don't like in the first place.

• **If possible, choose a show where you know someone or can get information.** If you have a connection to a story editor or a writer who has freelanced for a particular series, that's a major inroad. The relationship will help to get the sample scripts and tips about the show and will increase the chance (but won't guarantee) that the script will be read.

• **Choose a show that will be around** at least long enough to be considered a current show. Shows in syndication (other than first run syndication) are no longer in production — *M\*A\*S\*H*, *Moonlighting*, *Barney Miller*, *Family Ties*. A spec script for these is already dated. Shows that are at the bottom of the ratings or temporarily pulled from the schedule probably won't last long enough to read your script. They may already have been canceled.

Even shows that have been on six or seven years and are still doing well in the ratings can be a disadvantage. Producers get tired of reading the same things over and over. Agent Marcy Miller says, "It's a relief sometimes to read a spec script that's not a *Golden Girls* or a *Quantum Leap*." Other popular spec scripts at the moment include *Wonder Years*, *Murphy Brown*, and *Roseanne*. While these samples may show off your best writing, remember your spec *Roseanne* will now not only need to be as good as (or better than) the series, but better than the literally thousands of other *Roseanne* spec scripts circulating.

• **Pick the genre you (and others) feel that you are most talented in.** Knowing whether your strengths are one-liners, intricate mysteries, or pithy dialogue will help determine the best show for you.

• **Develop a variety of story ideas for each show** you are considering and factor these into your decision. Which story is the strongest? Which show brings out your best ideas? Which show do you enjoy thinking about the most?

## HOW TO GET INFORMATION

The Writers Guild requires that episodic shows provide background information to freelance writers who are members of the WGA before they come in to pitch. This required information includes a written listing of previous stories for the series. As example:

### REMINGTON STEELE
### MEMO TO PROSPECTIVE WRITERS

At the heart of *Remington Steele* lies a romantic mystery. Just who is this Mr. Steele and what is going to happen between him and Laura Holt? These questions spice up every episode and keep viewers coming back for more.

As a detective show, *Remington Steele* strives for sophisticated plots featuring intriguing characters with unusual problems. Stories strongly favor character over gunplay, engaging situations over intellectual puzzles.

### WRITING EPISODES

*Remington Steele* is a tough show to write because it is not bound to any formula or strict approach. This also makes it a challenging, exciting show to write. The only requisite is that each week Remington and Laura handle some sort of case. We are not committed to either a "closed" style mystery in which the audience only receives information as the detectives do or an "open" mystery in which the audience is several steps ahead of the detectives. Similarly, we are free to emphasize comedy or drama depending on the episode.

### STORY LINES

1. *License to Steele* (#2704)

(The Pilot Episode)

Convinced that being a woman might scare off prospective clients, private investigator Laura Holt invents a male "boss" and gives him the name "Remington Steele." All goes well until her creation shows up.

Laura has been hired to protect over two million dollars worth of jewels being delivered to car designer Gordon Hunter for a media event. However, various other individuals have designs on the jewels, including a handsome, mysterious stranger who keeps changing identities.

2. *Tempered Steele* (#0903)

Laura and Remington become involved with industrial espionage when they're hired to supervise the installation of a foolproof burglar alarm system.

Jim Meecham, an eccentric oil millionaire, insists that Remington personally supervise the installation of a fool-proof burglar alarm system to prevent trade secrets from being stolen from an electronics firm he has bought into.

When the high-tech alarm system fails to prevent a robbery, a friend of Remington's is killed. Furthermore, Laura and Remington are faced with a ten million dollar lawsuit that will destroy their agency and careers unless they manage to solve the case.

3. *Steele Waters Run Deep* (#2703)

Remington and Laura must find a missing video-game genius who has disappeared along with five million dollars and the plans to his company's newest video-game creation.

Albee Fervitz, president of the video-game firm, turns in desperation to Remington and Laura. They are to find his associate, who is the key to the missing money, the missing plans, and the successful merger with a major company, only 24 hours away. Meantime, one of the detective firm's other clients, Emery Arnock, gets drawn into the harrowing and humorous happenings.

The material the Writers Guild requires be provided its members includes character descriptions and other background information. If there is a ''bible'' for the show, that should be provided also. As example:

NOTES FOR WRITERS — *Scarecrow and Mrs. King*

Remember that we're not doing a conventional caper show here. Floating over whatever stories we do must always be the concept of ''what happens when Ms. Average is plucked from her suburban home and dropped in the midst of international intrigue.'' The use of Amanda on a case must always sound logical and harmless. In other words, she might be asked to pose as an assistant in a laboratory suspected of wrongdoing, but her sole function would be to write down the name of everyone who goes through door #101. Eventually, of course, Amanda can't resist seeing what's *inside* door #101, or she is innocently caught up in the intrigue, and the adventure escalates from there.

AMANDA has been divorced for about a year, and has spent most of her life making sensible choices. She has a college education, perhaps majoring in literature or some other field that left her without real preparation for the working world. Amanda's life at home must never be painted as dreary or a drag for her. She loves her home life, defends it against Lee's smirks, and insists that her responsibilities to home and children come first. If it come down to a Little League game or busting Carlos, the game comes first.

LEE was the only child of parents who died when he was quite young. He was raised by an uncle, an Army colonel, who dragged him all over the world from base to base. The Colonel and Lee never see eye to eye. (A hint as to the depth of their relationship: Lee always refers to his uncle as ''The Colonel.'' The Colonel always referred to his relationship with Lee as ''kid duty he pulled.'') The Colonel never approved of Lee's parents nor his hell-raising nephew, and Lee left home as quickly as he could, bouncing from port to port, adventure to adventure, acquiring sophistication and worldliness as he went. Possibly because of a lack of a strong woman's hand in his life, he has never had a successful or deep relationship with a woman.

The Writers Guild also requires freelancers receive a written or verbal listing of stories planned for the current season. Some story editors are good about providing information to freelancers — from sample scripts to a summary of previous plotlines. A phone call or a letter may be enough to generate these, if you treat secretaries and writers' assistants well. An agent can also call on the writer's behalf. Even then some shows send material only to writers invited in to pitch. Unfortunately, a number of shows have no written materials at all. (This Writers Guild rule is one that's not well enforced.)

The most important item freelance writers need from a show is sample scripts. Format varies from one show to another — the stage directions, the number of scenes per act, and descriptive attitudes for characters. *Moonlighting*, for example, used an ellipsis (. . .) to connect stage directions:

> . . . as a dizzy O'Neill picks himself up and staggers toward the door . . . Maddie opens it . . . he exits.

Most other shows use short sentences. *Trapper John* used *TRUCK WITH* as the camera followed a character; other shows use *MOVE WITH* or *THE CAMERA FOLLOWS*. These nuances of a script are not apparent from viewing the show. A spec script should read like other scripts from the show.

Most new shows also have screenings of the pilot for prospective writers. These are limited to writers being invited to pitch, but it can't hurt to ask to see or read the pilot before it's on the air. Pilots are also screened for advertisers in major media-buying markets such as New York or Chicago. Wrangle an invitation from a friend in the ad business. The rumor mill also runs fast and furious during pilot season. Find out which pilots are expected to be hot, and get your hands on a script so if you decide to spec the show you can be first in the door.

So how does a spec writer get information and scripts?

**Plan A.** Begin by contacting the story editors of the show, either directly or through your agent. A phone call is better than a letter since it is harder to ignore. A list of addresses and phone numbers of television shows in production (including the names of the story editors or producers) is provided in the monthly WGA Newsletter, which non-Guild members can subscribe to.

During your phone call be pleasant and direct, and don't apologize for calling. Ask for a couple of sample scripts, a summary of story lines, and any background material.

Some other advice:

• Praise the show. All film and television writers are hungry for affection. A well-prepared caller will even know which episodes the story editor wrote and praise them specifically.

• Offer to send a self-addressed, stamped, script-sized envelope for the material. If you make your initial request by mail, include this envelope with your inquiry.

• Don't ask if you can submit your latest script. At this point, you are only after information; don't mix purposes.
• Don't keep the staff writer on the phone any longer than necessary.

More than likely, you won't get to the story editor. Every writing staff has an assistant to the writers. This is a clerical position, often held by an aspiring writer. Be incredibly nice to the assistant; he or she can send you what you need directly. Often the assistant reads sample scripts and recommends them to story editors. Stephen Cannell (*A-Team*, *Riptide*) credits his entire early writing career to sympathetic secretaries.

If the show declines to send material, be gracious. There are other options. If the show does send material, immediately write a glowing thank you note or do something to ingratiate yourself to your new contact.

Once familiar with the written materials, you are allowed (at least in my mind) one more phone call — this one to say thank you, to get helpful hints and cautions about the stories not to do, and to get a recap of the storylines they are planning. Always ask which episodes the series considers to be its best.

Above all, don't wear out your welcome.

And if the show won't send you an anything? Time for Plans B through F.

**Plan B.** Through friends in the industry or other writers, try to locate a writer who has freelanced for the show. Ask to be introduced to this writer, then offer to take him or her to lunch for a little brain-picking. Writers who have freelanced a show should have sample scripts, storylines, hints, and suggestions. If there are materials available, insist that you pay the duplicating costs. Offer to return the favor by helping the writer locate scripts or information he or she needs. Don't ask if the writer will read your script when it's done; you're mixing purposes again. If by some miracle he or she offers to do this, grovel in appreciation.

**Plan C.** Watch the writing credits at the beginning of each episode and compare them to the staff credits at the end to determine which ones were written by freelancers. Then send those writers fan letters, care of the show or the Writers Guild. Be effusive about how much you loved their script, and ask for an autographed copy. Egos being what they are, most writers sign with a flourish and send it.

**Plan D.** Anybody connected with the show — actors, costumers, editors, secretaries, network types — has access to scripts. On most shows, at least one hundred copies of each episode are in circulation so that people can do their jobs. Ask a non-writer on the show to get you a script or to introduce you to a story editor. Any request for information that separates you from the mass of other freelance writers is an advantage. If your request is for a larger cause, even better. Writing for information on behalf of the Lodi Writers Association, the film class at Palomar College, or the Lompoc *Gazette* entertainment section will vastly improve your chances of getting the material requested.

**Plan E.** Find a big fan of the show. He or she will probably have episodes on tape and may even have scripts or know how to get them. A dedicated fan knows the story lines that have been done, the history of the characters, and many of the nuances.

**Plan F.** Failing all these, try your local library. Back issues of *TV Guide* list all the plots week by week. Many libraries (including those at the Writers Guild, the American Film Institute, or university film schools) have special collections that include copies of scripts and resource materials about the entertainment industry. Local writers' groups also may have the scripts you're looking for, or may know how to get them.

Always assume that it will take months for your scripts to be read. This philosophy will not only help your mental stability but will also discourage you from calling the show or studio every week. The best philosophy is to go on to the next script and forget about it. If good news comes, great. If no news comes, that's to be expected.


## PICKING THE RIGHT STORY

Developing a story for television is not a matter of writing a script about the first idea that comes to mind. A typical pitch session for an episodic series dictates that a freelancer bring in five to ten stories. The staff decides which one, if any, it will buy. You might as well get into practice. For each show on your list, develop a number of ideas. The process will force you into more imaginative story areas. Also bear in mind that none of these ideas is wasted. They may be useful for another show, a pitch meeting, or a future spec script.

One of the best ways to generate and test story ideas is to look at the stories the show has already done. There is always a pattern — certain kinds of stories and themes to those stories which the show knows it does well. On *Moonlighting*, for example, creator Glenn Gordon Caron was fond of telling writers that "the only two motivations that really work in their stories were lust and greed." *Moonlighting* did not do stories in which the characters were motivated by revenge, jealousy, or madness. Other shows have their own rules, and it's important to figure out what these are before picking a story.

In episodic television the strongest story approach is to start from the regular characters. What would you most like to learn about them? Chances are that is exactly what the rest of the show's audience would like to see, too; i.e., Scott Bakula (*Quantum Leap*) leaps into his own past, Sophia (*Golden Girls*) has a sister just like her. A clever approach is to do a story hinted at in a previous episode, but not explained — Hunter and McCall once slept together, Murphy Brown has a difficult mother or an ex-husband, Larry (*Perfect Strangers*) has a sibling he always competed with (who turns out to be a sister).

Character-driven stories, particularly about regulars or guest stars, provide the best drama and comedy. Inexperienced writers frequently make the mistake of concentrating on complicated plots instead of clean, interesting characters that can tell an emotionally compelling story. Producer-writer Anne L. Gibbs (*Webster, Alice*) also reminds writers to focus on the regular characters. "Don't do a story about an outsider; do a story about the regulars *because* of an outsider."

The test of a good episodic television story is:
• Does it have a beginning, a middle, and an end?
• Does it have good twists at the first and second dramatic act breaks?
• Does the story fit the form? If it's a comedy, can it be told in twenty-two minutes? Forty-five minutes for a drama? Is there

enough story to fill the time? Too much story? Can the dramatic twists be manipulated to the constraints of commercial act breaks?

• Does the story give the main characters a lot to do? Can the plot be told through them? Does the audience learn something new about the leads?

• Is the story set in a colorful area that will provide texture and movement to the script? This is important in hour episodic. In half-hour comedy, color can be added with a interesting guest character or colorful activities happening within the confines of the regular sets of the show.

• Does the story provide an opportunity for a "big moment" that will hook the reader during the first pages?

• Is the story original or have we seen it a hundred times before?

• Does the story require a limited number of guest characters? On many shows, for example, there is a guideline to avoid stories with more than three guest stars. Having more characters doesn't leave enough time for the regulars. Most series rarely introduce more than five guests per episode; the strongest scripts usually introduce fewer.

• Does the story translate into a compelling "log line" that can be pitched simply and directly with lots of implied conflicts and twists?

# CHAPTER EIGHT

# OTHER PRIMETIME TELEVISION

Although episodic series is the dominant form on network television, there are other network television forms that attract new screenwriters. Primary among these are made-for-television movies and pilots of new series. These are probably the two most difficult markets for a new writer to enter. Both forms are high on the prestige scale, which means new writers are competing with the most established television writers. All three networks approve writers for television movies and pilots.

A more promising primetime market is variety (*In Living Color, Tonight Show, Saturday Night Live*), which is open to the work of new writers, sometimes buying freelance skits or jokes. Variety writing includes special events such as the *Academy Awards* and *The Miss America Pageant*.

Additionally, there are broadening opportunities in primetime news (*20/20*, special documentaries), and in sports (*Monday Night Football*, Olympics coverage). All of these programs use writers. Sports and news programs are strictly controlled by the respective divisions at each network, not by the entertainment division. The status of reality programs such as *Cops* or *Rescue 911* is somewhat confusing. While they may tell or re-enact true stories as if they are news programs, reality shows are under the auspices of the entertainment division. (Discussion of the special writing requirements and rules for entry into sports, news, and reality shows are discussed in Chapter 11, p. 141.)

# TELEVISION MOVIES

The first made-for-television movie was aired on NBC in 1964. Since that time there have been over 2,000 of these films and the form has changed considerably. In 1989, for the first time, the cable companies (Turner, USA, HBO, etc.) made more television movies than the four networks combined. The subject matter has also narrowed; the sensational true story, usually involving mayhem and murder, has become the lifeblood. (The narrowing focus may also help account for a resurgence of viewer interest in theatricals in primetime. The television airings of *Fatal Attraction*, *Beverly Hills Cop*, and *Field of Dreams* were ratings successes despite vast exposure in video stores and on cable.)

Television movies (also known as "telefilms," "movies-of-the-week," "MOW's") and mini-series are expensive to produce compared to episodic television. The average licensing fee is fifty to one-hundred percent higher per hour for an MOW. Costs for mini-series such as *Winds of War* or *Lonesome Dove* can spiral to $4 million or more per hour. The high costs are compounded by the lack of a syndication market for telefilms. Studios are willing to deficit-finance television series in hopes of earning profits through reruns. But television movies are difficult to sell into reruns. The result is that many studios have not made television movies. This market has been left to the small independent studios or to in-house productions by the networks.

Currently, the networks are allowed to produce directly a maximum of three hours per week of primetime television. Most of this is devoted to the movie block and primetime news shows.

The economics of the television business has changed with the increasing importance of foreign markets. Because European television prefers movies, well-marketed American television movies have been successful there. Foreign sales are increasingly vital for companies that are deficit-financing their projects. This fact is attracting more and more of the major studios back into the television movie business.

The special problems of network television movies create many hurdles for a new writer. The networks are far more involved with the script for each telefilm than they are in the week-to-week writing on a series; they approve writers project by project. The system is often arbitrary. Some of the writers CBS approves, NBC will not; others who NBC loves, ABC blames for its latest disaster. Networks also like to be involved in the story development process which mitigates against spec television movie sales. In most cases, executives are much more interested in doing *their* version of the story.

Each of the three networks and most of the major production companies have readers for television movie scripts. While the percentages for selling a script through this system remain low, the exceptions are notable. *Do You Remember Love, The Promise* and *Long Journey Home* all began life as spec scripts. The percentages are much better in the cable market. Buyers like Turner and HBO welcome completed scripts, so they've created a brand new spec market for writers.

The competition to sell a television movie is intense. Barbara Gunning of Interscope Communications reports that each network hears ninety ideas a week. Of these, perhaps one-hundred-fifty are bought in a season by each network. On the average one in four is actually made; the odds for success, as a result, hover around two percent. Since television movies represent a top step in the prestige ladder, this means prominent writers and producers are being turned down. And even if a new writer's story idea or script is bought, the network may not allow the writer to do the script or the revisions. The widely-held belief is that the television movie and miniseries forms are too complicated and demanding for inexperienced writers.

## WHAT IS A GOOD TELEVISION MOVIE STORY?

The telefilm market is certainly the trendiest of all the forms of screenwriting. Stories are literally taken from headlines on the front pages of the local newspaper. What's hot and what's not changes quickly. CBS, for example, once known for its disease-of-the-week telefilms, no longer wants them. That network is now a leading buyer of the true story or "trauma drama" — the television version of true events, most often lifted from the headlines.

ABC is even more blunt — a purloined memo subsequently circulated all over town summarized a meeting with that network which quoted their television movie goals. All of the telefilms mentioned have aired since then:

## THE CONCEPT

This is what ABC buys. Described as "The ABC emotional imperative." It has to be a high concept (they do not want to know anything to do with the plot or story to begin with). It has to be relate-able, clear, and original, and the audience must have that emotional hook so that they know from the television log line (or eighteen-second promo) that they will either be entertained or moved in two hours.

## THE THEME

This is what ABC wants. Generally described as "heart" or "groin" — or preferably both! They do not need anything intellectual (that is not to say that intelligence is a subject to be avoided).

## THE AUDIENCE

Women between the ages of eighteen and forty-nine on Mondays; men and women between those ages on Sundays. A good guideline on the pitch is "What will happen if . . ." They gave me some "quintessential" ABC movies as benchmarks:

*Who Will Love My Children?* (What will happen if . . . Ann-Margret doesn't find homes for her children?) The ABC emotion here is heart rather than groin.

*The Making of a Male Model* (purely sexual and very high concept.)

*Paper Dolls* — The print ad showed two pictures: one of a couple of fresh-faced innocent young girls in pigtails, and the other of the same girls as overly made-up sexy models. The line was "Would you want them to do this to your daughter?" (This was heart and sex.)

*The Best Little Girl in the World* — If her daughter won't eat, a mother is going to starve herself to death. (What will happen if . . .)

*A Killer in the Family* — A docudrama about a man who conned his three sons into breaking him out of jail. They discover Dad is a cold-blooded killer.

*Something About Amelia* — If the young girl doesn't tell, her father will continue to molest her.

As evidenced from this memo, the one sentence summary or *TV Guide* "log line" is the key to selling a television movie idea to any of the networks. Given the plethora of telefilms each season, networks and production companies want to know how they're going to promote a particular film to attract viewers. Promotion consists of *TV Guide* listings, catchy ads, and short promotional spots. This is most effective if the "hook" for the audience is easily identifiable in fifteen seconds.

The memo also indicates that ABC has definite priorities for its telefilms. So do other buyers. The following memo from a studio to prospective producers and writers of telefilms underscores the perceived differences among the networks and cable companies. While the list is no longer current, it provides an interesting and blunt insight into how much telefilms are aimed at specific markets.

### TO: PROSPECTIVE PRODUCERS

We cannot stress the importance of doing your homework when developing MOWs for us. It is vital to understand each network's schedule and who and what is targeted.

CBS: aims at older, more rural viewers than NBC or ABC. Airs two MOWs per week. Sunday night is the bigger of the two and is the start night for miniseries. Because the miniseries is a bigger event, it tends to tie into issues, i.e., the Challenger, The Kennedys, Woodward and Bernstein. Tuesday night's presentation tends to be more oriented towards women. The network wants a one-line idea that involves an action, not a lot of description. Also likes gang romps with comedy series stars.

ABC: aims at urban and suburban up-scale viewers. Educated yuppies. Sunday nights are event-oriented. Monday nights are supposed to appeal to women.

NBC: Monday nights, oriented towards a male audience; Sunday night, female.

FOX: "Painfully high concept." Lots of comedies, but haven't had good ratings.

HBO: Yuppie, wants *NO* teens in scripts. Issues oriented.

SHOWTIME: Urban audience, wants foreign appeal, no comedy. Wants thrillers.

TURNER: Older audience, likes older stars, especially movie stars who aren't normally seen on TV. Big on issues, i.e., steroids, nuclear waste, ecological issues. Will do some historical films, i.e., *Billy the Kid*.

LIFETIME; Geared to a female audience. Will do smaller women's issues, but most likes woman-in-jeopardy where the woman takes control to solve her own problem.

USA: Will expand to twenty-four MOWs per year in the near future. Now doing action-adventure and exploitation. Lots of thrillers.

WHAT THIS COMPANY WANTS IN A PITCH FROM A WRITER OR PRODUCER:

1) A two-three sentence statement of the concept with action involved.

2) Who the main characters are.

3) The premise.

4) Don't pitch it if you don't have the rights.

5) The complete pitch should never be longer than fifteen minutes.

6) You can suggest casting or writers to write the story if you are only pitching the idea and not writing the script.


Sadly, these profiles indicate just how narrow the subject matter and intent of television movies has become. Bob Christiansen and Rick Rosenberg, producers of such television movie classics as *Queen of the Stardust Ballroom* and *The Autobiography of Miss Jane Pitman*, lament that they probably couldn't get either of those telefilms made today because they're not sensational or targeted enough to a specific audience.

Television also cannot compete with the production values, special effects, or box office stars of feature films. The television screen lends itself better to character studies with intense emotional conflict and a powerful yet simple dilemma posed by the situation. A television movie story is smaller and more intimate than a story appropriate for features. Simplicity is important. Television competes with the refrigerator, the telephone, and the other distractions of home viewing. A television movie cannot be so complicated that the viewer who misses a scene or two loses track of the story.

Very few television movies are comedies, although some try to inject humor into the intense drama. Most of the successful telefilm ideas fall into one of three categories:

**A true story.** The author has the rights from one or more of the participants. The story is even better if it was recently in the headlines. But since facts don't necessarily make for the best drama, scripts don't adhere to them. Ideas sold as a true story turn into scripts *based* on a true story. Any sensational new headline can turn into a bidding war for the rights. The saga of a mother in Florida who ordered her sons to kill their grandfather brought over a hundred inquiries about the rights and two competing telefilms on CBS and NBC.

**A book.** Often a best-seller, but not necessarily. Most studios that make television movies scan *Publishers Weekly* for announcements of new books, requesting the galleys of those that have promising television movie premises. Steamy novels are especially popular.

Securing the rights to a book is no guarantee of immediate success. Julianna Fjeld, a hearing-impaired actress, acquired the rights to *In This Sign* and spent ten years trying to interest studios and networks. With sponsorship from Hallmark, the telefilm was finally made by NBC as the Emmy-winning *Love Is Never Silent*, written by Darlene Craviotto.

**A star vehicle.** Stars with high "TVQ" (audience recognition/ popularity quotient) can make any television movie they want because networks believe certain stars provide an automatic hook. Many of them have deals with the networks and studios for just that reason. The major stars have readers who look for good vehicles. Who is high on the television movie list? Valerie Bertinelli, Jaclyn Smith, any major movie star (i.e., Glenn Close in *Sarah Plain and Tall*). Given the "women eighteen to forty-nine" target group, it's not surprising that almost all of the "bankable" television movie stars are women.

Stories on the "don't" list for television movies include: sports stories, disease stories (peaked in the '70's), frontier stories or period pieces (peaked in the '60's) and Biblical epics (peaked in '50's). Space or science fiction stories are discouraged because they look tacky compared to the high-tech values of the *Star Wars* trilogy, *Aliens* and other mega-buck features. Show-biz stories are also a low priority unless they are based on a bestseller or represent the biography of a major star — *Valentino, Malice in Wonderland* (Hedda Hopper/ Louella Parsons). Most stories set in the entertainment industry contain too many in-joke references for a television movie audience.

## HOW DO YOU SELL A TELEVISION MOVIE?

Begin by recognizing the special problems and requirements of the television movie form.

**Know your log line.** Be able to explain the premise succinctly and brilliantly. The hook should be apparent.

The best chance for a writer who has not been approved is to **write the full script**. Odds being what they are, a writer has a better chance of selling it than getting in for a meeting. Most agents give the same advice to their established episodic writers seeking to break into telefilms.

**Make sure the idea can carry** a two-hour movie and that it will fit the form. A television movie has *seven* acts, one short of the eight in the normal two-hour television block. The extra time is devoted to longer first and second commercial acts to allow more time to set up the characters and get the story moving. Most agents and executives agree that a spec television movie should be written in feature film format — no commercial breaks. The script is much more readable that way because of the special problem of six act breaks. Weak television movie scripts suffer from story interruptus — false jeopardies to bring the viewer back after the commercial. As example, a bad commercial break might be a noise outside that terrifies our heroine. (Women in jeopardy is the prototype television movie, after all.) An even worse choice is the first scene after the commercial, where she discovers it was just the cat. Make sure that there are enough good twists and turns in the story that a reader can see where all those breaks could potentially be.

Keep in mind that **television movies can involve lots of rewriting**. Ron Cowen and Daniel Lipman of *An Early Frost* did sixteen versions of that script over a two-year period before it was made. When director John Erman came in, he read each version and asked why they weren't shooting the first draft. The reason: network censors. Eventually, version twelve became the shooting script. Scripts can also be passed on to other writers. Darlene Craviotto, screenwriter of *Love Is Never Silent*, broke into telefilms by doing uncredited rewrites. Much like features, it is not unusual to have more than one writer on a television movie, particularly for the final polish.

The best strategy for new writers is to link up with an established producer in the genre. That producer can then take the story and the writer to the network to pitch the idea. Contact potential producers through friends. The personal referral approach is by far the best: once again, because of lawsuits, many producers are reluctant to hear ideas or read scripts from writers they don't know. The more realistic plan, if you don't know anyone who knows someone, is to watch the credits of telefilms of a similar style to yours and write a letter of inquiry to the producer or production company with a brief summary of the story idea in the text. The letter should identify the hook, whether the story is true, and verify that the writer has (or knows how to get) the rights. This approach is preferable to sending a treatment (unless it's specifically requested); even a short treatment will undercut the writer's chance of pitching the story to the producer. In-person pitching is always the better way to sell an idea.

The test of a good television movie story is:
- Does it have a beginning, a middle, and an end?
- Does the story have good twists at the first and second dramatic act breaks?
- Is it personal enough to hold an audience for two hours through household disruptions and the temptation to "see what else is on?"
- Does the story provide clear, sympathetic characters with complexities that can unfold over two hours?
- Does the story have a point of view — one character with whom the audience can strongly identify and through whose eyes the story is told?
- Does the story fit the form for television movies? Does it lend itself to seven commercial acts with pivotal interesting dramatic points at each break that will lure an audience back?
- Is the story set in a colorful area that will provide texture and movement for the script?

• Does the story provide for a big moment during the first five to ten pages that will hook the viewer or reader?
• Is there a motor or a "ticking clock" on the story that drives it along?
• Is the story an original idea or is it a cliche of the genre?
• Is the story salable as a television movie — a true story, a novel, a compelling contemporary issue? Does it have that all-important appeal to women age eighteen to forty-nine?
• Can the hook and concept be succinctly pitched in a sentence or two?

## MINISERIES

Also known as "multiparters" these are big productions (four hours or more) shown over several nights. The first miniseries was *QB VII* in 1975. *Roots* continues as the prototype and the highest rated miniseries of all time.

The rules for a miniseries are simple:

If you are not an established writer, don't bother.

A hot miniseries idea is either a major historical event or figure (*Nelson Mandela, Billionaire Boys Club, North and South*) or a smash best-selling novel (*Roots, Shogun, Lonesome Dove*). Get the rights, call us.

## EPISODIC PILOTS

Pilots look deceptively easy — create a bunch of stupid characters, put them in a stupid situation, then come up with a couple of pat story ideas and voila! — a television hit. It's an indictment of television that so many writers perceive new shows this way.

Most the new shows are rotten (I like to think that's why audiences turn them off so quickly). One of the reasons shows fail is that so few of them are really "new." The pattern for television over the years is to steal from itself. This year's hit show spawns next season's clones. It's easier to sell a show if it's "like *Cosby*" instead of "unlike anything on television ever." The latter frightens studios (who will have to deficit-finance it), frightens networks (who will have to sell it to their affiliates and advertisers), and frightens advertisers (because they don't think anyone will watch).

The whole system for pilots tends to result in writing by committee. A pilot is a particular victim of meddling from the moment it is first pitched to the date it gets a pick-up. The participants include producers, studios, networks, directors, agents, and actors. Since everyone has a stake in the product, they all have an opinion — thus creating the ultimate group art form. The amazing thing is that *any* pilot is good.

Let's begin by looking at the pilot process. Pilots are not sold from a written script; they're sold from a pitch — first to a production company, then to a network. They are not sold by new struggling writers and producers pitching stories; the pilot market is the province of the established. There is so much money to be made in a series that has a long run on television that the pilot market is where all the big guys compete. After all, they will get "created by" credit and money every episode, executive producer status, and if they are important enough, a percentage of the show in syndication.

In a recent season, the networks (through their separate episodic comedy and episodic drama divisions) heard some five thousand pilot ideas. Of these, roughly seven percent got a commitment for a pilot script. The majority of these commitments go to the producer/writers with the best track records — the people who have delivered hits before. The networks aren't buying ideas at this stage as much as they're buying the *curriculum vitae* of the person pitching, which explains why pilots are such a low percentage gamble for new writers.

Of these three-hundred-fifty pilot scripts, eighty were made (twenty-five percent). What happened in the interim? The studios and the networks probably offered every conceivable suggestion for changing the script — from making it funnier to making it more serious, from making the show an ensemble piece to creating a vehicle for a star.

When the pilot is finally completed it is viewed by executives at the network and then tested. Testing is done at preview facilities.

These screenings measure audience response for: appeal of the show overall, likability of the main characters, and the interest in seeing future episodes. In most testing facilities, the audience members use electronic devices to express their reactions throughout the screening. These readings register on dials in the control booth, so that the producers and network representative know at any moment in the show what the audience thinks (shades of *Network* and *Max Headroom*).

The results of these audience previews are then factored into network decisions about which pilots to "pick up" along with such criteria as demographics (the age groups the program appeals to), available time slots (where the network has weaknesses), counter-programming (what are good alternatives to the programs of other networks?), compatibility (is the show a good companion for other shows?), the mood of advertisers (which kinds of programs are selling well?), the track record and history of the producer with the network, and the executives' personal reactions to or career investment in each pilot.

At the end of this process, selected pilots get a series commitment. Of the eighty pilots made in the season mentioned above, twenty eventually aired. Five survived the first year. From the original five thousand ideas, this computes to a one-in-a-thousand success ratio.

Because the stakes for pilots are so high, many writers and producers sign "development deals" with individual studios and occasionally networks. They may get office space, secretarial support, and a weekly salary to develop ideas for pilots. As added incentive, they receive bonuses if they sell a pilot. But these contracts have also come to be known as "development oblivion." Even though the perks are nice, many writers/producers find the sales process too frustrating. "In retrospect," says producer/writer Deborah Zoe Dawson, "our development deal with Fox was probably a mistake. We didn't have the 'clout' to get a pilot made, and in the meantime all the other shows forgot we existed." Agent Beth Uffner discourages her newer writers from these deals. "Unless you're a major writer/producer that the networks are dying to buy from development can be tantamount to purgatory."

## WRITING A PILOT

The pilot script itself requires a sophisticated level of writing skill. That script must accomplish the following:

• Introduce the regular characters and provide sufficient background for the audience to know them and understand the relationships in a half-hour or hour episode.

• Set the franchise and tone for the show by telling a typical story. The pilot episode establishes the style of humor for the show, the way stories will be told, and the area and locations that audiences will see week after week.

• Show evidence of durability. This is known as the principle of "first and thirteenth." A good pilot introduces the concept for the show and sets up characters in the first episode while also functioning as the prototype for what the thirteenth episode will be like.

The best pitch for a pilot is to describe the main characters, detail the situation or ongoing conflict those characters find themselves in, describe the franchise for the series — how will they get into stories each week — and provide both the plot for the pilot itself and, if the network is still interested, five sample storylines for future episodes.

One of the common approaches to the pilot story is to focus on the moment when the regular characters either meet for the first time or are forced to live or work together. The pilot for *Golden Girls*, for example, began with Sophia's nursing home burning down, so she had to move in with the other three women. *Northern Exposure* began with Dr. Joel's arrival in Alaska. But Chad Hoffman (formerly of ABC) prefers which he call the "seamless pilot" — an episode typical of the show that weaves in the backstory without showing the moment of meeting. *Murphy Brown* began with all the key characters already in place at FYI. In later episodes we learn the history of how they came together.

New series may also evolve out of television movies that garner high ratings or critical acclaim. This was the case for *Cagney and Lacey* and *Twin Peaks*. (When this is planned, the movie is known as a "backdoor pilot"; when it's an accident, it's called luck.) Episodes of ongoing series may also serve this purpose for a network or studio — Richard Mulligan did an episode of *Golden Girls* as a potential pilot for *Empty Nest*. Shows are also created as spin-offs of regular characters from existing shows — *Knots Landing* from *Dallas*, *Family Matters* from *Perfect Strangers*. *All in the Family* holds the record for successful spin-offs: *Maude, The Jeffersons, Good Times, Gloria*, and *Archie Bunker's Place*.

Not all pilots are hour or half-hour shows. *Moonlighting's* first episode, in which Maddie discovered she owned a bankrupt detective agency, was two hours; so were the pilot episodes for *Simon and Simon* and *I'll Fly Away*. But these are exceptions.

There is a distinct season for pitching pilots which runs June through December when the networks declare themselves open to pitches. From January to March the networks are busy supervising the pilots they've committed to (some producers call it interfering), and the networks spend April and May deciding which pilots will go to series and which network executives are on their way up (or out). The search for midseason shows goes on year-round, so increasingly it is possible to pitch to the networks at almost any time.

Because the pilot process is expensive, all of the networks have experimented with alternative approaches. Some series such as *The Trials of Rosie O'Neill* are ordered off the pitch with no pilot because of the clout of the principals. Other producers are given a "presentation order" — a short segment of film, a bible for the show, key casting.

## VARIETY SHOWS

The variety form is one of the most versatile on television. There are variety series (both hour and half-hour), long form variety specials, talk shows (*Letterman* and *The Tonight Show*), awards shows, and one-hour variety specials (such as Bob Hope). Variety shows are most often done on tape with an audience and are the last form of television (other than news and sports) that is still done live. The variety series, other than talk shows, has been on the decline for years. There were sixteen variety shows on network primetime television twenty years ago. By January 1992, there was one: *In Living Color*.

Writers for variety programs are primarily sketch writers. They write comedy routines (two to eight minutes long) that emphasize broad humor. The sketch writer's best weapon is satire — finding humor in poking fun at well-known personalities, popular trends and current events. One staple of the genre is mixing two inconsistent elements — the Church Lady interviews a punk rocker or the homeboy who tries to use an automatic teller machine. The premises are too outrageous to sustain a half-hour story in a sitcom, but pointed, extreme humor is the keynote of good sketch writing.

There are a variety of jobs for screenwriters in this genre. Some shows, such as *The Tonight Show* or *Arsenio Hall*, employ a battery of writers — one group for the monologue, another for the sketches, and a third for questions and answers with the guests. Sorry, all that witty patter isn't improvised — much of it is scripted from pre-interviews before the show.

One of the most accessible markets for new writers is joke-writing. Every comedian buys jokes from the freelance marketplace. Through this system, freelancers get noticed and can become staff writers for their shows. The standard practice is to submit to stars through their agency. (The names of those agents are available from the Screen Actors Guild.) According to Maggie Randall, Joan Rivers's manager, any material submitted to a manager or an agent is almost guaranteed a reading. One-liners (minimal pay) are much sought after. There are even lists available (from Rivers and others) of potential subjects: "frustration with corporations," "dealing with teenagers," "embarrassing situations," etc. Writers will be required to sign a release before the material is read. New talents who catch the star's attention stand a good chance of being encouraged and nurtured.

Tom Perew, staff writer, (*The Tonight Show, Comic Relief*), on retainer with Bob Hope, began his career submitting material by mail (supporting himself by freelancing with greeting cards). Bob Kurtz, Kurtz & Friends Films, also ghostwrote for established comedians. He says a surefire entry is possible by connecting with a performer on the way up. "Hang around the Comedy Store," he says. "Money at the beginning of a career is terrible. Buy thirty gags, use three, pay thirty dollars." But all this can and has led to staff work. Mira Belimirovic (*Letterman, Saturday Night Live*) advises new writers to study a particular show, write sketches for the characters, and submit them with a cover letter to the head writer which introduces the material, the writer (resumé) and intended goals (critique, commissioned assignment, staff). The best timing is a few months before the year's production begins. Belimirovic went into a development position with the Muppets, and while the Henson organization uses staff writing almost entirely, they will consider unsolicited material by mail or through an agent. They, too, require a signed disclaimer protecting the producer from overlapping ideas. There is an eight-week turnaround for perusal, and a phone call then (but not before) is appropriate.

A good writing sample for a variety writer is not a full script, but rather a series of short sketches that are unbelievably funny. More than any other form of primetime television, variety shows tend to read and encourage new writers, and it is often possible to get feedback on submitted material.

Awards shows and special events (*Super Bowl Weekend, Grammy Awards, Miss America*) also fall into the variety genre. Shows such as the *Academy Awards* are granted waivers by the Writers Guild; writers are not paid. This is okay with most writers since the prestige of writing for these shows is the real pay-off. But lesser known events (even those where writers work for free) still can provide valuable contacts and experience. The first time my words were ever heard in public was a benefit for the Musicians Union where actress Esther Rolle read a statement I had written for her. Unpaid and uncredited, I was still thrilled.

CHAPTER NINE

# ALTERNATIVE
# MARKETS:
## SYNDICATION, CABLE,
## HOME VIDEO,
## PUBLIC BROADCASTING,
## DAYTIME SERIALS

There is a finite number of jobs for writers in network television and feature films, and that number has remained consistent in recent years. However, the explosive growth in cable, foreign markets, animation and industrials means those markets are booming by comparison to network television and feature films. For writers who would like to be paid to write as opposed to sitting around waiting for that movie to sell, there is a world of new employment opportunities to explore.

The so-called "alternative markets" (a Writers Guild description) may represent a smaller proportion of income to writers within the Guild, but provide some of the most promising entry level and long-term opportunities for new writers: these markets are less competitive and more accessible. Producers are more likely to share information and many actually encourage new writers to contact them. Alternative markets are also the markets in which the Writers Guild projects the greatest number of new opportunities for screenwriters.

There are five principles to keep in mind as you read about these other options for screenwriters:

**1. The rules for each market are specific to that market.** For example, a good writing sample for a daytime soap is different from that for game shows.

**2. Alternative markets do not pay as well** as the primary markets of network television and feature films; however, as many of the writing jobs available are staff positions, a regular income is easier to come by.

**3. Many of these markets are not covered by the WGA,** so working conditions may not be as protected. There probably won't be residuals.

**4. Feature and television agents don't represent writers in many of these markets.** Even in WGA fields such as pay-cable or home videocassettes, agents don't always keep up with the needs of the marketplace. Writers have to assume responsibility to research and make contacts in these fields on their own.

**5. Success in one of these markets does not necessarily translate** to the others. Newswriting, for example, will be of little help in first-run syndication. Similarly, soap credits in most cases won't do much to improve your employability in primetime television. Remember, "you are what you write." Exceptions to this pattern are noted where applicable.

## SYNDICATION

One of the most confusing concepts in discussing alternative markets is "syndication." The term is used to mean a number of things. When a show is "in syndication," it means that episodes are being shown outside of primetime network programming. A show is in "first run syndication" if it is producing and airing original episodes such as *Wheel of Fortune, Phil Donahue,* or *Star Trek: The Next Generation.* But most of the comedy and drama programs in syndication are *not* original episodes, they are reruns of series. Some of these shows may still be in production (*Wonder Years, Cheers*); most are not. The reruns are purchased for broadcast station by station. The sale is either cash for the right to a specific number of runs of each episode or by barter in which the production company receives a designated portion of the commercial time for each episode. The production company then sells this time in blocks to national advertisers who would not ordinarily place commercials one market at a time. This commercial time is valuable because non-primetime carries a third more commercials than primetime — three commercial breaks per half hour segment.

Since all television shows are deficit-financed in anticipation of future sales into reruns, the syndication market is important to studios — but most shows never make it to syndication. The reason? Not enough episodes. The cut-off is considered to be fifty-two episodes (roughly two-and-a-half years on the network). This allows a series to be syndicated weekly. Even better is one-hundred-fifty episodes (seven years) which allows the show to run daily for six months.

Syndication is also important to the creative people on a show. For any network episodes done after 1972, writers, directors, and actors receive money — "residuals" — each time an episode is shown. Residuals are adjusted to the size of the market and the number of times an episode has run. A successful show in syndication can provide an ongoing source of income for the writers; a show that only lasts a few months on a network will probably never generate rerun money. There are about two hundred national markets for syndication and the various guilds monitor these markets for their members to collect and distribute residuals.

The most successful syndication shows include *M*A*S*H*, *Three's Company*, and *The Cosby Show*. All are half-hour shows. In recent years, the market for hour shows has been soft: while *The Cosby Show* was setting records for syndication rights (over $500 million), *Cagney and Lacey*, available at the same time, sold into only a handful of markets and eventually was purchased by Lifetime. There have been exceptions: the one-hour shows *Magnum P.I.* and *Hunter* have done well in syndication ratings. And one-hour action dramas and soap operas still post strong earnings overseas.

Because shows such as *Taxi* or *M*A*S*H* are still on television, it is common for new writers to do spec scripts for these shows. But since neither is in production, a spec script for these shows is dated. That's why it's important before specing a show to keep track of which syndicated shows are first run — still in production for the networks — and which have finished first-run production. It is also helpful to keep in mind that syndicated shows have been re-edited to allow for more commercials, so the commercial breaks in reruns are not necessarily the commercial act breaks that appeared in the original script.

## FIRST RUN SYNDICATION: EPISODIC

Shows in first run syndication are new shows, produced specifically for the syndication market. Some are among the most popular shows on television: *Wheel of Fortune, Oprah Winfrey, Jeopardy*. These shows are also sold market by market.

For years, the only first-run syndication products were game and interview shows. Now a number of new series are in first-run syndication led by *Star Trek: The Next Generation*, as well as shows dropped by networks that continued off-network (*Baywatch, The Days and Nights of Molly Dodd*). A major player in the market is Fox Broadcasting, still rolling out a full schedule of programs in its bid to become the fourth network. The enormous success of shows such as *Married With Children* and *The Simpsons* has quickly vaulted Fox out of the syndication market and into full network status. There are also first run syndication *Movies of the Week*. Operation Prime Time (OPT) is the main buyer for projects such as *It Came Upon a Midnight Clear*.

The comedy and drama programming in the syndication market is no different from that of the networks, although the budgets are smaller, and writers are paid less because the market coverage reduces income to the studio. Fox shows choose to pay one-hundred percent of comparable primetime dollars per script to attract network caliber writers, but WGA minimums for other first-run syndications are fifty percent of primetime rate.

The writing samples required are full-length hour or half-hour episodic scripts. Network shows are excellent samples if the genre is closely related. The high-prestige syndicated shows such as *Molly Dodd* are considered transferable to primetime television, but many of the syndicated series are lightly regarded. Episodic shows in first-run syndication are virtually all under WGA jurisdiction.

# CABLE

Some of the biggest contenders in the television/film marketplace these days are the pay cable channels — Home Box Office, Showtime, The Movie Channel, Disney Channel, etc. Their influence is felt in a number of ways: competition with networks for viewing audience; co-financing of feature films (so that one pay-cable channel gets the first run of those movies). HBO has such a deal with Paramount: buying completed product from documentaries to specials, and licensing first-run programming just as the networks do.

The core programming of pay cable is still feature films, but the marketplace is changing. Pay cable doesn't live and die by the ratings; instead, the primary goal is to satisfy the viewers so that they will continue to subscribe. As a result, each pay cable company tries to establish an identity that distinguishes it from the others. HBO specializes in made-for-cable telefilms with feature stars such as Elizabeth Taylor and variety specials with Barbra Streisand or Liza Minnelli; Showtime is carving its own identity with direct-from-Broadway musicals and regular episodic series programming such as *Faerie Tale Theatre*. Other stations, such as The Movie Channel and Cinemax, have supplemented the standard fare with uncut, uninterrupted showings of classic films.

Pay cable companies compensate at rates comparable with networks so that they can compete for the same writers, actors, directors, and producers.

## BASIC CABLE

Initial cable service usually includes a variety of stations as part of the package that the viewer does not subscribe to separately. These are called "basic cable" and include: "superstations" such as WTBS (Atlanta), WGN (Chicago), and WOR (New York); other national cable systems such as the USA Network, ESPN (sports), CNN (news), C-SPAN (Congressional coverage), CBN (Christian Broadcasting Network), Lifetime (women's programming, health), Arts and Entertainment Channel (cultural programs); and local or regional stations. To date, there are nearly a hundred basic cable stations available, reaching about seventy percent of the nation. According to Marc Lustgarten (Bravo Channel), the future of cable is in "narrowcasting" to audiences who want more specific programming.

The range of programs in basic cable is eclectic — from episodic series (*The New Zorro*) to nature programs (*National Geographic Specials*) to sports. These stations are a booming market for old television shows (*I Married Joan, Burns and Allen*) and newer shows that didn't last long (*Buffalo Bill, Father Dowling Mysteries*). The stations are providing new life for reruns of hour dramatic shows (*MacGyver*). (Those shows may not be selling well in domestic syndication, but are prime cable fare.)

The payment scales for cable are much lower than for other syndication: *The Cosby Show* brought as much as $400,000 per episode in one market; the hottest hour shows sell for $100,000 into basic cable. Older shows sell for as little as $10,000 each. The market projects that shows on cable may eventually go into the larger syndication market: the audience base reached by cable is still small enough not to compete with syndication. That is the strategy for *Murder She Wrote*, which was sold to USA before going into the syndication market.

Ilene Kahn, Vice-President of HBO Pictures, says "The combination of pay cable and basic cable has a huge appetite." In addition to buying off-network programming, the basic cable industry also does an array of first-run programming. Budgets are consistently lower than the network equivalents; many shows are non-union. Most of them will look at new writers. These are often among the best regional opportunities. The rules of the industry change quickly, so luck favors those who do their research.

## MADE FOR CABLE MOVIES

Cable now produces more telefilms than the four networks combined. Leading the list is Turner Broadcasting, with period-piece films and issue-oriented material that have distinguished its offerings from the trauma-drama nature of network fare. Of particular note was HBO's *The Josephine Baker Story*, which garnered more Emmy nominations than any other program in the 1990 awards. Other major television movie players include Showtime, USA Network and Lifetime.

The aim for most cable companies is quality productions in the $2–4 million range, including biographies, period pieces, thrillers, romantic comedies and personal drama. Each company has its special priorities. Turner is especially interested in luring film stars who are not often seen on television. This includes older stars such as Charlton Heston or Gregory Peck. HBO is looking for big, prestige productions, particularly those with film directors attached, and seems willing to pay more for "event programming." Lifetime tends to buy women-in-jeopardy programming, but the woman should get herself out of the dilemma. And USA is especially prone to thrillers and the horror genre. All will consider comedy, but lighter fare is still a difficult sell. According to Ilene Kahn, the system is far more flexible than the networks: "There is no buying and selling period. HBO's story department is open all year." Additionally, companies such as HBO love to read full teleplays rather than just hear pitches. "We look for provocative projects that viewers cannot see on commercial television," said Kahn, who believes that there is particular future in "prestige little pieces (*Playhouse 90*-type shows) and low budget comedies."

Writers for made-for-cable movies such as Darlene Craviotto and Bruce Singer report extremely favorable experiences: minimal censorship, less studio and network meddling, and far more freedom in structuring the story. According to Craviotto, "It was a joy not to have to worry about the exact page count and the seven act format."

## EPISODIC SERIES

Cable companies look for series product that is an alternative to network fare — offbeat, often controversial. Programs on pay cable do not have to meet the censorship standards of commercial television, and so successful series include *Brothers* (with two gay regulars) and *Not Necessarily the News* (satire about current events). Most companies do not provide development money or pay for pilots. Instead the commitment is for production — as many as twenty-five episodes in the first order. Much like independent studios, companies like Showtime and USA hope that their series will eventually make it into syndication to generate additional revenue.

According to Dennis Johnson, vice-president of original programming at Showtime, "A writer with a series idea should come in with a producer. It helps to be aligned with someone who has a track record." Cable production companies are more inclined to read the work of new writers because they look for ideas and projects that are unusual, out of the mainstream. As with networks, good writing samples for cable are spec scripts from respected network series. Johnson liked a spec *Golden Girls* so much, for example, that he called the producer of that show and arranged for him to meet the writer.

Although union minimums for cable series are roughly sixty percent of network primetime rates, most shows pay equivalent to the networks in order to attract top writers. They earn some of that money back later when residuals are deducted from the over scale payment.

## LOCAL ACCESS

Federal law mandates that every cable company provide opportunities for local groups and citizens to use the airwaves in the form of access channels. Through this system anyone can apply for the chance to be on television and they do, through interview shows, aerobics workouts, and community theatre presentations. Any writer has access to these stations which usually provide the studio facilities for broadcast as part of the package. The writer/producer will need to come up with his or her own financing, material, and a written proposal for what the program will be. While not many people watch, some writers have found that cable access is a useful outlet in which to practice their craft and meet others in the local film and television community. Some enterprising writers have used their access shows to interview film executives, producers, and directors who are scouting locations, thereby creating contacts for the future. And some cable access hosts have gone on to national recognition as is the case with the *Hollywood Kids* (a favorite of Joan Rivers) or *Karen's Restaurant Reviews* (in which Karen spends most of the show kvetching about her life and often doesn't even mention the restaurant).

# HOME VIDEO

The home video market (videocassettes, compact discs, and laser discs) continues as the great unknown for the entertainment industry. The initial boom was in the rental of feature movie videocassettes as evidenced by the proliferation of video stores. There are an increasing number of television programs being released on cassettes (*Star Trek: The Next Generation, Honeymooners,* television movies such as *Sybil*). The most intriguing possibilities lie in made-for-home-video product that bypasses television and motion picture release entirely. The most successful "made for" programs to date have been music videos, exercise tapes, and children's programs. Now, other topics and programming are easing into the market. Some are how-to's on gardening, home repairs, and computers; still others are advice videos — how to save your marriage, how to do your taxes, good sex with Dr. Ruth. Speaking of sex, the home video porn market is booming. Nearly eighty percent of video stores have an "adult" section.

Writers break into the home video market by linking up with small independent production companies that have experience in the sell-through. Writers are hired for the ideas they pitch to the company, or they receive assignments for ideas the company already has. Unless the project is under WGA jurisdiction, there may be only minimal up-front money. Most video deals peg the writers' payments to the success of the video.

Much of this market flourishes in distribution channels outside the neighborhood video store. Direct marketing of cassettes through mail order catalogues and 800 numbers claims a sizeable share of total videocassette sales. While the quality of many of the early "sell through" tapes was poor, the field is becoming much more sophisticated.

*Billboard* magazine has four sub-categories for home video sales: health and fitness, business and education, recreational sports, hobbies and crafts. An average of one-hundred to one-hundred-fifty new videos are released in these combined categories each month. This rate is more than five times the number of feature films released annually.

There is also a potential market for made-for-video entertainment programs. Seth Williamson, vice-president of new product for videocassette at Paramount, said his company is looking for original motion pictures, limited series, and specials that do not air on television but instead can be directly released to the home video market. Some of the most successful programs have been video versions of romance novels, comedy specials, and non-union made-for-video slasher films that were never released in theaters. Many of these are low-budget independent productions or films made outside the U.S. According to romance writer Sydney Stone, for example, the Harlequin/Silhouette romance home videos are filmed in Canada using Canadian writers. Because the market is still unpredictable, studios such as Paramount look for producers who want to co-venture, and therefore assume some of the financial risk.

There has been a tremendous increase in new companies formed to develop video product. It is an industry still in the development stages. New writers are welcome, but they should beware of potentially exploitative working situations. Williamson advises, ''It's smart to approach the home video business as a writer/producer rather than just a writer.'' This not only helps a writer protect his or her project, but it also shows a company that the writer is willing to share the workload and the risk of getting the video made and distributed.

The home video field is by no means confined to videocassettes. In Japan, laserdiscs (also known as laservision) is the number one source for home videos, surpassing videocassettes. Most observers predict that in the U.S., the laserdisc will replace the videocassette in the coming decade.

Writers with ideas for ''how to'' tapes, story concepts that might appeal to an in-home audience, or projects that are uniquely suited to this market should contact production companies of videos and discs directly. The are also an increasing number of books and specialty magazines telling ''how to'' succeed in the ''how to'' business.

# PUBLIC BROADCASTING

The Public Broadcasting Service (PBS) is a loose federation of three hundred non-profit television stations across the country. Known as "public television," this system of commercial-free stations is supported by government funding, grants from corporations and foundations, and local pledge drives that garner subscribers and individual donations.

Programming for PBS is designed to be enlightening and cultural; the system was created to provide quality programming without the pressure of maintaining the high ratings necessary to sustain advertising rates. The trade-off for this freedom is a struggle for operating and programming funds. PBS stations are at a distinct financial disadvantage in competing with their commercial counterparts, but WGA minimums for writers are comparable to networks for national programs. Some projects are prestigious and can lead to work in commercial film and television, but PBS writers complain that it is difficult to parlay credits in public television to other screenwriting markets. Conversely, successful commercial writers do PBS projects at rates substantially below their normal "quote" for the chance to do high quality work without the pressure for mass appeal.

PBS programs arrive at stations for broadcast through one of the following routes:

## NATIONAL PROGRAMMING

These are projects selected for broadcast by PBS — produced by individual stations or by independent producers for national broadcast, and funded by some combination of PBS, Corporation for Public Broadcasting (CPB), corporate and foundation grants. National projects include the ongoing dramatic series *American Playhouse* and *Wonderworks*, as well as limited documentary series such as *The Africans*, *Vietnam*, and *Eyes on the Prize*. Requests for funding from either PBS, CPB, or the national endowments (NEA — National Endowment for the Arts; NEH — National Endowment for the Humanities) are submitted at specific deadlines, set several times annually by the respective agencies. Decisions for allocating public funds are made by panels of professionals chosen for each submission round in conjunction with the agency staff. Most grants from the public agencies represent only partial funding of a project. Programs are also sold once a year at the station affiliates market.

Both *American Playhouse* (primetime adult drama) and *Wonderworks* (primetime family drama) are managed by consortia of stations with central development offices and executive producers. The main *American Playhouse* office is in New York, but scripts and productions come from all over the country. The series has also established American Playhouse Theatrical Features; films by APTF pre-released theatrically before PBS airing include *Testament, El Norte, Native Son,* and *Longtime Companion.* Financing packages are put together as in the rest of the industry, with PBS taking the exclusive network (free television) rights. Single dramas range from sixty minutes to three hours; to date, miniseries have been three to seven hours. Completed plays, original screenplays, and literary adaptations are considered, as well a proposals or treatments.

*Wonderworks* has offices in New York, Pittsburgh, and Los Angeles. It also considers adaptations or original material for sixty minute slots only. Stories focus on children and pre-teens and aim for full family viewing.

Station members of these consortia are:

*American Playhouse* — KCET, Los Angeles
        SCETV, South Carolina
        WGBH, Boston
        WNET, New York
*Wonderworks* — KCET, Los Angeles
        KTCA, Minneapolis
        SCETV, South Carolina
        WETA, Washington, D.C.
        WQED, Pittsburgh

Submissions may be made to any of the member stations or directly to the series' central offices.

Many of these national projects are produced by local stations, and most large-scale projects come to PBS with an endorsement from a member affiliate. Only about a half-dozen stations produce or

package national programming in any quantity. Some of the most prominent producers and their fields of specialty include:
• New York (WNET) — public information programming (*The Brain, Heritage, Civilization and the Jews*), and drama, dance, and music (*Great Performances*).
• Boston (WGBH) — nature and science programming (*Nova*), public affairs documentaries (*Frontline*).
• Los Angeles (KCET) — drama (*American Playhouse* and *Wonderworks*), science (*Cosmos*), public affairs (*Secret Intelligence*), comedy (*Trying Times*).

## LOCAL PRODUCTION

Any PBS affiliate is a potential sponsor of a project. Almost every station, no matter how small, produces programs that are not distributed nationally. Such programs may be documentaries, public affairs, interview shows, special events, children's programming, or comedy/dramatic specials. Writers may contact their regional station for additional information.

## COMPLETED PRODUCT

The PBS system also buys completed product, both foreign and domestic. The most prevalent of these have been programs from the United Kingdom, including series such as *Benny Hill* and *Monty Python's Flying Circus*. Miniseries such as *The Jewel in the Crown* and *Paradise Postponed* were produced with British companies by *Masterpiece Theatre*, managed by WGBH in Boston. The PBS system has also acquired completed domestic programs such as *The Day After Trinity* and *Seeing Red*. Most national PBS programs are done under WGA auspices, depending on the producing entity. Most local programs outside the major markets are not covered by WGA.

# DAYTIME SERIALS

The "soaps" are an unusually specialized market, both because they tend to be based in New York (only three soaps shoot in Los

Angeles) and because the mathematics is unique to the form. As in primetime serials, the hour structure for a soap is five developing stories in each segment — one begins, one ends. Stories are not told in episodes, but in weeks. Each of the stories has one or two major plot points per week. There are also half-hour daytime soaps which have three developing stories per episode. A half-hour soap has three commercial acts; an hour soap has six. There are four to six scenes per act.

Most soaps are organized as follows: the executive producer (often the creator, who supervises the show overall), producer (responsible for production activities), head writer (frequently the co-creator, who supervises the writing staff), breakdown writers (who prepare scene outlines known as "breakdowns" for each episode), and associate writers (who turn breakdowns into dialogue). All writers are WGA. A typical hour soap employs three breakdown writers, who alternate episodes, and five associate writers who each write one episode a week. The schedule is a killer. Unlike other forms of television, the soaps run daily, fifty-two weeks a year. That means that each associate writer is writing an hour episode every week. Bridget Dobson, executive producer of *Santa Barbara*, says "You have to be sort of crazy to write soaps." For several months, she and her husband wrote a hundred pages a day, seven days a week.

The associate writer receives the page breakdown for an episode and has five days to submit the full script. Most staff writers live in the same town in which the soap is produced, but there are west coast writers working on east coast soaps. Soaps write eleven months ahead for the overall view, seven months ahead on a story outline, and two weeks ahead for scripts to air.

Most soaps read the work of new writers year-round. There is a high burnout rate among staff, and replacements are needed quickly. The emphasis in a soap script is on romance, mystery, humor, drama (usually life and death.) Good dialogue skills are at a premium. Stephanie Braxton (*Guiding Light*) encourages mystery writers and romance writers, in particular, to consider the soaps. "You need the ability to write larger than life when dealing with the nitty gritty of daily existence."

If you know someone who will read it, the best writing sample is a series of scenes for the particular show. Or try to get an assignment to write a sample script. The show provides information to be included, but don't expect the script to air since it will be doubled by a version of the same script written by one of the regular writers. Shows will also read samples from other markets, such as feature films or television episodes. For additional information, contact the staff of the soaps you watch.

Periodically there are training programs to develop new soap writers — Procter & Gamble, ABC, and CBS have all been sponsors. By developing contacts with working writers in this market, new writers can keep abreast of these opportunities and sudden job openings on each show.

Certain agents are knowledgeable about soaps. For more detailed information, there is a book about this market, *Writing for Daytime* by Jean Rouvenal. Stephanie Braxton cites a number of advantages in soap writing: "Scripts get rewritten less because of the time pressures, there's relatively steady work, and scripts air within four to eight weeks of writing." She advises, "The only way to write soaps is to genuinely enjoy them. Let people know you want to write soaps and be enthusiastic."

CHAPTER TEN

# ALTERNATIVE MARKETS:

## REALITY PROGRAMMING, NEWS PROGRAMS, MAGAZINE AND INTERVIEW SHOWS, GAME SHOWS, DOCUMENTARIES, INDUSTRIAL EDUCATIONAL TRAINING FILMS

### REALITY PROGRAMS

No television programming wave has caught on more in the '90s than the proliferation of reality programming. Shows such as *Rescue 911, Unsolved Mysteries, Totally Hidden Videos,* and *America's Funniest Home Videos* meet the three basic needs of network television these days: they're popular, they're (relatively) cheap, and, depending on the format, they can be produced in great volume without regard for actors' schedules or a lengthy script development process.

Scripts for many reality shows are done after footage is shot or assembled. The actual script consists of host narration or voice-over. Even the dramatic re-enactments are culled mostly from research notes with story lines that emphasize visuals and interviews rather than dialogue. If segments get too slick, after all, they lose the edge of being "real."

The form has been the mainstay of television since its inception. Shows like *You Asked for It, Ripley's Believe It or Not,* and *That's Incredible* laid the groundwork for the current boom. The reality of reality programming is that it is a much broader field than the narrowly defined concept in vogue at the networks. Reality programming, by definition, is anything non-fiction, and so includes news, documentaries, investigative reports, talk and magazine shows, game shows, award programs, and sports — in short, anything that is real as opposed to made-up. Nevertheless, when the entertainment industry discusses reality programming, it means shows with a central theme divided into short, free-standing segments — some actual, some dramatized: *America's Most Wanted* (the stories of three criminals on the loose), or *Cops* (incidents in the week of the Pittsburgh Police Department). Also falling within the definition are "clips" shows such as *Candid Camera, Bloopers and Practical Jokes,* or *America's Funniest Home Videos,* which string together short clips and videos.

The rules for this market are closest to news and magazine shows, and many researchers, writers, and producers of reality shows have moved over from those fields. Of little transferability to reality shows are credits or writing samples in sitcoms, dramatic series or features since most reality shows are produced in segments and each has its own segment producer, director, and researcher. Segments are mixed and matched to create full episodes. As material is based on actual occurrences, clips or interviews, the role of writer is similar to that of researcher. The writer finds ideas for segments, proposes them, does the research, and then turns the material over to the segment producer and director for production. As a result, most reality shows are not Guild signatories, at least in the early stages. Analyst Chuck Slocum of the WGA says that production companies sometimes sign with the Guild after receiving extended episode orders, when they begin to appreciate the flexibility the Guild allows reality programming, and the benefits the Guild brings to writers on the series. Successful shows also boast larger staffs that may distinguish between pure researchers and writers. *Unsolved Mysteries* currently employs twelve researchers and three writers.

Tom Fuchs (*Crimes of Passion, Ripley's Believe It Or Not*) says that the bulk of reality programming work is basic research reports that summarize the available material, resources, and key points from articles, witness or participant transcripts and interviews, opinions of experts, and other background information. This information is then distilled into four forms:

**The host blurb.** These are on-camera at the beginning and end of the show (Dan Rather on *48 Hours*), or between segments (William Shatner on *Rescue 911*).

**Voice-over.** This is the narration heard during the clips or while a re-enactment is in process. Reality shows try to avoid much on-camera dialogue during action sequences, preferring instead on-camera witness or expert interviews.

**Dramatic re-enactments.** These are scripted carefully to show the key moments of a story, with much of the explanation of what we're seeing handled in voice-over.

**Dramatic monologues.** These are sections where the host tells the story using props that were involved. On *Ripley's* Jack Palance often dressed as characters in the stories to dramatize the points being made.

Writers for these shows must be self-starters who are able to find stories and create their own leads. This is no place to be timid — writers must be comfortable making cold calls, tracking down leads, and calling friends for assistance. Tenacity is the trait that is at a premium.

Stacy Schneider of *Unsolved Mysteries* lists five key skills needed to do research for these shows:

- The ability to listen and distill information.
- The ability to ask the right questions. "Every crazy wants to talk to you. A writer needs to be able to decipher the truth."
- Phone endurance and good phone manners.
- Basic library skills — know where and how to find the source material.
- The ability to translate information to the written page.

Lynn Laurence, also of *Unsolved Mysteries*, adds three other critical skills:

- A good vocabulary.
- An awareness of what's happening in the world so you have a context for your research.
- Computer skills. Much as in news, the ability to store, sort and edit information is critical.

**How to break in:** Because most reality shows are not WGA signatories, few agents know much about this market. Once again, the writer is on his own. The key is to study the structure and style. It is appropriate to call a show and ask for sample segment scripts to see how the form looks on the page. All the writers and researchers we talked to were eager to share insights about a market that is still overlooked. All agreed that the best samples would be written segments for the particular series the writer has targeted. These samples are the best way to prove a writer's ability to capture the storytelling style and tone of that specific show.

Some shows, like *Unsolved Mysteries*, will accept query letters and pay a modest finder's fee for submissions used. Lynn Laurence suggests unearthing an obscure, fascinating story appropriate to a particular reality series and writing a query letter. While it is unlikely you will be involved in the segment if the idea is bought, you will have begun a relationship. The staff will be open to entertaining further queries from you and may even be able to arrange a pitch meeting.

Many writers and segment producers entered the genre as apprentices or interns working for free — ingratiating themselves to the staff, and then interviewing for paid positions as they opened up. Lynn Laurence's try-out for associate producer of *Two on the Town* consisted of submitting one hundred segment ideas (one- or two-line concepts) and identifying a replacement for her job as production manager.

There is good news for "out-of-town" writers. Some reality shows are outside the Los Angeles/New York axis, such as *America's Most Wanted* which is produced in Washington, D.C. — and that's where staff is hired. The industry predicts that more of reality programming will be generated from regional centers in the next few years.

# NEWS PROGRAMS

Writers at the network news departments and at network-owned stations such as Los Angeles and New York are under WGA jurisdiction. Those at NBC, its affiliates and many of the independent stations are National Alliance of Broadcast and Engineering Technicians (NABET). Most writers for local stations are not covered by any union.

Established news writers are often represented by agents who specialize in this field, but agents do not represent smaller markets. News writing requires a strong sense of current events and knowledge of resources for research and investigation. In regional stations, the news anchors frequently are responsible for writing their own material. The style is different from newspaper and magazine writing; the emphasis is on short, dynamic summaries of news items. The average time per news event is only thirty seconds. The writing has to capture the emotion, humor, or importance of a story in what amounts to a *Reader's Digest* format in language comfortable for a news anchor to read aloud.

The writing sample required is usually a series of sample fifteen- to sixty-second news reports. Bob Compton (KNBC News, Los Angeles) says the requirements are specific: "Be fast, good, have clear writing skills, and bring something to the piece."

Prospective writers may be invited to the studio and put in a room to prepare news reports from the wire services. Inexperienced writers can intern (for no pay) in the news departments of a local station to develop skills and background. Eventually, the interns may be hired by that station or use their credits to move to another station or market as a paid staff writer. An excellent approach is to apprentice as part of a college work/study program.

# MAGAZINE AND INTERVIEW SHOWS

While network news programs such as *60 Minutes* and *ABC Special Reports* are under WGA or NABET jurisdiction, most syndicated magazine interview shows are not. These include *Oprah!, Hard Copy*, and local/regional programs. These shows do not hire writers, but rather producers, segment producers, and associate producers who "just happen to write." These producers end up writing introductions, guest questions, and segues. In small markets, one producer may do all of these tasks. In the smallest markets, the host may write everything.

The advantage to a writer is the opportunity to learn a variety of skills — writing, producing, even directing and phases of production. Writers have an edge on competing for producer jobs because of their writing skills. The production schedule for these shows is a notorious killer. Many film six or seven shows a week, doubling up episodes so that all the taping is done in three days.

According to supervising producer Darlene Hayes (*Phil Donahue, Montel Williams*), "Everything happens yesterday." Writers with a knowledge of production do especially well. On a typically successful daily show there will be five producers (one per episode each week) and five associate producers, working under a supervisor or executive producer whose job is akin to air traffic controller.

Writing is confined primarily to introductions of guests, summary research on the day's topic, sample questions for the host drawn from pre-interviews and research, and the ever-popular promos. The magazine/interview market is so competitive these days that the fifteen-second promos for each episode are critical to attracting audience. Hayes describes the challenge as "How can I get the sexiest hook in the shortest possible sentence?" Episodes with entertainment-oriented guests require more written material than those that are issue-oriented.

The writing skills needed remain the same: the ability to write in succinct, colorful, compelling, dramatic language that fits the tone of the show and the personality of the host. Good samples for this genre include news writing, short documentary scripts, reality show segments, advertising copy, and commercials. Many shows have intern programs, and this is an excellent way to experience production firsthand and develop professional relationships.

Writers sometimes overlook their other options in the magazine/interview market: public relations and promotion departments. *Donahue* and *Oprah!*, for example, have departments for both. In these departments, writing skills are a prerequisite. Public relations is responsible for information that goes to the public and press about the show, its star, and the staff. This information includes bios, news releases, and speeches. The promotion department handles information that goes out for commercial purposes, including *TV Guide* loglines, newspaper ads, and television promos. Public relations and promotion provide an excellent opportunity for a writer to get noticed as producer material for the show.

Credit on magazine and interview shows are transferable to other programs in this market, but mean little in episodic television or features. Producer Hayes, for example, winner of three daytime Emmys, arrived in Los Angeles to discover that to be a primetime writer she had to do spec scripts for sitcoms.

## GAME SHOWS

Writers are paid to create the games, write the questions, and punch up the answers of contestants on shows like *The Love Connection*. There is even a career to be had in writing descriptions of the prizes ("Yes, Pat, this elegant bedroom set . . ."). The positions are full-time and, in most cases, not under WGA jurisdiction. Writers are often hired as "researchers" to escape WGA contract. There may be as many as six or seven writers on a show such as *The Family Feud* which aired twice a day.

New writers are hired through interviews and an assessment of writing skills. Previous work on game shows is the preferred writing sample, but failing that, applicants may be asked to submit material specific to the show — questions for the game, sample prize descriptions, or patter for the host. This can be a controversial practice, since on more than one occasion questions written by applicants have turned up on the games, even though the writer was not hired.

Many companies that produce game shows are open to new writers and freely answer questions and provide information. Interestingly, most are also willing to hear pitches for new game show ideas from just about anyone. Pitches are screened over the phone; if the idea has potential, its creator will be invited to come in to pitch to the staff after signing a release form to head off lawsuits. The company may option the idea and put the writer on salary to develop it or put it into their own development system.

Be warned that developing a good game show is not easy. There are some basic rules. The game has to be playable within eighteen minutes with an exciting "bonus" round at the end. It must be compelling for the home viewer (the "hook" in game show parlance), and it must be exciting for both contestants and viewers. The best ideas are based on childhood games — *Hollywood Squares* is tic-tac-toe; *Wheel of Fortune* is hangman. Marilyn Wilson of Dick Clark Productions emphasizes that the game is the most important element. "We don't want to know the scoring system, the staging, or the gimmicks. We want to know what the game is."

Robert Noah, executive producer of *Sale of the Century*, says "Job openings on shows come up quickly and have to be filled fast." Consequently, many producers interview anyone who inquires even if there is not a job opening at that time. Wilson suggests that writers follow the trades: "When you read that a company is doing a pilot, contact it immediately with writing samples."

Some of the newer opportunities for game show writing are on cable stations seeking original, low-cost programming. MTV, Nickelodeon, USA Network, and Lifetime have all experimented with their own versions of game shows such as *Double Dare* and *Supermarket Sweep*.

## DOCUMENTARIES

The image of documentary film-making is that of the purest form of screenwriting. A writer/producer with a burning need to tell the world about a particular issue spends years bringing a project to fruition, invests his or her life savings, and commits everything to putting the message on film. In this case, the reality is close to the myth. The success of most documentary film-makers is born out of their passion for their subject.

There is a thriving market for documentaries that includes public broadcasting, local independent stations, cable, home video, and even theatrical release. And it is possible to make a living specializing in this market.

The bad news is that the primary demand is for completed work: projects that are already written, produced, and financed. As with many of the alternative markets, writers become producers, directors, even narrators. Documentary writers become fund-raisers as well. They raise money through grant proposals to the Corporation for Public Broadcasting (CPB), the National Endowment for the Arts (NEA) or the National Endowment for the Humanities (NEH), and state arts and humanities councils; requests to corporations, foundations, charitable organizations; and from individuals. Successful appeals are usually in the form of pitch presentations with accompanying treatments or a demo reel. Through these presentations some documentary producers are able to garner distribution contracts before completion of the film, an invaluable tool in the fund-raising effort.

Steve Brand, a film editor at ABC News, spent seven years completing *Kaddish*, a critically acclaimed documentary about the experience of growing up as a child of a Jewish holocaust survivor. Brand received support from the National Endowment for the Humanities, but was finally forced to scrape together $60,000 of his own funds to finish the film which played in art circuit theatre around the country.

Similarly, Steve Okazaki conceived of and directed *Unfinished Business: The Japanese American Internment Cases*, which was nominated for an Academy Award. Okazaki found funding for this personal project from the Corporation for Public Broadcasting and private sources. The film has done well in sales and rentals to schools and libraries.

The Writers Guild newsletter has published a number of upbeat reports on the future of the documentary. One such article stated, "The straight documentary is getting a major rebirth — you guessed it — via videocassette." One program, *The Mysteries of the Titanic*, came out first on cassette, then went to television. "Today, writers in and out of the Guild are being given assignments to write sponsored industrial documentaries on powerful social subjects — AIDS, pollution, computer ethics, and government contract fraud," says writer Kirby Timmons. Major new sources for television exposure include the Arts & Entertainment Channel, the Discovery Channel, and HBO. The latter financed the acclaimed *Dear America: Letters Home from Vietnam* and *Stories from the Quilt.*

The processes for conceiving, funding and distributing documentaries are complicated. The best advice to writers interested in this market is to contact the various organizations that support independent film and documentary producers. Among the most prominent are:

• **The Film Arts Foundation.** Serves film and video makers through Northern California as well as members in other regions of the country. Among its services, FAF provides low-cost equipment and facilities rental, non-profit sponsorship for fundraising efforts, monthly classes, and a regular newsletter. Julie Mackaman, development director, urges prospective documentary writers/producers to contact them early in the process, so Film Arts Foundation can get would-be producers pointed in the right direction.

> Film Arts Foundation
> 346 Ninth Street, Second Floor
> San Francisco, California 94103
> (415) 552-8760

• **International Documentary Association.** This membership organization recognizes the importance of documentaries through an annual award show, film festivals, workshops, and seminars. There is a monthly newsletter free with membership and a "Survival Guide."

> International Documentary Association
> 1551 S. Robertson Blvd. #201
> Los Angeles, California 90035
> (310) 655-7089

• **Association of Independent Video and Filmmakers (AIVF).** A national membership organization based in New York. Publishes *The Independent,* which provides information on production, funding sources, film festivals, and strategies for planning and selling independent film and videos. AIVF also offers insurance programs, advocacy on behalf of independent filmmakers, screenings, seminars.

Association of Independent Video and Filmmakers (AIVF)
625 Broadway, Ninth Floor
New York, New York 10022
(212) 473-3400

In addition, writers are advised to write to networks or PBS for a script from a documentary in order to see how they are put together. Pay particular attention to the story-telling structure of documentaries. The best are not a dry listing of facts or unconnected sequences. The best documentaries tell compelling stories with a clear beginning, middle, and end.

# INDUSTRIAL/EDUCATIONAL/TRAINING FILMS

Many screenwriters are too starry-eyed at the Hollywood/New York connection to see or consider opportunities to write screen images outside traditional network television or feature films. The largest producer of media product in this country, for example, is not Universal Studios or NBC, but the federal government. And the largest amount of film produced is in the rapidly expanding informational film market. Millions of dollars are spent each year by the various levels and departments of government, by social service and political organizations, and by industry for training, educational, and instructional films. Some of these films make their way into mainstream markets via cable, PBS or video stores, but most are for local consumption. And somebody had to write them.

This was the realization of the Writers Guild in 1988, when a side letter was added to the Minimum Basic Agreement to allow Guild jurisdiction over informational films. The terms of the agreement are unlike those for any other area of Guild jurisdiction. No minimums are established and companies themselves have the option of executing the letter of adherence. The terms are binding upon the company for that project only. According to WGA information films committee member, David Vowell, ''In comparison to the rights and protections guaranteed by the Minimum Basic Agreement for writers working in other areas, it may not seem to be much. But for information film writers, any recognition represents a major gain.''

The specifics of that gain are that writers will be able to use informational film experience as credits towards joining the WGA and maintaining eligibility; the signatory company will make pension and health contributions for the writer; and in the long term, it is anticipated that there will be some standardization of rates and working rules.

So why is the Writers Guild so interested in this new jurisdiction? Because, according to WGA analyst Chuck Slocum, the informational market is "the most accessible, diverse and dispersed market for WGA writers in the U.S." The Guild found that many of its members were already working in this market without Guild benefits. In many cases, informational films provided the main source of income for writers while film and television were supplemental. Some very successful Guild writers work in informational films including Brent Maddock (*Short Circuit*) and writers/producers Ken Cinnamon and Karen Wengrod (*Who's the Boss?*).

Estimates of the market for informational films are: $15 billion in annual sales, twenty-five percent of all video sales, fifty thousand currently available titles. Additionally, there are at least fifty companies, including GTE and Sears, that maintain private satellite networks to produce and buy informational films for use as sales tools, to conduct employee training, and to function as internal video newsletters for employees.

The informational film market is often summarized as the three "I"'s:

- **Informational films:** similar to documentaries, they present information in an interesting, entertaining way.
- **Instructional films:** information is presented in a structured manner to teach an audience a given set of concepts, skills or procedures.
- **Infomercials:** a combination of an informational film and a commercial. Sometimes called "sponsored videos," they present information as part of a sales pitch for a product or service.

Major clients for informational films include:

- **Government:** Almost every division of federal, state, and local government produces training materials, public service films, and promotional pieces.
- **Corporations:** An increasing number of corporations have established in-house audio-visual departments. Some produce dozens

of films each year through the marketing or public relations departments, including those films designed for sale to other companies
on generic topics such as workplace safety or effective
communication.

• **Audio/visual production companies:** There are lots of these companies in every major city that bid on projects or are on retainer with
individual groups or companies. Some are too small to hire freelance
writers.

• **Ad agencies, public relations firms, graphic design firms:** They
have contracts with specific clients.

• **Non-profit groups:** Hospitals, research organizations, charitable
institutions, and political groups are major producers of informational films both as part of public education efforts and also as fund-
raising tools. Some production companies specialize in this market.
Writer Sunny Fader (*Quincy*) finds this market particularly reward-
ing. "Unlike ordinary 'show biz,' you will be treated with respect
and often great love. The most important qualification to work with
the non-profit sector is a genuine concern for the issue you're writing
about."

With the growth of the industrial film market, there has been
increasing specialization. Cindy Skalsky was described by one producer as "queen of the industrials" — a title she accepts "with a
great deal of suspicion." Her specialty has been the automotive industry, which seventy years after introducing the sales film as a way
to promote new car models for far-flung dealerships, is still one of
informational film's most voracious consumers.

The pay scales for informational films are substantially less than
for comparable network television or feature film programming and
may vary widely. There is a consensus that basic rates average $200
per minute of film time or a flat rate of $5,000 for a twenty-two
minute film. This, by the way, is almost identical to the WGA rates
for a thirty-minute or less low-budget documentary. Pay is contingent on additional work that might be required. Since many informational films are part of a larger training presentation it is not
unusual for the film writer to be involved in development of supplemental training manuals, workbooks, or print materials; or-
chestration of live meetings or demonstrations where the film will
be screened; development of multi-image presentations which mix

film, slide projection, live stage activities, and participant activities. WGA analyst Slocum points out that live industrial presentations are also eligible under the WGA letter of adherence.

Most writers in the industrial film market describe the requirements of the writing itself as identical to those of any good film script. According to Slocum "drama, comedy, interesting characters, recognizable situations, and unexpected plot twists are all basic expectations of viewers no matter what form they're watching." Larry Tuch (*Quincy, Columbo*) concurs: "Informational films are not slumming. They are no longer boring, poorly imagined films we watched in biology twenty years ago. The best are carefully crafted, tell a story, and present information in a way that is compelling and not linear."

In a move still further away from the old, boring image, the new generation of informational film is interactive. Frank Binney, an Academy Award documentary film-maker, spends much of his time designing interactive videodiscs for museum exhibits. Museum patrons touch the screen of a monitor to indicate which subject they wish to explore. From there, the viewer controls the flow of information by making choices. According to WGA informational films committee member Michael Utvich, the key to the success of such a program is its depth. The writer must constantly anticipate the range of choices a viewer might make and create the material to answer them. The technology is already in widespread use in airports providing travelers with information about local areas of special interest, at malls where kiosks provide interactive information on stores, and at trade shows where clients can ask the tough questions about new products. Who answers those questions? Often, it's the corporation president (on tape, of course). Writer Kristen Anderson (Health Net) may well represent the most in-demand hyphenate of the future: she is a writer/computer-graphic artist.

## HOW DO WRITERS BREAK IN?

As with most of the other alternative markets, informational films are not represented by agents. Step one is to research the local industry. Check telephone listings for production companies, audio/visual companies, government agencies, local *Fortune* 1000 companies that might have their own audio/visual departments, advertising agencies, and public relations firms. Remember that this industry is centered in metropolitan areas outside Los Angeles and New York, so there may be a booming business in your community — it's just a matter of finding it.

Through these companies, try to identify the individuals who work within the field. Producers, directors, and writers of informational films in a regional market usually know each other. There may be a trade or membership organization you can join. Also, many informational film writers belong to writing groups. Some groups, such as Scriptwriters Network in Los Angeles, have subcommittees and events that address the needs of the industrial film members.

There are also a number of regional directories, newsletters, and trade publications that list companies involved in advertising, production, and support services. Contact your local film board to learn about these directories. For government contracts, Charles Wallace, who has produced over five hundred informational programs for various governmental agencies, suggests contacting:

- The National Audio Visual Center
  8700 Edgeworth Drive
  Capitol Heights, Maryland 20743
  (301) 763-1896

NAVC publishes a directory ($10) which lists the agencies that contract for writing and/or production services. A national membership organization is also recommended:

- International Television & Video Association
  6311 N. O'Connor Road
  LB 51
  Irving, Texas 75039
  (214) 869-1112

ITVA publishes directories of active producers and has a variety of regional affiliates. There are also courses available at many universities and colleges.

Above all, those working in the informational film industry encourage new writers to consider that market as a serious option to dead-end jobs. Industrial films can pay the rent while the writer waits for that first big feature break. "After all," says Charles Wallace, "You will get paid. For writing."

# CHAPTER ELEVEN

# ALTERNATIVE MARKETS:

## ANIMATION, CHILDREN'S PROGRAMS, FOREIGN MARKETS, RADIO, PLAYWRITING, COMMERCIALS, SPONSORED PROJECTS

### ANIMATION

All forms of animation employ writers, but, surprisingly, animation writers are not under WGA jurisdiction. As a result, there are no residuals and pay scales tend to be lower than the equivalent product in other markets. Also, much of the animation process has moved to foreign markets — Taiwan, Korea, Ireland, and Latin America — because of lower labor costs. However, the production companies are still based in the U.S. where the scripts are written.

The market has grown beyond Saturday morning cartoons. It extends to features, commercials, industrial and educational films, primetime series (*The Simpsons*), primetime specials (*Charlie Brown*), segments of children's shows (*Sesame Street*), and the booming new market of computer graphics (music videos, network promotions, and computer animation). The success of films such as *Who Framed Roger Rabbit?*, *The Little Mermaid*, and *Beauty and the Beast* have fueled tremendous growth in the amount of animation product. By all accounts, animation is one of the fastest-growing segments of the entertainment industry.

The core audience for Saturday morning cartoons is six-to-eight-year-olds. As a result, these shows have to have clear characters, an easy-to-follow plot, and jokes that can be seen as well as heard.

While most production executives in children's programming are women, nearly eighty-five percent of the writers are men. As a result, there's an effort to encourage more women to explore animation writing. Anne Simon (ABC Children's Programs) believes women can add "warm, nurturing feelings children need" to the script. The executive suggests specing an episode for a show, then approaching the production company (Hanna-Barbera, Ruby-Spears, Filmation, etc.). Formats and sample scripts are sometimes made available when writers request them. A warning: lawsuits have been a particular problem in animation. Bob Kurtz (Kurtz and Friends Films) hates unsolicited scripts because ideas so often coincide with projects they have underway. Kurtz prefers to meet writers in person who sign a waiver and *then* he will hear their ideas. Similarly, Susie Marks at Disney says that they no longer consider unsolicited material. Writers for Disney projects come almost entirely through friends or recommendations.

Disney and Sullivan Studios (*An American Tail*) are both major producers of animated features. Budgets are $16–20 million, and films are often developed by buying the rights to published books. These projects rely heavily on humor, "but not the Saturday morning kind," says Susie Marks. Both the humor and writing in long-form animation should be subtle and character-based.

The possibilities and future of animation have not gone unnoticed by other major studios. Universal partnered with Hanna-Barbera for *The Jetsons: The Movie*, Fox has had a feature length version of *Tom & Jerry* in process for a number of years, and nearly every studio has at least one or two animated features or television series in development. The activity has attracted the attention of writers and producers who might have disdained the market in the years pre-*Roger Rabbit*. Some cross-over writers include Caroline Thompson (*Edward Scissorhands*), Isaacs & Levine (*Cheers* to *The Simpsons*). My animation education came when I was hired to do a final polish rewrite on *The Jetsons: The Movie*; it was a sort of crash course on how animation writing is unique. To begin with, good animation writing must be extremely visual. The best moments are not in the dialogue but in the drawing. According to Anne Simon and Jenny Trias (ABC Children's Programs,) writers need a good visual sense and the ability to translate humor to images. "If it's not in the script, it won't be on the storyboard, and, therefore, it won't be on the screen." After all, anything is possible. George Jetson can do a quadruple flip and land back in his chair.

A writer has to let his imagination go. A script that does not take advantage of the unlimited possibilities of the medium is not an animation script. I learned this on my first rewrite. "We love the new dialogue." gushed the producer, "but our people don't know what to draw." I had given them a live action script, not an animated one.

This does not mean animation writers throw out all principles of dramatic structure. On the contrary, the pace of good animated features is so frantic (try diagramming *Roger Rabbit*), that structure, theme, and plot become even more important. Writers should study an episode of *The Simpsons* to see clear, inventive use of the three-act structure.

Because of the need for visual details, animated scripts tend to have far more stage directions than a live action script. Those stage directions should provide lots of movement so the pacing is fast — and they can't be subtle. Subtle is simply too hard to draw. After all, there are voices to interpret a writer's work, but no faces. Sound effects are important. The writer must add the odd noises and exaggerated sounds that amplify the humor or the plot of the story.

Most animation houses also sub-produce for advertising agencies of clients who provide finished scripts for industrial and educational films.

A telephone inquiry will ascertain which studios will work with freelance talent. According to Janet Macotie (development at Hanna-Barbera,) her company works almost entirely with in-house talent, but will add freelance writers during a hot season. Both freelance and staff are chosen from an open resume file; samples of written or produced work are sought. Hanna-Barbera also runs a free, semi-annual training program for prospective animation writers. As interest in animated product has increased, so have the companies that supply it. Very popular are computer animation companies that provide cartoon animation and special effects for films such as *Terminator 2*.

Additionally, some production companies and shows buy completed short films. Producer Edith Zornow of the Children's Television Workshop (CTW) says her staff will screen any submitted reel of sample animation, since most CTW animation is sub-contracted. There are also a number of festivals and competitions that showcase animated material and provide valuable exposure and recognition for the creators.

# CHILDREN'S PROGRAMS

Live-action children's programming takes three major forms: on-going network/PBS series (*Sesame Street, Mr. Rogers' Neighborhood*), after-school specials, and the children-oriented cable stations such as Nickelodeon, the Family Channel, and Disney. On-going series have a staff of writers who generate scripts for the show in collaboration with the host or other talent. Much of the material may be improvised during the taping. The producers of these series don't buy freelance ideas, but they do interview writers for future staff openings. Children's Television Workshop in New York has a writers' workbook available. Staff writers on nationally syndicated programs are covered by the WGA; those on local programs are not.

All three networks, PBS, and some companies active in the syndication market produce specials for children. These are most often one-hour and designed for telecast in the afternoon. The best approach is to identify the production companies who specialize in this market by watching samples of the form on television and then contacting the companies directly. Eda Hallinan, a recent director of children's specials at ABC, said she would consider unproduced writers but not unrepresented writers: "I need to know someone beside your mother thinks you can write." A good sample script is a longform — no half-hour samples. "Someone with a light touch is welcome."

The audience for after-school specials is primarily teenage girls and young women. Any thought-provoking subject can be dealt with — teen pregnancy, AIDS, alcoholism — as long as *it involves the protagonist of the story* (usually a teenage girl) and not her immediate family or best friend. Network executives assume they have a new audience every four years, so they don't mind repeating a subject if a different "take" can be developed.

The biggest new markets for children's programs are the burgeoning children and family-oriented cable stations — the Disney Channel, Nickelodeon, the Family Channel. Their programming is a mix of reruns of old programs (*Lassie, Davy Crockett, Flipper*), remakes of old series (*The Mickey Mouse Club*), cartoons, and new series and specials. Economics dictate that new programming be low-cost, so kid-hosted talk shows and game shows are popular, but there are efforts to develop original series (*The New Zorro, Hi Honey, I'm Home*).

## FOREIGN MARKETS

The impact of globalization of American business has been dramatic in the film and television industry. Non-U.S. companies now own many of the major U.S. studios — 20th-Century Fox (Murdoch of Australia); Universal (Matsushita); Columbia (Sony); and MGM (briefly, Paretti of Italy). Beyond these mega-acquisitions, there have been scores of smaller purchases and investments in independent companies, production facilities, and suppliers. Most observers believe the acquisitions have provided much-needed infusion of capital, but there is a question about the consequences for the product that will be generated.

American producers are unaccustomed to sharing power and control. In the past, foreign companies invested money in American films — not ideas. The idea was "only we know how to do it, thanks for the bucks, we'll tell you how it turns out." No longer. Foreign investors are increasingly insisting on participating as equal — or greater than equal — partners. A co-production these days means just that.

As a result, America lags behind the rest of the world in its co-production efforts. No major work is produced in Canada, Australia or Europe that is not a co-production among several countries. The product is too expensive, there's too much risk, and no individual country has a large enough market to consistently afford its own programs, particularly telefilms and hour series.

Until recently the United States was the exception. While our industry is heavily dependent on foreign box office for films, a theatrical did not have to be a big hit overseas to make money. Now, however, U.S. box office has been flat. By the early '90s the foreign market share had exceeded fifty percent. Suddenly, foreign audiences became not only the gravy for American films, but the critical factor in a film breaking even.

Similarly, in television, American companies have been able to produce series for U.S. networks with a goal to break even on the network telecast and turn a profit in syndication and overseas sales. But the domestic syndication market, especially for hour shows, has nearly collapsed — and other countries are rushing to place quotas on the amount of American television allowed to air in their primetime in an effort to encourage local production. American producers, as a result, are under pressure to co-produce series that can evade the quota restrictions.

Nowhere is the increasing importance of co-productions as apparent as in the revival of the television movie business. Theatrical-length presentations are very popular overseas; for U.S. producers, pre-sales and co-productions provide the vital funds necessary to turn a profit. Many American telefilms even play initially in foreign markets as theatricals. As co-productions with Canada, Britain, or Germany, these films compete for the licensing fees of the prime-time marketplace.

There are further changes far beyond co-productions. For the first time, American networks are buying foreign productions to air in primetime. This was the case for *Love and Hate,* by Suzette Couture, a Canadian production with no American participants, which aired on CBS in 1991. CBS has also experimented with co-produced series in its late-night slots. A wheel of five action/adventure shows produced variously by Canadian, Spanish, French and U.S. companies has provided first-run programming at vastly lower licensing costs. Not that the quality of these series is any good, but they're cheap.

Is this good news or bad news for American writers? Well, the outlook varies, depending on the genre.

## FEATURE FILMS

American films so dominate the world box office, both through the style of story-telling and the strangle-hold on distribution, that it is unlikely we will see blockbuster foreign films cutting into the American share anytime soon. The heyday of the foreign film in the U.S. market was the '60s. Only *Cinema Paradiso* in recent years has enjoyed the success of those earlier efforts. Exceptions include occasional English-language films such as *Crocodile Dundee, Hope and Glory, Chariots of Fire*, but without an American producer to guarantee distribution these efforts are risky.

Foreign markets and ownership will have an impact, however, on the *kinds* of films Americans make. The prevailing wisdom is that action-adventure films translate better to overseas markets. Films such as *Hudson Hawke* — at best, marginally successful in the U.S. — made much more money overseas. High-quality productions are in demand. U.S. writers will continue to have an advantage in the international feature marketplace because of the American story-driven movie style, but the market for comedies and dramatic films may be limited. There has already been an impact on stories featuring female stars: the prevailing wisdom, subject to much controversy, is that only male stars can open a movie overseas.

## TELEVISION MOVIES

Many American companies that had dropped out of the television movie business have now re-entered, and an increasing number of their projects are co-productions, especially with Canada and England. This change has worked to the special benefit of writers, directors, production personnel, and actors from those countries because the nationality of each of those elements is a factor in qualifying as local production. Since television movies emphasize dialogue and character over plot, the advantage of the American writer is not as great.

## SERIES

The biggest difference between American programming and that of other countries has been in series television. Historically, foreign companies have tried to do series television as if they were doing motion pictures: long shooting schedules (rather than the seven days of an American hour show), and limited orders (six to ten episodes rather than twenty-two). But lengthy production periods make the cost of the individual episodes prohibitive, and show orders don't allow expensive start-up costs to spread over the full run of the show. When companies operated with sizeable government subsidies, these problems could be overlooked; now the proliferation of commercial channels throughout Europe and Asia makes that style of doing television too expensive.

Another major difference between American series television and these other markets has been the nature of the product itself. The sitcom, for example is a British and American invention. Relying on word-play and humor, sitcoms have not found a wide overseas audience. Retaining the rhythm of the humor and dialogue is too difficult to translate. Far more successful exports have been action shows like *Hunter* and soap operas. *Dynasty* and *Dallas* were big hits overseas and a number of American daytime soaps such as *One Life to Live* play in primetime abroad. Therefore, it is in these genres where foreign companies have made the most serious attempts to break the American monopoly.

One of the biggest such efforts has been in France, with production of the steamy soap opera *Riviera*. The original production was set up by Americans — production personnel, directors, writers — and they trained their French counterparts in the American style of production of a soap opera.

*Lucky Luke*, a one-hour comic western that I helped create for European television, took a different tact. The series is based on a popular European comic book series about the American west. Producers Terence and Lori Hill chose to shoot in New Mexico, in English; however, the key production positions were filled by Europeans: the line producer, art director, assistant director, costume designer, and animal trainer. From the outset, the principals sought American writers with experience or samples in the one-hour form to ensure that scripts would have the structure and pacing of an American production. My contributions were to help set up the franchise for the show; i.e, the creation of a base for the series, development of the regular characters, and establishment of the style and tone of the story-telling. *Lucky Luke* had been pre-sold throughout Europe. The intent was to sell the series to the American market for profit — the reverse of the traditional pattern.

## HOW TO BREAK INTO FOREIGN MARKETS

There is no question that there is increasing interest in American-style writing, and increasing opportunities for American writers. However, finding the legitimate companies that might buy your idea can be frustrating. Even more than in the U.S., the foreign entertainment industry runs on relationships and personal connections. In most countries, there are no agents for writers, no Writers Guild, and, consequently, no minimum standards for payment or working conditions. Convincing a foreign company to become a Guild signatory (as was done with *Lucky Luke*) is often the reason WGA members have not been able to land foreign assignments. There is erroneous fear of American unions. In some cases, it is justified. Horror stories are rife about writers not paid, expenses not reimbursed, and promises not kept when working for foreign companies outside union jurisdiction. Be careful.

Many of the larger agencies have agents charged with tracking foreign developments: they attend film festivals and markets, meet with visiting executives from foreign companies, and monitor the activities of key companies. Even smaller agencies will have connections with particular companies in each market and will know, at least to some degree, of upcoming opportunities. Most knowledgable of the foreign markets, however, are independent producers and production companies that have been successful in the pre-sales and co-production businesses. Some major companies such as Carolco, DeLaurentis, and Cannon have built their reputations on foreign connections.

For the new writer without access to these resources, the best approach is to look at your personal connections. Do you have friends and relatives in other countries who could introduce you to members of the film community? If you work in a non-entertainment business, are there work connections abroad that could be parlayed into introductions?

Also highly recommended are visits to international film festivals and the myriad of film markets, both inside and outside the United States, where there is the chance to meet aspiring producers and foreign production companies who are also trying to get "inside."

# RADIO

Some writers are surprised to learn that radio writing is under the jurisdiction of the Writers Guild. Before television radio was the public medium and it has a long history of drama, comedy and informational programs — many of which eventually moved to television (*Jack Benny, Amos & Andy, Playhouse 90*).

Radio today is mostly confined to music, news, talk shows and call-ins; radio drama and comedy shows have fallen on hard times. Most radio executives say that no writer is making a full-time living in radio. Instead, information programs such as *All Things Considered*, radio talk shows, and the patter between top forty hits are written by the announcers.

The stations that buy radio drama look for product that is already written, directed, and taped. Even then, the option fees are minimal. National Public Radio (NPR) with three hundred member stations, for example, is in the premiere position in the country to buy original drama, yet their average rental/option payment is less than $200 per program — far less than the cost of producing the project.

The irony is that airtime would be available if there were more product. Producer Charles Michelson buys the rights to old radio shows and sells them to a variety of stations. He doesn't have enough shows for the demand, but has found that funds to produce new ones are not available. He adds, "there aren't many people left today who know how to write for radio; they don't know what sound effects to use, for example, or how sound effects are made." Steve Barker (BBAT Productions) suggests *The Techniques of Radio Production* by Robert McLeish (Focal Press, 1988) as a good training guide.

Some stations import foreign radio programs. Station KCRW in Los Angeles, for example, airs as much radio drama as any station in the country. It has a special arrangement with the British Broadcasting Corporation (BBC) because it can't get the product here.

In the meantime, what does a writer with a hot idea do? Plan to produce the show yourself. Raise your own funds. And even if it is aired, Mary Lou Finnegan of NPR cautions writers/producers that they probably won't recover their costs.

Financing is possible, says writer Ken Goldman, if "you can convincingly explain how your production will further the arts (government grants) or bolster Mobil Oil's image (corporate grants)." According to Steve Barker, funding sources are the same as for theatre, and there are no designated funds for original radio drama. As a result, would-be radio writers often hook up with local theatre groups to offer both a staged production and subsequent broadcast.

The advantage of this approach is that the writer ends up with produced tapes. This has been Ken Goldman's strategy. He now has samples of his work for BBAT, Janus, and local radio. Those productions can then be considered for NPR and eventually be eligible for the premiere radio festival, the *Prix Italia* Contest, which showcases the best of international radio production. This can lead to foreign sales, where there is a substantial market, especially through state-subsidized companies such as the BBC.

There is also a limited amount of freelance work available doing short sketches for radio show hosts. These may be parodies of current events, scripted interviews with unusual guests, or dramatic re-enactments (always funny). The notion is exactly the same as variety show writing for television, except sketches are no longer than one- to three-minutes. Writers can try their luck querying popular local morning-drive deejays, or go national with companies like American Radio Company in New York. This is the group that produces Garrison Keillor's work, and it pays for material used at up to $200 a minute.

CARL SAUTTER

Goldman also reports a future for audio drama: "Cassette distribution is slowly shaping up as an outlet for dramatizations of books and for original drama. Companies specializing in advertising or skits that keep your ears busy while on hold on the telephone use writers; the pay is $50–75 per thirty-second bit. Comedy radio and cable audio are new markets and the airlines are entering the market. Some airlines have added old radio drama as one of the in-flight audio channels. Why not some original work?"

## PLAYWRITING

While plays may not be screenwriting, every screenwriter fantasizes about writing the definitive American theatre piece. Although, in fact, many write plays between screenplays, more and more playwrights are crossing into screenwriting. The best known include Harold Pinter and David Mamet.

Playwriting is an excellent potential training ground for the screen. In its first season, *St. Elsewhere* sought out playwrights to do episodes in hopes of raising the level of writing on television. A number of playwrights have adapted plays for film or television. Authors of successful productions, even in small theatres, get noticed by producers and are invited in to pitch television and/or film ideas. While the successful adaptation of such plays as *Driving Miss Daisy* has expanded the access playwrights have into the film business, a play still is not considered a representative writing sample for film or television by most agents or story editors: playwrights end up specing scripts like everyone else.

The center for theatre continues to be New York, but regional theatre is strong and is one of the best opportunities for writers to meet other writers, directors, and producers.

As a play emphasizes character and dialogue, it is a valuable way for a writer to improve these skills. In Los Angeles, some screenwriters do staged readings of their screenplays in order to improve pacing and dialogue. Other screenwriters raise money to do full productions of their unsold scripts, hoping someone will notice and buy it for network consumptions. More likely, however, is that the *Los Angeles Times* will blast the production as a sitcom (which of course it is) — a blasphemous reference that is about as damning a criticism a play can get.

Plays are under the auspices of the Dramatists Guild which is based in New York. The Dramatists Guild is not a recognized union; it is a membership organization that develops standards for payment residuals and protection of material. There is no collective bargaining agreement for playwrights. Unlike screenwriters, playwrights own their own material.

# NOVELS

Novels are a major source of material for both features and telefilms. Much like playwrights, many novelists take up screenwriting to improve their standard of living.

Novelists are sometimes given (or demand) the first chance at writing the screenplay adaptation of their books. More often than not, however, networks and studios discourage this because the pattern has been that writers who gave great novel don't give good film. Maddy Horne (CBS) has found "novelists aren't used to getting notes." Most likely the rights to a book will be optioned, and a screenwriter will write it.

A notable exception to this pattern has been the anthology shows such as *Twilight Zone* and *Amazing Stories* which sought out well-known mystery writers for some episodes.

The hardest part of the adaptation process is deciding what not to use. Novels tend to be internalized, giving the reader access to a character's thoughts and motivations. These internal actions must be externalized in a screenplay through visuals, dialogue and reactions. Adapters of novels often face cutting many of the elements they most liked in the book. Additionally, stories usually need to be trimmed and simplified, peripheral characters eliminated, and the pacing of the storytelling, escalated. For a novelist to have this kind of perspective on his or her own work is rare. For the writer debating whether to first write the novel or the screenplay, the advice is the same: write whichever is your original vision and for which you have the most passion.

# COMMERCIALS

Writers for commercials are hired by advertising agencies and are ad executives, not screenwriters. Some of the larger national accounts employ highly paid writers. A special gift for slogans and brevity are required. Ad agencies will want samples of commercials as part of the interview process. The work is sometimes transferable into news, on-air promotions, and magazine shows. A writer who thinks the three-act structure can be avoided should think again. The best commercials tell a story with — you guessed it — a beginning, middle and end.

Many writers have moved into the film business from advertising, not the least of whom is Glenn Gordon Caron, creator of *Moonlighting* and director of *Clean and Sober*. The emphasis on word economy, visuals, and pace in commercials serve writers well in other forms of screenwriting. Additionally, the commercials market, along with music videos, is one of the hottest training grounds for new directors. As those directors crossover, they often bring other co-workers with them.

# SPONSORED PROJECTS

Networks, studios, and producers are not the only outlets for writers. There are many companies ancillary to the television and film industry who also look for media projects. The best known are Hallmark Greeting Cards (*Hallmark Hall of Fame*), Procter & Gamble (daytime soaps), AT&T (which provides twenty percent of the corporate funding to PBS), or Sprint (interactive television 900). There are others (toy manufacturers, cereal companies, oil producers) that have a stake or exploratory interest in the media, particularly in the new technologies such as home video. And hundreds of advertisers have become directly involved in home video programs either as producers or subsidizers of projects. These companies have development offices that read scripts, hear pitches, and meet with writers and producers. The companies are hard to find; not even agents know about them. But new writers who do stumble in are well received. Phyllis Wagner and Louella Caraway wrote a computer game based on the television show *Dallas*; Bruce Graham (Greenroom Enterprises) has learned to go directly to corporations such as Mobil with projects; the Operation Prime Time movie *It Came Upon a Midnight Clear* was done directly for Coca-Cola.

The best way to find these companies is to ask around. Assume that any company active in home electronics, marketing or media development, or a company that buys lots of television advertising is a possibility. The people to contact in non-media companies are in the public relations or special projects divisions.

## HOW TO BREAK INTO THE ALTERNATIVE MARKETS

The advice is similar to other forms of screenwriting. Start with what you like. What forms do you know, watch, have contacts? Research the market — analyze the style of the genre, what the product does and doesn't do. How do these needs match your skills? Try to find written samples to understand both the format and the difference between what is said and what is written. Look also at the opportunities in your particular region. Are there local commercial production companies? Computer animation firms? A strong PBS station? Because of the pricey nature of doing business in Los Angeles or New York, many of the alternative market companies are deliberately based elsewhere.

Most important, find someone working in the particular genre in which you're interested. This is especially necessary in the alternative markets because they are so specialized. An insider will be able to tell you much more than any reading or watching. Note the names of writers, directors, production companies or sponsors on shows or products and contact them directly. Look for specialty publications (such as *Direct Sales, Cassette Marketing* or computer animation journals) that focus on the fields of most interest to you. Attend trade conventions or conferences to see technologies and meet their creators. In short, match your skills and interests to a market and do your research.

To oversimplify the life of a screenwriter:

- Television comedy means **writing funny**.
- Television drama means **writing clearly**.
- Movies mean **writing visually**.
- Alternative markets means **finding them before somebody else does**.

CHAPTER TWELVE

# HOW TO WRITE BETTER THAN ANYONE ELSE

1. Pick a smart market.
2. Learn the special demands and requirements of that market.
3. Look at all the elements of a script and aspire to do them all equally well.

## THE ELEMENTS OF A SCRIPT

Markets, dramatic structure, and visual writing are only the beginning of the requirements of a good script. Following is a checklist with some of the questions a writer has to consider to be truly competitive.

**The market:** the genre in which the script is competing. This affects length, structure, and pacing. Is this the right market for the writer? For this story?

**Idea/notion:** the basic idea the writer came up with that inspired this script. Is it strong enough to compete? Is it original — an idea no other writer would come up with?

**The story:** Does it have a beginning, a middle and an end? Is it a successful blending of:

> **Plot:** the events that happen. Are the plot points compelling? Is there enough to fill an entire script? Is there momentum throughout? And . . .

> **Theme:** the answer to the question "what is this movie about?"

157

Does the theme bring emotion to the plot? Give it substance? Does the theme grow out of the personality/experiences of the main character?

**Structure:** how are plot and theme integrated? Are there strong act breaks with dramatic twists and surprises? Are these the best possible act breaks? Has the writer cut the boring parts?

**Characters:** are the main characters compelling? Do we care what happens to them? Are they propelling the story or are they hapless bystanders? Are they original voices or caricatures? Do they have a clear arc through the script, with a beginning, middle and end?

**Supporting characters:** are they original voices or caricatures? Do the important ones have an arc with a beginning, middle and end? Do they overwhelm the main characters? If so, should the movie be about them?

**Subplots:** are there subplots? (There should be.) Do they grow out of the main story, parallel it? Are they the right subplots for this particular movie? Is the amount of time spent on them in proportion to their importance to the film?

**Structure:** how well do all these elements integrate? Are the plot and theme compatible? Given the theme, has the writer picked the best possible plot?

**Setting:** where does this film take place? Is it unusual or intriguing? How does the setting impact the story and characters? Are there more interesting locations that would further the theme of the script? Is it visual?

**Scenes:** are they interesting? Do they have beginnings, middles and ends? (We don't have to see all three . . .) Are the scenes inventive? What would make particular scenes livelier?

**Dialogue:** is the dialogue crisp and not overwritten? Do the characters talk to each other and not in cliches? Is the dialogue visual? Does the dialogue move the story along without discussing the plot?

**Stage directions:** are the stage directions interesting and readable? Are they overwritten (i.e., like a novel) so that there's too much black on each page? Are they fun to read?

**Visuals:** as one reads this script, does he see the movie? Are the dialogue, stage directions and characters colorful and specific?

**Format:** is the script in the right format for its market? Is there straightforward scene writing (no camera angles, no director's notes). Is it well-typed, no spelling errors, clearly printed?

Below is a memo circulated at NBC to provide guidelines to executive and readers in analyzing either submissions or script assignments in process. The questions apply to both feature and television and emphasize how important *all* the elements of a script are.

## SOME QUESTIONS TO PONDER WHILE ANALYZING MATERIAL

1. What written material are you analyzing — novel, non-fiction book, biography, treatment, miniseries manuscript, script, play?

2. What is this intended to be — miniseries, movie for television, comedy or drama series, cable project, feature, etc.?

3. Would this written material translate well in cinematic terms as well as in characterizations and central plot line? Or is there too much that is internal (the machinations in the central protagonist's mind, for example,) or shown through narration, the novelist's words describing settings, and characters?

4. If this is a play/script, is it balanced in terms of external action and internal action (the psychological concerns of the characters, and the progression there . . .)?

5. Do we believe these characters? Are they realistic (even in comedy we must accept what they do as being motivated out of a reality base . . . even in farce, they have to be relatable human beings who would, given these circumstances, behave in this manner . . .)?

6. Do we sympathize with their concerns, and are their concerns valid and interesting to us? Do we care about the outcome?

7. Do the characters change or grow during the course of the material, or are they stilted, unable to move forward emotionally? Do they take action, or have things merely happened to them? If they are central characters, do they propel things along, create momentum in the plot line?

8. Is there conflict, something to work on, in the story line? Is it both external and internal with these characters?

9. Does the story rely on hardware — gimmicks, gadgets, naked bodies — or is something of merit and entertainment value being said here?

10. Is there some humor, even in drama, to prevent the story from veering into stereotyped melodrama?

11. Does the dialogue presented aid these characterizations or hinder them? Would this potentially good story line with some solid characters be enhanced by a rewrite, perhaps, another writer who could better envision how these characters would truly speak? Do the different characters have distinctive voices, or does everyone, even the little children if there are some, speak with one voice?

12. Is the story line contrived and predictable — something we can immediately decipher the outcome of — or is something relatively fresh and unexpected taking place? Is it contrived, pat, or refreshingly different?

13. Is the resolution positive, or does the action merely trail off in an unsatisfying manner? Are we satisfied with the ending here; has the ride been worth it? How could it have been improved?

14. Have we been dealing with warm, fully dimensional human beings all along who are combinations of good and admirable qualities, and some negative traits, too, or are these caricatures and stereotypes of people, and not three dimensional human beings at all? Are their situations of jeopardy trumped up or real and involving, and do we care that they are ultimately saved? Do we like the leads? Why?

## TAKE THE FIRST STEP FIRST

Every writer has strengths and weaknesses. Nobody is equally skilled at every part of the script process. Some people have a gift for natural-sounding dialogue or writing jokes. Others can weave a dynamite mystery, create characters, write thrilling chase scenes. Still others specialize in clever premises or in developing issue pieces. All screenwriters learn to improve their weaknesses, but knowing what you do well helps determine which markets to pursue initially.

Are you a movie buff? A couch potato? A news junkie? Odds are that the form of screenwriting you most watch is what you know the best, and consequently the best place to concentrate early efforts. It's probably also what you'll most enjoy, and you can find out if you really like writing. There's plenty not to like — the isolation, the long hours in front of a word processor, the rejection and the rewriting.

The best way to assess your strengths and weaknesses is to begin writing, but not necessarily a full script. Most writers begin tackling full scripts long before they're ready. As a result, they don't pay enough attention to learning the mechanics: how to tell a story, create compelling characters, develop natural-sounding dialogue or write clear stage directions. First-time writers often try to do everything at once; a first script can be a mishmash of every possible mistake.

Instead, try doing exercises that isolate particular skills to find out what you do well and where your writing needs improvement:
• Spend an evening writing a scene of dialogue between two characters you create.
• The following weekend, write a thrilling chase sequence, maybe a new ending for *Thelma and Louise*.
• At lunch, do an outline for a murder mystery.
• Pick a favorite situation comedy and list dozens of possible situations that could be stories for the show.
• Write a stirring summary speech for a courtroom scene about an issue close to you.
• Write a five-minute routine for your favorite stand-up comic.
• Invite a small group of writer friends over, watch a sitcom, then come up with new jokes for the episode you just watched. Which jokes worked? Which didn't? Which jokes did you improve upon? You are simulating the process of "punching up a script," the ritual for every situation comedy series.

By undertaking these varied activities, you'll start to understand your rhythms as a writer — when you work best, what activities come naturally. Most important for a new writer, you'll realize that a good writer has more than one idea. By moving from one project to the next, you'll force yourself to develop perspective and learn to let go.

The next step is to edit. Go back to the early exercises and reread them with a critical eye. Tear the scene apart, rewrite it, polish, play with it, experiment with ways to make the scene better. Practice reading your work as if you've never seen it before. And, cautions producer David Lee (*Cheers*), "Don't fall in love with your own material."

## PICKING A STORY

Story ideas are everywhere, if you use whatever special insight your own experience can provide. If you are a nurse, for example, do you have an understanding about a patient's emotional conflict that you can bring to the script? If you're a horse racing fan, was there a colorful character at the track whose story you could tell? As a divorcée, do you understand the pain and humor of separation better than other writers?

A promising source of stories, of course, is newspapers and magazines. The trendiest ideas are on the front page and are probably the ones everyone is pitching. Look instead for the little headlines, the human interest stories, the letters to *Dear Abby* — human stories with built-in conflict and surprises.

Don't hesitate to spend a lot of time researching the story. You may find elusive plot twists during interviews or at the library. In preparing the "Leprechaun" episode for *Moonlighting*, we read every Irish folk tale we could find and watched *Darby O'Gill and the Little People* at least a half dozen times. We discovered Irish incantations, rules, and etiquette for leprechauns, and cadences for the characters — all of which were used in the final script. I've also been to ice-skating competitions, a meter maid convention, and a chocolate festival, all in the name of research for story ideas. Many working writers hire a researcher to help with the legwork because studios are often reluctant to absorb the extra expense. Studio research departments are helpful in finding magazine and newspaper articles, but that's about it. My favorite research is to find people to talk to. You can glean details, attitudes, characters, dialogue, and story from the right interviews.

Remember that, above all, a story by definition has a beginning, middle, and end. This is not the same as an "area" or a notion. *An area* (also known as arena) is a setting — i.e., Laura and Remington join a circus, enter car racing, play in a tennis tournament, etc. Although colorful areas can contribute texture and interest to the script by taking the regulars to a chocolate festival, a satanic cult, or a Beverly Hills spa, areas by themselves do not constitute a plot. The bane of every detective/cop/adventure series, for example, is the *Who Is Killing the Great Chefs?* story idea. Writers arrive at a meeting with ten versions of the same story. One may be who is killing the champion skiers? Who is killing the prostitutes? Who is killing the eligible bachelors? It doesn't matter who's being killed, it's the same story. All the writer is doing is changing areas. The "who is killing?" formula becomes a new story when a good twist is added: *Remington Steele* added a twist by making Mr. Steele one of the eligible bachelors. The NBC pilot *Jake's M.O.* added a twist by asking who is killing randomly? and is it really random? It wasn't; the killer was using a mathematical formula. These twists made both stories a departure.

Similarly, a *notion* is just a piece of the plot; i.e., Maddie and David have to get married. This is an engaging premise pitched to *Moonlighting* by a number of writers. But the idea was never bought because writers weren't able to find the rest of the story — a logical explanation for why, the dramatic twists, a believable ending.

Unfortunately, writers tend to ask for input only when the full script is done. The best time for a writer to solicit opinions is during the story stage. Try pitching story ideas to friends, family, and other writers. Do you get the "ooooh" response? Is the premise compelling? Do they see the conflict? Is there a strong theme? Are the characters interesting? Is the plot too complicated? Were they surprised by the twists? Is it a good story for a movie, a particular television series? Practice by watching television episodes and then retelling them in succinct, concise form.

It is easier to fix story problems before there is a full script. At story stage, a writer is more likely to get honest feedback. When a friend sees all those neatly typed pages of a full script, the impulse is to criticize details such as dialogue or character names rather than the basic structure. All the shuffling of dialogue in the world is not going to help if the basic story has gone awry. And film and television are always at their best when telling clear, simple stories.

## CHARACTERS

Screenwriting requires clear, easily defined characters. Given the constraints of time and multiple plots, television characters in particular must be easily understood by an audience that is only half-watching. Feature film characters can be more complicated, but not confusing. Characters should not be one-dimensional, of course: however, contradictions in their personalities have to be presented clearly and succinctly so the audience will understand what's going on.

Every major character should undergo some change during the story — start at one emotional level, go through complications, and end up at a different emotional level with a new attitude. This is called an arc — a beginning, a middle, and an end in each character's story. In the leprechaun episode of *Moonlighting*, the three main characters (the leprechaun, Maddie, and David) each had a distinct beginning, middle and end in the story. The leprechaun began the episode by giving up all worldly pleasures to protect her pot of gold full-time. Her beliefs are confirmed when there really is a pot of gold, but by the end she realizes she doesn't want to be a leprechaun anymore. David thinks she's easy money (beginning), finds reason to believe her (middle), and finally finds out the gold doesn't belong to her (end), Maddie refuses to believe (beginning), comes to feel that if there were leprechauns, she'd be one (middle), and is heart-broken when the truth comes out (end).

One tendency in screenwriting is to develop cartoon characters — good guys who are too good — bad guys who are despicable. A hero is more interesting if a flaw is apparent and a villain is more compelling if he or she has an aspect of vulnerability. This development extends to supporting characters as well. The dumb blonde next door should have flashes of insight; a maitre d' can be a source of humor if he's allergic to polyester, the tough police chief might have a green thumb. The best characters have layers — qualities, attitudes, and backgrounds that come out one layer at a time as the stories unfold.

Most screenwriting classes and books recommend doing a detailed bio on each of the main characters. This biography can be simply a paragraph or as involved as three to five pages. The biography should identify the motivations, perspective, and history of the characters. Where did they go to school? Do they have brothers and sisters? What is their favorite color? Anything can go into a bio that helps the writer get an image of that character. These backgrounds are purely for the writer's use and are never shown to anyone else. Only a few elements from even the lengthiest histories will be used in the script. But the experiences and attitudes of the character overall will give the writer the manner in which the characters talks and interacts.

Writers often prepare shorter bios with a clear hook for each character to use as notes in pitching. This allows the writer to summarize the important personalities in a project in a line or two that is memorable to the listener.

The strongest stories grow out of the characters and are propelled by them. Which means that the more a writer knows about the characters at the beginning of the story process, the more the characters themselves will determine the story twists and plot points. The strongest pitch will introduce the characters in the context of the story so that they are easier to remember. I've learned that, in features especially, the first introduction of a key character should be as memorable as the writer can make it. That first scene sets up that character for the next two hours.

Independent film-maker John Sayles also offers an excellent rule for his own work: an audience will only accept up to three changes in point-of-view in a film; otherwise, the storytelling is too fragmented. That means that every scene has to be from the perspective of one of those three (or fewer) characters. Showing all those scenes from the POV of various bad guys may hurt the drama and momentum.

Also be wary of the "you must have an antagonist" rule that is popular in screenwriting classes and seminars. Caroline Thompson (*Edward Scissorhands, The Addams Family*) debunks this notion flat out: "Create characters that can tell a good story. Not all good stories have a bad guy." Who's the villain in *Tootsie?*, *Gone with the Wind?*, *Driving Miss Daisy?*

## PLOT OUTLINE

Take two or three of your most promising ideas and use the characters' descriptions to develop the major plot points in each story. These plot points (or beats) are not scenes, but rather the steps and information necessary to tell a particular story. Stay away from too much detail; concentrate on the story points only.

As an example, below is the rough plot outline for the first act of the black and white episode of *Moonlighting*, "The Dream Sequence Always Rings Twice:"

1. A man thinks his wife is having an affair.
2. He hires the Blue Moon Agency to investigate.
3. David and Maddie discover the wife's not having an affair.
4. They meet the man, at an old nightclub he's thinking of buying, to tell him the news. He's furious. He wanted grounds for a divorce.
5. He decides not to buy the club. After all, he doesn't want his wife to share in the profits.
6. He storms out, leaving David and Maddie with the depressed owner of the club who can't sell it.
7. The owner laments the future of a building with so much history. He tells David and Maddie about a murder that happened there, involving a singer, her husband, and a trumpet player. The singer and the trumpet player both went to the electric chair, each claiming the other was responsible.
8. Afterwards, Maddie and David realize they disagree about who was to blame for the murder.
9. The disagreement turns into an argument. Maddie feels the woman was a victim; David thinks the trumpet player was set up.
10. Maddie storms home, still upset about the argument with David.
11. She falls asleep. In a dream, in black and white, Maddie becomes the singer in the '40s. The nightclub owner is her husband.
12. The trumpet player arrives at the club — it's David.
13. The singer is helplessly drawn to the trumpet player.

14. He finally traps her in a passionate kiss . . . she has no will to resist.

END OF ACT ONE

The advantage of a plot outline such as this is that the writer can test whether the story holds up from beginning to end and if each story point is logical. Just as important, the writer can decide where the episode or movie should start. The rule is *start the script as close to the story as possible*. The black and white episode didn't begin at story point Number One as outlined above, but rather at story point Number Four. The early information became backstory conveyed through dialogue in the first two scenes.

Starting a screenplay close to the heart of the plot allows a writer to skip the earliest beats of a story, which tend to be explanatory rather than visual; get to that big moment within the early pages; and concentrate on interesting complications and character attitudes through the middle of the script. A weakness of many scripts is that they take too long to get to the actual story. Typically, the plot turn on page thirty is the problem the story is about, and should have been introduced by page ten with a new act break at page thirty. This restructuring gives the writer an additional twenty pages to further escalate and explore the story.

## ADDING SUBPLOTS

Match your story to the structure of the market you've picked. Determine how many stories are told in a typical episode of the television show or genre of movie.

In a feature film, there is the main story, a subplot that most often is the arc of one or both of the main characters (such as a love story), and separate smaller subplots or arcs for the other important characters. Generally, all subplots in a film grow out of the main story and intersect with it. This is substantially different from the use of subplots in television, which often bear no relationship to the main story. Comedy films have more subplots to keep the pacing fast; an action-adventure film has no more than one or two subplots because the focus is on the action sequences of the main story. In an ensemble film with four or five stories of equal importance, don't worry about subplots — you have enough story problems already! In television sitcoms the norm is one main story and one humorous subplot. In television action-adventure shows there is usually one plot-heavy main story and a minor runner. In most other forms of hour drama there is a main story, a subplot, and a humorous runner. In other genres, study samples of the form to determine the appropriate number of stories.

Spend time analyzing the genre you hope to write for and the patterns will be surprisingly easy to figure out. At this point, think mathematics. Your script should follow the mathematics used by the particular market. A spec script is not the time to break new ground in the structure of a film or television show unless a writer has good reason to be so confident, such as an assignment or an Academy Award.

Determine which story ideas are main stories and which will work better as subplots or runners. Mix and match. What happens when main story Number One is matched with subplot Number Five? Does this give more interest to the script than stories Number One and Number Three together? Is there a more intriguing subplot for a particular character? Is there enough humor? Have you missed a subplot hidden in one of the character's bios? Can one plot affect the other? In a feature, does each subplot you've chosen feed into the main story and help its momentum? Is there a better subplot lurking in the story you didn't notice the first time around?

As a rule the effective matching of stories does one of four things:

1. The main story and subplot show us **two different views** of the same circumstances. One story may be the murder and all its complications, the other may be the developing relationship between the two leads. The first story provides the primary jeopardy, the other provides insight into their sexual tension. This was the mix of stories in *Romancing the Stone* and *Tootsie*.

2. The **stories intersect at some point** and help to resolve each other; i.e., two seemingly opposite people with their own stories end up helping each other. This is a popular structure in television and in opposites attract features, as love stories (*Witness, Pretty Woman*) or buddy film (*Lethal Weapon, Thelma and Louise*).

3. The two **stories parallel** and somehow comment on each other. *Cagney and Lacey* might be dealing with a teen pregnancy case, while at home Lacey is worried about her son's dawning sexual awareness. In *Moonstruck*, the Olympia Dukakais subplot subtly commented on the primary story of Cher.

4. The subplot and/or runner **relieve the tension** of the main plot. In an episode of *Trapper John, M.D.* about AIDS, the runner was raising tropical fish for stress-reduction. In the first editing cut, the director eliminated the runner entirely to allow more time for the main stories, but eventually decided the episode was too unrelenting. The fish story was put back in for relief.

## SCENE OUTLINE

The next step is to prepare a scene outline which translates the story beats for plots A, B, C and D into the form of the show or market you are writing for. When a writer is on assignment with a television series, the scene outline is worked out step-by-step with the staff of the show. Scene outlines are the bane of a screenwriter's existence (right up there with pitching). These outlines are narrative writing, and explain clearly and concisely what will happen in each scene and why. It's impossible to show the nuances or subtleties planned for a scene. And yet, putting in too much detail muddies the story and can make the outline hard to read and slow-moving. The writer has to learn to put in enough to show the plot and subplots, as well as the growth of the characters, the tone of the sources of humor and/or drama. Then, when it comes to the story meeting, take your lumps. The outline process almost never goes well.

That's one of the reasons why a scene outline is a bad way to sell a story. My advice is: either pitch the story from a short treatment or write the full script. The former gives the writer the chance to sell a concept with visible enthusiasm; the latter shows writing skills. An outline shows neither.

One good rule is not to put in pieces of dialogue. Outline dialogue reads stilted, partly because it is out of context and partly because an outline is blunt, direct writing, exactly the opposite of good dialogue. Don't write "Michael says, 'I have a problem' ''; write, "Michael realizes he has a problem." The latter accomplishes the same goal but doesn't imply that you'll be putting dippy lines such as "I have a problem" into the script.

A second option for scenes that defy narrative description is to put in a sequence of dialogue so that individual lines are not standing alone. In sitcoms, this technique can be used to show a joke that can't be shown in narrative. There is also another trap when including dialogue in outlines: you may become wed to your precious words, making it that much harder to cut them later.

The formats for a feature outline and a television outline are identical with the exception that a television outline reflects the commercial act breaks, and a feature outline, the dramatic act breaks (although this is optional). What is no longer optional in features is the scene outline itself. Bayard Maybank (Triad Artists) notes a major change in attitudes. "Now many of the studios *require* an outline from their producers, which means the producers must require one from the writer." Previously, feature writers could skip the outline phase by going through a series of story meetings. The results were then pitched to the studio, rather than submitted in writing. Writers Guild rules allow for two versions of the outline before the writer is green-lighted to first draft, and these days production companies are taking advantage of that. The intent: to have more input into the story process, early on.

A television scene outline is required during the episodic process and is one of the steps at which a writer receives payment. WGA rules allow a writer to do two versions of the outline in hour episodic; one version in half-hour.

Half-hour comedies average only three to five scenes per act. These tend to be full scenes, each with a beginning, middle and end. The conflict is introduced into the scene, complications arise, and they produce a result, but not a solution. In a typical scene from *Golden Girls*, Dorothy's ex-husband shows up (introduction), he's going in for surgery (complication), Dorothy feels sorry for him (result). The solution comes in a later scene: he'll stay with the women during the recovery period. A typical scene outline for a half-hour show will run ten to twelve pages (double-spaced, with extra spaces between scene paragraphs). As you do your outline, remember how important it is to keep the story moving.

In hour episodes, the outline form will be five to twelve scenes per act. If there are less than five scenes, the stories are probably not complicated enough; if there are more than twelve, the story has too many beats for episodic television and will seem choppy. Write only scenes that the audience absolutely has to see in order to understand the stories. A typical scene outline for a one-hour show will run ten to fifteen pages (single-spaced, with double-spaces between scene paragraphs).

Some producers prefer double-spaced outlines so they can make notes more easily. Ask for sample outlines for any show where you have an assignment to see their format of choice.

In hour drama or features, the writer can do scenes that start in the middle — i.e., Maddie and David are already fighting in the car when a scene begins. The audience does not need to see the early build. Or, a scene can cover two locations — the argument begins in the parking garage, and without missing a line suddenly cuts to the lobby of the Blue Moon Detective Agency.

To better understand the structure of a particular television show, spend time dissecting episodes. Take notes and outline what's happening.

1. How many scenes does each episode have per act? Most shows have a definite pattern. In some hour dramas it is as specific as 8-8-5-8. The third act tends to be the shortest because it is the final set of complications.

2. How many scenes are devoted to each story? In what order are they presented?

3. Which settings or locations are consistently used in the show that should be incorporated into your script?

4. How many scenes involve the leads? Does the story ever cut away to the guest stars by themselves? On *Moonlighting* the only cut away was in the opening scene — after that, the script stayed with Maddie, David, Dipesto, or Herbert.

5. Which story does the show start with — the "A" story? The runner? Which story does the show end with?

Some shows use short two- or three-minute introductions at the beginning of each episode. These are bumpers and often have nothing to do with the story that follows. Other shows use tags — a one- or two-minute scene at the end of the episode which reflects on the story completed and the lessons learned. Shows such as *Roseanne* and *Growing Pains* often use both a bumper and a tag in each episode. Bumpers and tags are designed to be cut for syndication where more commercial breaks are allowed. If *The Dick Van Dyke Show* had included a bumper, the syndicated version would not have to start one minute into the show.

Study samples of the various genre in features. What are the dramatic act breaks? What is the average number of scenes in each act? Are there lots of short, choppy scenes or long, languid ones? Do scenes most often start in the middle or at the beginning? What is the transition from one scene to the next? Do scenes tend to get longer or shorter as the film progresses? Film outlines run in the twenty- to forty-page range, and are often double-spaced for easier reading and to allow room for a producer's notes. Even in situations where an outline is not required, such as spec scripts, the scene outline is a good tool for structuring stories and establishing the overall pace of a script.

A good scene outline establishes:

1. **The number of scenes** per commercial or dramatic act.

2. **The plot points** that will be covered in each scene (therefore mapping out how the various stories will be told).

3. **The important information** to be covered in each scene.

4. **The locations.** These should be a mix of interiors and exteriors in a film show or feature film, and the various interiors in a sitcom. The regular sets and locations in a television show should be used extensively: e.g., the living room in *Golden Girls*, the high school in *Beverly Hills 90210*. Sitcoms provide special limitations — three permanent sets and no more than two swing (or new) sets.

5. **The attitude of each character** in the scene — the way he or she approaches the scene. This attitude is best if it's specific. Rather than writing "Maddie is angry with David," we know much more about the scene from "Maddie can't believe David is only concerned about his pay raise." This attitude is often described as a goal or

motivation; it should be clear what each primary character is trying to accomplish in each scene.

Additionally, every scene should have three elements:

**Conflict.** Characters should not yell at each other every moment, but there has to be tension. This may be in the form of sexual chemistry, two characters operating at unstated cross purposes, or one character not trusting another. Drama is conflict. Every scene should have characters with distinct and conflicting goals/attitudes.

**Purpose.** Every scene has to move one of the stories forward. If not, cut it. If a scene only makes a slight contribution, merge the vital information into another scene.

**Focus.** But be careful not to put too much story into any one scene. If too much information comes out, a scene can get muddled or static. Tease the audience with the story; dole it out one piece at a time. In "The Bet" episode of *Moonlighting* written by Bruce Singer, Maddie says she's fed up with David being immature (the problem). He storms out. Maddie then goes to his office and offers to bet that he can't act like a mature adult for a week (the solution). The problem and the solution were presented in two separate scenes with movement in between.

Some of the best advice I've ever heard about scene-writing was from playwright David Mamet. He credits his writing success to a simple principle: "Get into every scene late and out of every scene early." In other words, envision your scenes without the dull openings — characters walking in, words of introductory chit-chat. Get to where the point of the scene begins. And get out without neat wrap-ups, buttons or repeating information. Create tension for an audience by leaving us not quite knowing what just happened here.

Once a rough draft of the outline is done, it should be reviewed to make sure:

- **Information is emerging** in the most interesting possible places (the storytelling is not predictable.)
- The **script is not linear:** we do not spend scene after scene with the same characters or the same plot.
- **We see only what we have to** see in order to understand what's going on.

- Information and **story points are not repeated.** A script reads better if the writer assumes the reader got it the first time. This includes the rule of three jokes — it's funnier if the joke builds. A running gag in one episode of *Perfect Strangers* was "the dance of joy." The first time Balki dances because Larry allows him to keep a stray dog; the second time Balki teaches the dog how to dance; the third time Balki asks the dog if he likes the people who now want to adopt him. In response, the dog does the dance of joy. The script does not repeat the same joke each time, it builds to a bigger pay-off.

## FEATURE FILM SCENE OUTLINE

Debra Frank and I submitted a thirty-three-page outline for *My Step-mother Is an Alien* to ensure that we, the director, and the production company were all talking about the same movie. We weren't. Good thing we found out before writing the full script.

This is our version of the early scenes of that movie:

### ACT ONE

(1) RESEARCH LABORATORY — DAY
A huge Jet Propulsion Laboratory type facility with lots of security and high-tech government research programs. But this particular lab is in the back corner of a back building next to the xerox and shredding machines. Clearly, the research done here is not one of the priorities of the company. On this particular afternoon a storm moves in and the sky is temporarily darkened.

STEVE is a dedicated scientist who has been trying to make radio contact with life in outer space for the last ten years with no results. He sends out sperm whale mating calls, termite noises, anything that might provoke an answer. His partner, RON, meanwhile, is watching television — alternating between *Phil Donahue* and *Wheel of Fortune.* He watches *Donahue* to prove he is a sensitive man (a good way to pick up chicks) and *Wheel* because: "Vanna has a hot tush."

As Ron switches to *Wheel* the category is "A Thing." At the exact moment a contestant guesses "The Law of Gravity," LIGHTNING hits the transmitter. Sparks fly and the power to the lab goes out. Unable to get the equipment on again, Steve and Ron finally give up and go home.

(2) INT. SECURITY CLEARANCE
Steve and Ron exit through several security gates (like those at the airport). As Ron watches other scientists leaving their labs, he laments about their dead-end project. He'll never move up in the company. Steve suddenly remembers he left his groceries back at the lab and returns to get them.

(3) INT. RESEARCH LAB — CONTINUOUS
As Steve retrieves the groceries from the refrigerator, he realizes that there is a message on their long-silent machine. The aliens have finally answered in some strange code. He rushes to the window to try to catch Ron, shouting that we made contact! But Ron is oblivious as he drives out of the parking lot, listening to the advice of Toni Grant on the radio.

(4) EXT. MILLS HOUSE
JESSIE (age 13) is playing basketball as THEO, her basset hound, barks encouragement. Steve drives up. He excitedly shares the news about finally getting an answer from outer space; Jessie is proud of him. He challenges her to a quick game of one on one.

(5) INT. RESEARCH LAB — THE NEXT DAY
Steve shows Ron the graph. Ron is stunned. He makes Steve promise not to tell anyone about this until they decode the message and figure out how they made contact in the first place. Steve is reluctant; their higher-ups have a right to know. But Ron convinces him if they can't explain how they did it, they'll look foolish.

(6) A DAZZLING PAIR OF LEGS . . . then we see LIPS, EYES, and other provocative BODY PARTS, as we hear TWO WOMEN talk and we learn about the mission.

Through a window we see EARTH . . . and we realize that we are on a SPACESHIP. There is a brown haze around the planet. The Voice in Charge laments that it used to be the prettiest planet in the universe, but earthlings have ruined it. Now they'll ruin the rest of the universe; they have vital information that will help them finally get into outer space. The Voice in Charge can't believe someone could be so stupid as to answer a message from Earth. The Voice explains that Venus Theory — as soon as earthlings decide there's no life on a planet, they move on to the next one. If they know there's life out there, they'll never leave us alone.

When the conversation is over, a HAND picks up a red leather purse (BAG) and snaps it shut to complaints of "be more gentle" and we realize the Lips have been talking to the Handbag.

The same format is used for television movies; however, act breaks are indicated.

## HOUR EPISODIC SCENE OUTLINE

The following excerpt of an outline is from *Beverly Hills 90210*. Note that there are more details provided in a television outline than the feature film version.

ACT THREE
*The Following Week*

(18) INT. NEWSPAPER OFFICE — DAY
Andrea has finished her article on sports language, but Brandon insists on reviewing it. It's going in his sports section after all. And for the first time, Brandon gets to critique Andrea's work. He make the most of the opportunity until he sees . . .

Trisha waiting at the door. He invited her to come by the school for lunch.

(19) EXT. THE HIGH SCHOOL — DAY
Brandon shows Trisha life outside the bubble. They walk through the halls of West Beverly . . .

(20) EXT. LAWN OF HIGH SCHOOL — DAY
Lunch-time. Brenda has taken her new obsession with retail sales beyond the walls of the boutique; now she is offering advice to everyone in the group: Donna really should wear a lighter blush; Steve . . . even men need to think about using a moisturizer; and Kelly . . . there's the most adorable outfit! Dylan is not the only one who doesn't much care for the new Brenda, which is why they are all relieved when Brandon and Trisha walk up.

The group can't believe Trisha's missed out on the joys of junk food . . . talk about deprived. They come up with a plan — a junk food lunch in honor of Trisha's freedom. Everyone will get their favorite disgusting food from the cafeteria. Is there time? That's why they call it fast food. We also know that it's a great way to get away from Brenda, who is now deciding Trisha's best colors. SHOCK CUT TO:

(21) A BURRITO
This could be Trisha's greatest moment of glory. She tastes a burrito for the first time. And from among the hamburgers, potato chips, snack pies, and milk shakes the kids have brought her . . . this is her favorite.

*Friday Night*
(22) INT. ICE RINK — NIGHT
Brandon picks up Trisha for her first official date ever. She looks fabulous — perhaps a little older than we've seen her before. So what would she like to do? Go dancing. But that's a problem, remember? The one thing Brandon doesn't do is dance. Trisha offers that he loves to skate though, right? Of course. She turns on the tape machine with the music from one of her

routines and offers her arm. They'll ice dance for her first official date.

And in a wonderful romantic sequence the two move gracefully across the ice. It is sweet and playful and incredibly innocent. And for the first time in his life, Brandon is beginning to understand what romance is.

(23) INT. BOUTIQUE — NIGHT
Brenda works on her biggest sale yet. She convinces the woman to upgrade on every item. Then Deirdre returns from her dinner break. She recognizes the woman and offers that she'll take over. Not wanting to cause a scene, Brenda backs down then watches helplessly as Deirdre takes credit for the entire order — which means she gets the entire commission. Brenda can't believe it.

(24) INT. ICE-SKATING RINK — NIGHT
Brandon and Trisha finish their dance only to realize that they are being watched. By the coach. But this time his tone is not upset but urgent.

It seems a lot of important people have their future riding on Team Trisha. In an unusual move, the Skating Federation granted a waiver for her to compete at Regionals. The politics of skating strike again . . . only this time in her favor. Trisha is thrilled. The bad news: she has less than a week to pull herself together. If she hopes to have a chance, she's going to have to start now. Trisha hesitates — what about their date? But Brandon doesn't waiver — of course she has to do this; the date can wait. She's very sorry, but Brandon understands. And yet we can see that he's also crushed.

## HALF-HOUR EPISODIC SCENE OUTLINE

The following excerpt of a half-hour outline is from *Murphy Brown*, written by Russ Woody. Note that scenes in a situation comedy tend to be even longer, contain more indication of dialogue and emphasize humor.

"KYLE"

(A) INT. FYI SET — EVENING

Between live segments of the FYI broadcast, Murphy picks up notes and coffee and steps from the FYI news desk to the interview chairs where a small, nebbish man in his mid-thirties is being miked and prepped. He stands when she approaches and accidentally knocks her coffee down the front of her blouse. All the while, Isaac Hayes sings, "Never Can Say Good-bye." Miles is terror-stricken as a veritable SWAT team converges on the set with dampened cloth, portable hair driers, etc. The stage manager is now counting down until they're back on the air. Miles is taking some sort of medication. Last touch-ups are done to Murphy's blouse, the music ends as do the main titles and Jim addresses the camera to introduce Murphy Brown and Kyle Crabnatter.

With perhaps some black and white photos, newspaper excerpts, etc. Murphy explains that Kyle Crabnatter was wrongfully arrested fifteen years ago by New York City police and charged with bank robbery. Then in 1978 his sentence was extended when he was charged with taking part in an ill-fated escape attempt. Murphy explains that he has since been exonerated of any connection with the robbery. (A guilt-ridden cop confessed to framing Kyle because they were unable to pin the robbery on anyone else and their captain was screaming for a bust). That's all backstory — the thing is Murphy worked hard, persevered, busted her butt to clear this guy . . . and he's grateful. In fact, he's overwhelmed by all the attention — he never expected it. Through the interview we learn that Kyle has, his whole life, been blamed for things he didn't do. What he touches turns to shit. As a result, he seems to have become somewhat fatalistic about life. He's grateful to be out, but doesn't really expect it to last long because as soon as someone, somewhere, sometime robs a bank, the police are going to hunt him down and send him back to prison. Kyle probably also lacks many social graces — he hasn't been part of society in a long time. Asked if he's bitter, he says no, it would have happened sooner or later anyway . . . and he met a lot of interesting people, was blamed for some interesting stuff during his tenure in the hole. Kyle might also mention that a great many of the guys are big FYI fans and would jump at the chance to meet and molest Murphy . . . while others seem to have a predilection for Frank.

The interview finishes, the show wraps and all say a tearful good-buy, good luck to Kyle.

(B) INT. BULLPEN — NEXT DAY

Corky is up to her neck with the story she's working on (killer mice of the central and western United States), while Jim is doing this or that (some sort of B-story thing — maybe he's invested in some sort of conglomerate stock?). Murphy is on the phone talking to her latest secretary. She's telling her that the two-week vacation in her contract does not come into effect until the secretary has actually shown up at the office. Murphy hangs up, pissed, as Frank enters with a boyish grin, tells her about a tip he got on a horse. Odds are twenty-to-one and his inside line says it's a sure thing. Some others are listening. Frank says the horse, Lucky Streak, has been carefully tested for personality traits — high-spiritedness, aggressiveness, type-A personality. Lucky Streak was trained by a new method including a diet of red meat and coffee. This horse is gonna blow the doors off horse racing as we know it. Frank asks Murphy if she wants in on it. Murphy says no.

Miles enters a little peeved at the American public because the numbers for last night's show were very low. Miles is trying to figure out why, speculating, whatever, stumped . . . when the elevator dings and Kyle enters, hat in hand to say hello. Murphy greets him as all say hello. She asks how his first day of freedom went. He says it's gone pretty much as he expected. He's been to twenty different places applying for work and no one will hire him because he has no skills . . . and probably because he tells them he's not worthy of any job they might have. But, he says, it's no big deal, he's not worried because he expects any day now to be arrested for some other crime he didn't commit. With that he pretty much tells everyone to have a nice day and splits.

A dark cloud has just visited and left behind an ubiquitous shadow on the minds of all — except Murphy, who's calling the secretarial pool. Miles says it's terrible. The others agree and, after Murphy hangs up, he mentions that they should do something to help Kyle out. After all, they were the ones who got him out of jail in the first place. Murphy says she's sure he'll be okay and that they really wouldn't be doing him any favor by stepping in and doing this stuff for him. Murphy says he'd probably want to secure a job on his own, rather than feeling even further in debt to them. But, more importantly, she adds, it's a matter of not overstepping their roles as journalists.

Miles pretty much ignores everything she's said and says he's got a great idea.

(C) INT. BULLPEN — A COUPLE DAYS LATER
Kyle is at the secretary's desk in front of Murphy's office, hunting, searching for various letters on the typewriter's keyboard. Murphy, we realize, is further behind in her work with Kyle's help than she would be without it. For several hours now, Kyle has been typing a letter of Murphy's to the Secretary of State. Kyle is kind of pissed that the keyboard is arranged catch-as-catch-can instead of alphabetically. He spent the better part of junior high learning the alphabet and now it seems it was all for naught.

Frank approaches and reminds Murphy that Lucky Streak is making her maiden race that afternoon and it's still not to late to get in a sure-fire profit. Murphy is not intrigued, but Kyle is and wants to put some money down.

Jim steps over to ask Kyle about something that Kyle has screwed up for him (the B story thing) as two men roll the xerox machine out and truck it to the elevator where Corky emerges, and asks what happened to it . . . everyone looks at Kyle. Oh. Corky was already more than a little annoyed after some footage of killer mice attacking a German shepherd in Utah was lost because of Kyle.

There's some other stuff here about things going wrong and all the bad luck that has fallen on FYI in the last couple of days, Also, maybe someone is reading the Telex machine and mentions that the First Central Bank was held up that morning and the culprit is still at large. A few people look toward Kyle, who says he's been in the office all day . . . typing the Secretary of State letter.

## WRITING THE SCRIPT

Bearing in mind that a scene outline is a discussion tool, discuss it — with the staff of a show or studio if it is on assignment, with friends and fellow writers if it is a spec script. Blunt, direct criticism is important at the outline stage because the writer has a last chance to fix problems before writing pages and pages of scenes that may not be necessary or don't tell the various stories clearly. If there was a "No Service for the Next Hundred Miles" sign posted during the script process, it would be here.

After this, you're on your own. Write the script. I don't recommend stopping for criticism once you've waxed poetic with dialogue and stage directions. Asking for a critique of individual scenes is an exercise in frustration. The reader is criticizing the scene out of context. As a result, only the dialogue can be critiqued. This is of limited value until the reader can look at all the dialogue and all the story. Once you've started, keep writing until you have a whole script.

There are some exceptions. There is nothing wrong with rethinking the plot while writing. Every writer does. But you'll probably find that doing a revised plot outline and asking for critiques of it is a more effective way to solve your problems than showing someone a partial script and asking how to fix it.

Occasionally, there are individual scenes that are tough to write. This is the time for my one *absolute rule* — go back a step. If you can't nail the dialogue, it's probably because the attitude of the characters is wrong; if you can't nail the attitudes, it's probably because the plot's going askew; if the plot's going askew, you either need to rethink the plot or cut the scene. The problem is almost never the step the writer is stuck at, it's the step or two before. Now is the time to draw on all those writing classes, seminars and books — natural sounding dialogue, clean stage directions, character histories, movement within a scene, get in late/out early.

Viki King (*How to Write a Movie in 21 Days*) offers some of the best advice in this regard: "Write from the heart and edit from the head." During a first draft, relax and let the personal voice flow. Don't try to edit yourself while you do the first version of scenes. Let your personal voice guide you. If you think too much, you'll never finish. Instead, move forward, confident that you can go back and fix it later.

## A CHECKLIST FOR REWRITING YOURSELF

Any smart screenwriter knows that the biggest part of the writing process for a television or movie project often is the rewriting process. So get a head start on all those story editors, producers, studio types, and writers who will follow by unmercifully rewriting yourself. The best way to rewrite is to be as distanced from the project as possible, reading it as if for the first time, not predisposed to a single line, plot point or joke. Yeah, easier said than done. At any rate the following criteria might help:

1. Every scene should have a purpose. If not, cut it.

2. Every scene should have conflict. If not, add tension or cut the scene.

3. Every story and subplot has to have a beginning, middle, end.

4. Every major character should have an arc — beginning, middle, end. If there are sudden transitions without a logical basis, the story will be melodramatic.

5. Every character has to have a purpose both to the story and to the scenes they are in. If not, cut them from the scene or consider merging them with another character in the story.

6. Every major plot point should be logical and consistent. Have the plot twists been set up so that they are believable? Have the elements introduced at the beginning of the script been paid off by the end?

7. Immediately rewrite or cut any scenes, dialogue, or characters that are on the nose — too obvious or that we've seen or heard a hundred times before.

8. Determine if scenes are in the right order. Would the story be more interesting if some of the scenes were reversed or if infor-

mation were held to a later scene? Is the right information in the right act? If there are long passages of character establishment in dramatic Act Three, they should move to Act One.

9. Does the story and structure of the script fit the genre it's intended for? Can it compete with other spec scripts in that market?

10. For a script with a lot of comedy: are there funnier lines? For a script with a lot of drama: does the emotional conflict have sufficiently high stakes?

11. Is the script in the right format for the market? (See Appendix A.)

# CHAPTER THIRTEEN

# IT'S DONE —
# NOW WHAT?

Picked a smart market . . . did the research . . . great story . . . detailed outline . . . well-drawn characters, pithy dialogue . . . right format . . . rewrote and rewrote . . . other writers like it. Now it's time to submit your script. But to whom and how?

First, resist the temptation to send the script to everyone you've ever met. This will not only cost a lot of money, but will irritate the people who receive it. Most of them won't be able to do you any good, anyway. Be selective. If you were smart in the beginning, you wrote the script knowing *exactly* who would read it when it was finished. That's because you wrote the script to a specific market. (If you didn't, this might be a good time to review Chapter Two.)

Your target list of connections should include:

**Agents.** A writer does not have to be signed with an agent to submit the work. An agent can provide a cover letter for the script and make the submission. He or she gets ten percent if it sells; if it doesn't, you're not cluttering up the client list. And you're not committing to an agent before you know if he or she is at least reasonably well-connected.

**Other contacts.** Executives at studios, producers, and writers and friends who can recommend the script (and you) to shows and producers in that market. These contacts can be almost anyone connected to the entertainment industry, as long as they read the script first and are willing to put their own reputations on the line.

# AGENTS

Probably no aspect of the life of a screenwriter is more clouded by misinformation than that elusive commodity known as the agent. Myths are rampant at all levels of the industry. New writers complain, "If I could just get an agent, I could sell this script," writers who finally get an agent are certain that "now the job offers will roll in," and writers who have agents but still aren't working say, "it's my agent's fault."

The truth is that most agents are merely brokers caught between writers with something to sell and producers who, sometimes, are looking for projects to buy. Contrary to popular belief, an agent is not an employment agency. An agent does not hand out work. Having an agent is not the same as having a career. New writers, even those with agents, create their own work through good writing samples, friendship, word-of-mouth, or smart handling of contacts.

Actor Henry Polic (*Webster*) advises actors that perhaps one in ten jobs they get will be generated by agents. The percentage is similar for writers. A freelancer has to meet people, do additional spec work if necessary, and gather information about job possibilities if he hopes to work regularly. Writer Russ Woody (*Murphy Brown, St. Elsewhere*) found his first six writing assignments on his own. His agent negotiated the contracts. Writers who are realistic about how the process works will be a joy to any agent.

Agents don't broker power as much as they play a life-size version of *Jeopardy* — they try to match answers (in this case, writers) with questions (the needs of producers). The game is a notoriously high-pressure one for which agents receive a ten percent commission on the writer's gross earnings. In order to parlay these commissions into a suitable lifestyle, agents must either go with writers who are working or those who through their writing samples show exceptional potential to work. Established writers are in demand: it's easier to find them work and the payoff is usually greater.

This misunderstanding about who gets who work — the agent or the talent — has created the classic love-hate relationship. The conflicts begin with new writers who complain that agents aren't giving them a chance. Agents counter that the writing samples aren't good enough. Writers with agents complain that they don't get them work. Agents counter that the writer's credits aren't good enough. If their career is going well, most writers did it themselves. If the career is going poorly, "I'm thinking of changing agents." Meanwhile, the agent for a successful writer got him his big break, but the same agent says of an unsuccessful client "he has a bad reputation."

A smart agent is time-efficient, picking clients who will generate the maximum amount of income with the least amount of agent energy. It's important to remember that most agents are at their best negotiating a deal and at their worst trying to find work for someone with no credits.

There is a hierarchy among agencies based on the prestige of their client list, perceived clout within the industry, and history. The three hundred signatories to the Writers Guild range from the mega-agencies such as Creative Artists Agency (CAA) and International Creative Management (ICM), to one-person agencies that operate out of the agent's home. To become a signatory, an agent must agree to abide by Guild rules regarding minimums, working conditions, and rights for the writer. Additionally, the agent is not allowed to negotiate contracts with producers or companies who are not signatory to the Guild Minimum Basic Agreement (MBA). A standing WGA committee reviews agencies' compliance with these rules and complaints against individual agents. WGA members are not allowed to be represented by non-signatory agencies.

Almost every agent, regardless of the size of the agency, will look at new work referred by one of their clients or someone in the industry whose judgment they respect. The smaller agencies and independent agents are more likely to read work by new writers without referrals.

Big is not necessarily better in the agent business. A *Los Angeles Times* article once profiled fifty of the town's top agents. The list included players from agencies large and small. The size of the agency is not as important as the skills, reputation, and client list of the individual agent. A new agent in a huge company may have far less clout than a well-respected one-person office. Some of the smaller agencies are pound-for-pound the most influential.

Agencies can be grouped as follows:

**Mega-agencies.** CAA, William Morris, and ICM are generally acknowledged as the big three with Triad a close fourth. These agencies have separate divisions to represent actors, writers, producers, directors, and the music business. The literary departments at these agencies average up to fifteen agents or more. Each has his or her own client list and also represents writers/producers and writers/directors. An agent in one of the mega-agencies will represent fifteen to thirty writers and often pools clients with other agents. Their biggest selling point to clients is the clout they wield in negotiating mega-buck contracts and getting projects made.

**Mid-size agencies.** Writers and Artists, Intertalent, and Innovative are representative. Many have long histories. The literary division is three to four agents, each representing an average of twenty to thirty clients. Their biggest selling point to clients is extra attention and personal service. They are often referred to these days as "boutique agencies" because many specialize. The Kaplan/Stahler Agency, for example, is known for its stable of sitcom writers. Many of their big name clients have a long-standing relationship with the agency from the early days before the writer was known, and loyalty is an important bond.

**Small agencies.** The vast majority of agencies are one- or two-agent offices. Most deal only with writers or writers/producers. They range from the very respected to "Who? From *what* agency?"

Small agencies tend to be more willing to peddle their clients for freelance television episodes than agents in the larger firms who focus on prestigious big bucks markets. The disadvantage of a small agency is that agents often have a large client roster, as many as fifty clients per agent. This is necessary because the average earning power of freelance clients is so much lower. Agent/client loyalty is also a factor. Some of these agencies will look at work submitted by new writers without referral. These may also be the agents with no clout; signing with one of them may be a waste of a writer's time and energy.

**Entertainment lawyers.** They also function as agents for writers. Most do not find work for their clients, they negotiate deals and review contracts. This is at a lower rate than the ten percent agent commission, often either five percent of the writer's gross or a fixed fee. Writers with agents are well-advised to have an entertainment lawyer review any contracts — including the writer/agency agreement. Entertainment lawyers can be helpful in finding an agent.

**Personal managers.** Managers provide specialized services, such as press releases to the trades or accounting services for payment of bills and promote their clients as opportunities arise. Managers normally receive fifteen percent of a client's gross income. Managers are popular with actors, providing career guidance and an industry profile. Some also represent writers. They are not regulated by the Writers Guild and function most often as an addition to an agent. Managers try to assume the dominant role in shaping a career, so the relationship between managers and agents can best be summarized as tense. Technically, a manager may not solicit work for a writer or negotiate deals, therefore their job is most often an advisory function. Most writers find that having both a manager and an agent is overkill; after all, the combination means giving away twenty-five percent of the writer's gross income.

The established agents in large firms deal primarily with the heavy hitters: major writers of features, television movies, three-picture deals, and packaging (putting together a writer, director, and major star who are all clients of the agency). This group is then sold as a package to a studio or network, for which the agency receives a packaging fee. Most agencies ask three percent up front, three percent deferred, and ten percent of the gross off-network sale. Proponents of packaging claim that the system increases the chances of a film or television project being made.

For new writers, the promise of packaging may be akin to the emperor's new clothes. Packages are rarely plucked from the lower echelons of the agency's client list. After all, the agency wants their packaging percentage; a writer without substantial credits can be a liability in selling the package. Agent Maggie Field doesn't believe in packaging. "Invariably one of the components of the package gets sacrificed. Who's the most expendable? Certainly not the big-name actor or the big-name director. My experience is that it's always the writer." Agent Robb Rothman (United Talent) says, "Even writers in television who have reached the executive producer level often get sold for less than their real value in order to service the agency package."

Smaller agencies, which some established writers prefer, have strength based on their contracts. They may be adept with television movies, for example, or have a relationship with a particular studio. These strengths are apparent by analyzing the kinds of writers the agency signs and the places where those writers get work.

Any successful agent practices a certain amount of blockbusting. They get one client into a production company, studio, or show and develop a relationship that enables others to get in. This is especially true when the agent has a client in a producer or story editor position. They call the client directly to lobby on behalf of other clients.

A new writer can safely assume that his best chances for snagging an agent are either the smaller firms or new agents and trainees in large firms who are just beginning to build their client roster. Most new writers don't get the agent they want. They get the agent who will have them. As a result, writers are as fickle as actors when it comes to agent-hopping. It's assumed that the agent you start with is not necessarily the agent you'll keep for life.

Agents also leave — jumping from one agency to the next. Their clients usually have the option of going with them or staying at the agency. If an agent leaves the business entirely (many go into production,) the writer stays with the agency.

The standard client/agent agreement is a written contract spanning two years, one year for a new writer. An escape clause mandated by the Guild provides that if the agent does not generate work for a client during any consecutive three-month period, the writer may ask to be released from the contract. The writer is then free to shop around for another agent. The reverse also happens, however: agents periodically drop clients who aren't generating income. Even established writers get dropped, either because their employability seems to have peaked, or because they have proven too difficult to deal with.

## HOW TO FIND AN AGENT

The single most important piece of advice every agent agrees on is: don't bother until you're ready. There's no point in going to agents until you have completed scripts that are good enough to compete. The materials an agent reads in deciding whether to sign a writer are the same materials the agent will use in submitting that writer for work. The same script a writer uses to get an agent is the script the agent sends on to producers as a sample. If an agent doesn't care for it, why on earth would he or she take the risk of hoping somebody else will? If the writing samples are not competitive, the writer isn't either. According to agent David Dworski, it's that simple: "If you write well, you'll get an agent." Agents rarely will read a second submission if the first was weak. "Take your time," advises Robb Rothman. "Go through an extra draft or two. It will do wonders."

The best sign that the work is good enough is when another writer recommends you to his or her agent. Referral is the system by which most agents sign most clients.

The agent will want to see two writing samples, often of different genres. The reasoning is threefold: to discourage the one-script-wonders who are out peddling the first thing they've ever written; to make sure a good script isn't a fluke; and to analyze the writer's employability in various markets. Most often, the two scripts requested will be one from episodic television and a feature movie, unless the writer is clear he or she specializes in one or the other.

During the course of a meeting or telephone conversation, the agent may also ask for a list of credits, basic biographical information, and even a list of who you know (this makes their job easier). If you get a chance to talk with the agent, be prepared to explain why you want to be a screenwriter, the kinds of projects you want to write, and your long-term goals. Dworski can identify a good prospect from this first conversation. "Is this writer adult, competent, focused?" Don't keep the agent on the phone too long — their time is their most valuable asset.

Be warned that agents tend to hang up quickly on writers who want to do everything: i.e., writing/directing/producing/starring in their own movie. Similarly, agents are wary of writers who can write anything and offer writing samples from every conceivable genre. It means they are all over the map and may not write any one thing well. Some agents who specialize in a particular market will specifically ask for samples of the same genre; i.e., two comedy features or two sitcom scripts.

Referrals to agents may come from producers, directors, or studio executives. It's in the interest of all parties involved that the referral comes from someone who has read the material.

It is possible to go to some agents directly without benefit of referral. The Writers Guild maintains a current listing of signatory agents that can be obtained by contacting either the East Coast or West Coast WGA offices. The list is free if picked up in person; a small fee by mail. About twenty percent of the agents listed are located outside of Los Angeles and New York. The list indicates which agencies will consider unsolicited material from writers, which will consider unsolicited material only as a result of references from persons known to it, and which will only accept material specifically requested by its agents.

As an alternative, Robb Rothman suggests that writers watch lots of television and film and get the names of writers whose work they respect. Then call the WGA, ask for the agency department, and ask for the name and telephone number of that writer's agent. "You may not get by the agent's secretary, but this will at least give you an understanding of which agents represent the type of writer you want to become."

For agencies indicating an openness to new material, the Guild recommends that writers call or write the agency, detail their professional and/or academic credentials, and briefly describe the nature of the material to be submitted. The agency will then advise whether it is interested in receiving the material or not. The writer can also decide if this agency is worth the trouble. Most of the agencies on the Open to Submissions List are not. Some are hobby agents who hope to break into the industry by finding a writer who'll do the real contact work; others have thinly veiled money-raising scams such as classes, script consulting or contests they encourage clients to pay for; and some just enjoy the authority they wield over their so-called clients. The horror stories are rife: endless free rewrites for an agent who has no idea what he or she is doing; thousands of dollars spent on a script consultant who turns out to be a business partner of the agent; bogus screenwriting contents where the sponsors keep the entry fees and the winners get a certificate (if that); agencies that sign clients and mysteriously disappear overnight.

Some writers report that even years after disentangling from wanna-be agencies, the agents were still passing around scripts claiming to represent the writers. *Be careful.* Don't be so desperate to get an agent that you lose your judgment. Don't be fooled by false promises or leads. One of my particular pet peeves is the agency surveys done by screenwriting magazines and newsletters. They are a popular feature and, to the credit of most newsletters, they encourage feedback from writers and drop listings if there are too many complaints. But let's be realistic. Why would any agency submit themselves to a deluge of unscreened phone calls and scripts when it's easy to generate volumes of material by mentioning to a few key industry contacts that the agency is looking for new material? If the agent has no contacts to do this through, how effective is he going to be? Far better for a writer to spend the same time and money developing his or her own personal contacts, so that when the material is finally ready, the writer has people who can read it and provide referrals to mainstream agents.

What are the odds once your script does get read by an agent with some clout? About four-hundred-to-one, reports Karen Perew of the Evergreen Agency. That's the number of scripts she estimates she reads to find the one client she'll sign. Rick Ray, one of the founders of Triad, says "It's easy to discern true talent. You read four pages by Alvin Sargent, and you know you're dealing with somebody who has a gift. It is equally easy to perceive somebody with no talent. The real problem comes with the ninety percent in the middle."

The worst possible approach is to send whole scripts without even contacting the agency first. This is akin to trying to teach a pig to dance — it's a waste of time and it irritates the pig. A similar waste is to send a mass mailing to each of the three hundred agencies listed. Many have coded their addresses on the Writers Guild list so that envelopes are easily identified and sent back unopened. It is better to send individual letters to agents at selected agencies or to make phone calls. Rothman also advises being friendly with the agent's secretary. "The secretary may slip your script into the agent's weekend reading and get you a good shot."

It's important for new writers to be aware of the potential pitfalls of even legitimate agents. Some agents, for example, collect far more clients than they can possibly serve. The operating theory is "the more clients, the better the chances one of them will find something." Some agents blanket shows with writing samples from every client, rather than selectively matching particular writers to a show. The blanket strategy usually backfires and none of the scripts is read. Remember, a script under submission to a show doesn't mean much. A script that is being read by a show is news. The real clout of an agent is his or her ability to get material read. Agents do that by having good reputations. A producer knows that if a particular agent says a script is good, it probably is. An agent's reputation becomes the writer's calling card.

New writers shouldn't be too eager to sign with any agent who'll take them. Even beginning writers owe it to themselves to know something about an agent before signing:

- A partial client list.
- Where those writers are working or have worked.
- The genre in which the agency specializes.
- Who will represent the writer — the head of the agency who took him to lunch or the trainee just hired?
- Compatibility of the agent with the writer. The two have to be able to communicate and jointly plan strategies.
- Responsiveness of the agent. Does he or she return phone calls? Show up on time for meetings? Not take phone calls while meeting with the writer?
- The validity of the advice the agent provides. Often, agent advice takes the form of "do a spec episode for this show," "write a comedy," etc. A smart writer double-checks this advice with other writers before blindly starting yet another spec script.

Don't necessarily rule out an agent who takes a while to read your materials — although the agents with the best reputations read submissions within a few weeks. A reading period longer than that may be an indication that the agent is over-extended, disorganized, or not interested in new clients. In any case, no agent reads scripts the day they're submitted, so be patient. A good agent spends his or her day on the phone or in meetings. Script reading is done at night and on the weekends. If the news is good, you'll probably get a phone call. If the news is bad, you'll get a letter and your scripts back.

What material to send? Whichever scripts criticism has indicated that people like the best and which, if you're lucky, are the same ones the agent asked to see. Don't send more material than requested. Less is more. Most agents feel they can tell if a writer can write after the first few pages. If they don't care for the material, they don't read much further. Attach a cheerful and professional sounding cover letter. A sample follows:

Agent name
Address

Dear (agent's name):

Thank you for taking time to look at my work. I've enclosed a *Trapper* script and a television movie. The latter has been well received, but is considered a hard sell because of the dismal ratings that sports-related stories have been receiving on television. It's a fair sample, however, of the kind of projects I like to write.

Television writing is an interesting addendum to a career that has spanned non-profit arts, the unions, and magazine writing. I thought some background might be helpful.

Currently, I am a consultant with a variety of theatres and arts groups (LA Stage Company, the Odyssey Theatre, the CAST Theatre, National Endowment for the Arts) and West Coast contributing editor for *SAVVY*, a business magazine for professional women. Previously, I worked for the performing arts unions (SAG, Equity, WGA, DGA, etc.) doing special projects such as the Media Awards for the Disabled and the SAG Benefit at the Hollywood Bowl. Before that, I was the founder/executive director of a large arts complex — the Pasadena Community Arts Center — which sponsors training programs for visual and performing artists, community arts festivals, and theatre productions.

Through these varied activities I've met a cross-section of people in the entertainment industry so it was perhaps inevitable I'd try my hand at television writing. I joined the Writers

Guild three years ago off of a fluke sale of a story idea to *Secrets of Midland Heights* at Lorimar. This last six months, however, represents the first serious effort to work in television.

I particularly like hour episodic and the light action genre. Some of my best contacts are at *Remington Steele, Fame, Jesse* (new CBS series) and *Crazy Like a Fox* (CBS mid-season). In half hour (which I've not tried my hand at) there are strong connections with *The Jeffersons, Webster,* and *Family Ties.*

The relationship with the staff at *Trapper* has been terrific. My current assignment for them deals with international marriage brokers who import Asian wives — a story they seem quite enthusiastic about. I anticipate another script or two for them this season.

I suspect I have a couple of years lurking in episodic television ahead of me as the craft gets more polished. On the long term, television movies hold the most appeal as they provide an opportunity to mix some of my issue-oriented background with such a powerful media form. Television movies such as *Adam, Something About Amelia,* and *Sybil* represent the level of writing to which I aspire.

Thank you again for your time. I look forward to the chance to talk with you.

My best,
Carl Sautter

Make yourself as attractive a commodity for an agent as possible. Let him or her know your contacts, interests, and any relevant background. Above all, send the best script you have and don't expect notes. Agents, for the most part, do not like to act as editors and do not have the time to give detailed criticism. As for query letters, they should be *much* shorter and to the point. These people don't know you yet, after all. You are trying to get them to read your script. So don't bore them in the letter. Freelance Screenwriters Forum, a national membership organization, sponsors an annual query letter competition for letters designed to attract interest from agents open to submissions. Overall, founder David Groh has been dismayed at the poor quality of the correspondence submitted. Some letters have not been in proper letter format, many had misspellings and typos, and few could summarize their script succinctly so that the story made sense. With permission of the Forum, here are the two winners of the 1991 contest with selected comments from Groh.

Ms. U. Willa Pikthis
Picnomenal Success Agency
102149 Blockbuster Avenue
Burbank, CA 91522

Dear Ms. Pikthis,

I have recently completed an original feature film script entitled, *Heart of Silence*. It tells the story of a man forced to confront his own divinity when his dead daughter rescues him from suicide. The stage version of this story, entitled *Cry of Silence*, won the 1989 Kumu Kahua playwright's award from the University of Hawaii. The script is one-hundred-four pages.

*Heart of Silence* has been reviewed by a professional reader, who commented: "An intelligently written script, professionally written and in proper format . . . Your characters, particularly the husband, were well-drawn and realistic." Dalene Young, a professional scriptwriter said the material was, "moving, believable, and dramatic."

I have also completed an original feature comedy entitled, *Queen Kong*. It is a send up of *King Kong*, in which the hero is the love of the female beast. It runs one-hundred-ten pages. Both scripts are available upon your request as a hard copy or on disc in WordPerfect 5.1 for IBM.

In addition to additional works of my own, I am also interested in working on rewrites and collaborations. I am able to travel to take meetings in Los Angeles.

Thank you for your consideration.

Aloha Pumehana,
[Screenwriter No. Five]

*Comments From David Groh*

Screenwriter No. Five set up an expectation for great things to come. The peach paper with professional letterhead and clean, dark print (apparently a top-notch typewriter, though possibly a laser printer) gave this image. This letter would be read once opened.

The first sentence cuts right to the heart of the matter, and leads directly into a comprehensive one-line synopsis of the story. The reference to the readers and their comments offer good endorsements for the script. The first two paragraphs definitely maintained my interest. However, one major flaw involved the discussion of *Heart of Silence* being derived from a stage play of unknown origin. The writer did not mention whether the rights to the original story were already secured.

The *Queen Kong* paragraph could use the same synopsis format as the description of *Heart of Silence*. Stating ''the hero is the love of the female beast'' makes for trouble — how can ''the love'' be ''the hero.'' That concept is certainly not presenting anything in visual terms. And pitching a second story can hurt the first.

The last paragraph trips from the start on a redundancy — ''In addition to additional,'' though it does end professionally. Except I'm not sure why she offers a disc.

The score:

If opened, would it be read: Yes — definitely

If started, would it be finished: Yes

If finished, would the script be requested: Possibly, although the *Queen Kong* synopsis and lack of clarification of the rights to *Cry of Silence* and *Heart of Silence* may keep many replies from coming.

Dear _____,

Some weeks are better than others. Abigail Goodman is having a bad week. Fresh from graduate school, she moves to Boston to start her first real job. She meets a would-be suitor who can't quite get his foot out of his mouth, a bag lady who speaks in sing-song rhyme, a sexually indiscriminate boss, and a long lost member of the Goodman clan — Hepsibah.

But some family reunions were never meant to be. Some relatives are better left forgotten. Especially if the relative has been dead for three hundred years. Especially if she now seeks revenge for her wrongful murder during the 1692 Salem witch trials.

Abigail has a thing or two left to learn about blood relations. Nothing could ever prepare her for such a welcoming.

I, on the other hand, would welcome the opportunity to show you the script for my horror/action film, *The Welcoming*. Having completed four screenplays, and consulted with two professionals in the industry — a Disney project developer, and an award-winning independent television producer — I feel I am ready to approach your agency about possible representation.

Please let me know if you would be interested in seeing the screenplay. Thank you very much for your time and consideration.

Sincerely,
[Screenwriter No. Nine]

*Comments From David Groh*

Screenwriter No. Nine took my favorite approach: jumping into the story without any boring introductions. This writer captures my interest from the start (although the cheap paper and unclear typeface make for a tough decision on whether to make the initial read).

Its originality of style forced me to finish every line — I would expect the same from the script. (An SASE would help secure the reply). Some cautions: 1) No one keeps track of how many scripts you've written; they only care if this one is any good; 2) Mentioning script consultants raises the questions: why didn't they recommend the writer directly?

The score:
If opened, would it be read: Possibly
If started, would it be finished: Definitely
If finished, would the script be requested: Very likely.

## WHAT HAPPENS WHEN YOU HAVE AN AGENT?

Once a writer has an agent, it is reasonable to expect:

**Periodic updates** (every two weeks is fair) on possible job leads and submissions or the lack thereof. Agents hate daily phone calls even from their most prominent clients.

**An occasional face-to-face meeting** — perhaps every two or three months. Please note: nowhere is it written that the agent always pays for lunch.

**Substantial duplication bills**. In most smaller agencies, the writer is responsible for xeroxing his or her own scripts for submission. Agents usually ask for five to ten copies for this purpose.

**Assistance to the agent**. New writers are at a disadvantage, so they should not expect to sit back while their agent does all the job hunting. A smart writer tries to find his or her own work and updates the agent on contacts and possibilities. Once a contact is made, a good agent takes over and makes sure the material gets read.

**The agent negotiates contracts**, promotes the writer at every opportunity, and follows up on leads. According to the WGA, a writer should expect the following items to be settled by an agent during the negotiating process for a script assignment:

- Start date/option date
- Compensation/payment schedule
- Writing schedule
- Reading periods
- Optional writing services
- Production bonus/purchase price
- Contingent compensation
- Series sales bonus/royalties
- Sequel/remakes/MOW/spinoffs
- Residuals/reruns
- Series services
- Novelization/publication rights
- Turnaround
- Exclusivity
- Research/travel expenses
- Pension/health/welfare
- Theatrical release/producing/directing services

- Office space
- Profit participation

As you read this list, don't get too excited. Freelance writers in the early stages of their careers don't get profit participation or office space.

## HOW TO MAKE AND USE CONTACTS

While I like to believe that contacts can't make a career, friends in the right places certainly create some of the lightning every writer needs. Sources within the industry provide scripts, information about job leads, and guidance. Friends can recommend a writer to agents, provide support during the discouraging times, and offer trusted criticism. They can also get your material read by somebody who might buy it: writers/producers often ask other writers they respect for leads to help staff their show.

The process of meeting people and cultivating relationships within the industry requires some sensitivity. It isn't a matter of meeting a producer at the car wash and asking him for a job. In fact, that's probably the fastest way not to get one.

Remember, anyone who is reasonably successful is deluged with writers, actors, and others clamoring for advice and help. Unfortunately, many story editors, producers, and writers have learned, through bad experiences, to be wary of new writers. Horror stories abound about writers who, after a casual meeting, begin merciless series of phone calls to the staff of a show. This behavior eventually backfires to the writer's disadvantage.

The actor or writer who uses these tactics has not only lost a potential contact, he or she has begun developing a bad reputation. All of us in the industry are regularly reminded just how small an industry this is. Saying that someone recommends you when they don't *will* catch up with you.

A good example was provided at a seminar where the producer of a well-known television show expounded on his desire for openness. He had instructed his writing staff to look at new work; if they liked a writing sample, he pledged to fight with the network to give the new writer a break. The moment the seminar concluded, he was deluged with writers pressing business cards, sample scripts, and asking for his home phone number. He couldn't believe the feeding frenzy he had created. And, suddenly, the wall of aloofness that so often separates the established from the struggling came crashing down. I doubt any of those writers got their material read by that producer, and I'm sure he never made those comments in public again.

Therein lies the dilemma that all hungry writers face. First, how do you meet people who may give you advice or help your career? Secondly, when you do meet someone, how do you behave?

**Rule One. Don't throw out basic etiquette.** People who have social skills often lose them in the presence of any agent or a network executive. No one has the right to interrupt a dinner conversation, recite his resume, or pitch her latest story. Emmy-winning producer Paul Waigner (*Beverly Hills 90210, Hunter*), facing a cocktail party full of aspiring show-biz types, will introduce himself as a grip to avoid such encounters. Director Roland Joffe at a black-tie dinner for the Hawaiian Film Festival insisted he was one of the waiters and began serving champagne to prove it.

**Rule Two. Don't overestimate what someone can do for you.** A successful freelancer may be able to read a script and recommend you to an agent, but he cannot get you work. A producer in a situation comedy is probably powerless to help a writer who wants to be in features. Most story editors have nothing to do with casting, and so can do little to help an actor.

**Rule Three. Real relationships will do more good** in the long run than friendships of convenience. If someone is determined to be the new best friend of a studio executive, simply because that person is an executive, he's wasting time and energy. Invest in people you care about and who care about you. As you or they move up, you can help each other — for the right reasons.

Where do you find friends in the entertainment industry? For writers, the easiest places are writers' support groups, film festivals, screenwriting classes, seminars, and conferences. Other writers are invaluable both to a career and to mental health.

This notion runs contrary to an attitude rampant among both aspiring and established screenwriters — the notion that other writers are competition or that they'll steal ideas. If that's a writer's primary concern, he or she is in the wrong business. Even if an idea or two is lost along the way, the advantages of trading scripts with each other and learning to take and give criticism far outweigh the risks. The unemployed writer you gave an *Empty Nest* script to last year could well be the story editor this year. The reality is that all new writers are on the outside and anything a writer does to help other writers will come back around.

Writers tend to enjoy trading the bad stories and not the good ones. A writer I helped some years back with job leads is now a development executive. She has recommended me for features repeatedly. An assistant director that Paul Waigner helped to attain his first directing job later recommended Waigner for a vice-president position. Another old saying in Hollywood is that everyone is either moving up or out. Secretaries move up. Unemployed people get jobs. Studios and networks are purged of executives so regularly that Robb Rothman describes the process as "the executive *du jour*."

## OTHER PLACES TO MAKE FRIENDS

**Non-writing jobs in the industry.** These may include secretary, production assistant, crafts services, or script typist. Working on a show or on a production lot will bring you into contact with other people in the industry and provide valuable insights into the business side of the business. This town is filled with successful writers who did just that. Lissa Levin (*A Different World*), Juanita Bartlett (*Rockford Files*), and Vickie Patick (*Do You Remember Love?*) all started as secretaries. Almost every employed writer in Hollywood did something else — production assistant, reader, go-fer, agent trainee — before he or she finally wrote that breakthrough script. The first break has often come from the very people they met when working as a secretary.

**Related services to the industry.** These services may be public relations, accounting, research, etc. There is even a legendary group of now-successful actors and writers who were tour guides at Universal Studios in the late '70s. Through the years they helped and supported each other. Most are now major contenders — writing television movies, feature films, and, in some cases, producing their own projects. That lowly group of tour guides turned out to be terrific contacts for each other.

**Non-profit art groups and theatres.** In every city there are arts organizations looking for volunteers. Particularly promising are small theatres where one is likely to find other writers and producers. Here, there may be an opportunity to do a staged reading of a script or submit a play for production.

**Other non-profit groups.** The entertainment industry has been described as ''cause mad.'' Whatever the cause or disease or political candidate, someone from show biz will be involved. These groups need volunteers. Pick a cause or an issue you care about and volunteer your time.

**Sports.** Health clubs and aerobics classes are social centers in most cities. Whether the game is racquetball, tennis, basketball, softball, volleyball, bowling, or *tae kwondo*, there are classes, leagues, and tournaments to join. Almost all include plenty of people from the business.

**Neighborhoods.** *People* Magazine not withstanding, the entire entertainment industry does not live in Beverly Hills, Malibu, or New York's Upper East Side. And for the others, neighborhood associations, tenant groups, and local community groups are good ways to meet them. Ann Gibbs and Joel Kimmel (*Alice, Webster*) had their first script read as a result of walking Joel's dog. A fellow dogwalker turned out to be on staff at *The Mary Tyler Moore Show*.

There are some writers who have developed ingenious ploys. Russ Woody did a magazine article interview with the producer of a popular sitcom. The article was submitted to various magazines for consideration and was, in fact, finally published. In the meantime, however, Russ got hints for writing a spec script for that sitcom and his material was read. Writer Martin Zwiback went far beyond interviews. Fed up that no one would read his feature script, he threw a copy of it over Katharine Hepburn's fence. Flash forward to the news that she actually read it and eventually the movie was made: *The Ultimate Solution of Grace Quigley*. But don't take this as advice to polish your shot-putting skills. The more likely reaction from actors, directors or producers who find their backyards littered with screenplays is an arrest warrant and a long memory.

## HOW TO USE BUT NOT ABUSE

There are a few guaranteed ways to send any producer, director or writer fleeing in the opposite direction:

- Call more than once a month.
- Show up at dinner with a script for them to read.
- Pitch that latest story idea during intermission at a play.
- Beat them too many times in tennis.
- Use them as a reference for a job or an agent without their permission.
- Be *too* friendly when you've only just met.
- Invite an employed industry type to a party of your unemployed friends.
- Invite them to a poorly-staged reading of your latest work or to a bad theatre production starring your best friend, the actor.
- Get testy because they canceled a meeting or are late.

Remember, asking someone to read a script is not a little favor. There is a minimum of two hours' reading time (if it's a feature), another hour of angst while they figure out what the hell to say about it, and yet another hour or two if they decide to give notes. If done right, it's a five-hour favor.

## THE STORY OF A (SMART) NEW WRITER

A while back a young writer was referred to me who so impressed me with the manner in which he handled the whole process that I thought it a useful scenario to pass along. His name: George Saunders. Yes, it's his real name.

**Scene One:** *The phone call.* George called and said he had been referred by his aunt. He reminded me that I had met her at an ice-skating competition in Cincinnati. (Smart move one: George reminded me who this lady was.) Next, he told me that mostly he was calling to say how much he loved my work. (Smart move two:

writers love praise.) Then he did an extraordinary thing: even though I had made an offer to his aunt to give him some advice, he explained he would understand if I was too busy to talk to him. (Smart move three: he let me off the hook.) I was intrigued. How could I help him? He responded with a list of thoughtful and specific questions. (Smart move four: he knew exactly what he wanted to find out from me.) We set an appointment. He offered to come to my office. (Smart move five: never ask contacts to come to you. And if for some reason they do, for God's sake serve good wine or pay for lunch.)

**Scene Two:** *Setting the meeting.* The day of the meeting George called to confirm. (Smart move six: he made it okay for me to postpone.) In fact, I did reschedule. By now I was both impressed that he was smart and grateful that he was understanding. The day of the next meeting George called again. (Smart move seven: he was consistent.)

**Scene Three:** *The meeting.* Of course, George was on time. He had a list of questions, and listened attentively as I offered advice in subjects he hadn't considered. He didn't argue, "No, I tried that" or "An agent told me the opposite." (Smart move eight: he made me feel like he was listening so I was careful to say things that I actually believed.)

As I cited examples of my experience, George said, "Oh, I read that" and "I really liked that script." I began to realize that this kid had read *everything* I'd written — the *Moonlighting*s, that first obscure *Trapper*. He went to the trouble to locate those scripts through UCLA. (Smart move nine: by now, I figured George would be a network executive soon and in a position to help *my* career.) And then he offered to get me copies of a couple of movie scripts I mentioned that I'd love to read. (Smart move ten: this guy didn't just take information, he was willing to offer it, too.)

Then perhaps most amazing of all, at precisely one hour after the meeting started, George announced that he realized how valuable my time was and thanked me for my help. Usually the hardest part of advice meetings is how to end them. But not with George. (Smart move eleven: keep the meeting short.)

**Scene Four:** *The follow-up.* A few days later, the scripts I lent George were returned with a pleasant thank you note. There was still no request to read his work or even to get together again. (Smart move twelve: wait to be asked before you press a script on someone. I would have been crushed if he'd made a mistake at this point.)

In the months that followed, George still did not call me. He returned the rest of the materials with a second thank-you note.

So what happened to George Saunders? Despite being smart and doing his research, even George has had a struggle. He began writing with a partner (another smart move), John Bryant Hedberg, and they did five spec scripts without result. How do I know this? Did George call with weekly updates on his latest depressing rejections? No, he dropped me notes and cards a couple of times a year with updates.

Most important, he and John kept writing. Finally, the diligence and patience paid off. They did a rewrite on a film for Cannon and were subsequently hired to write a comedy feature. And George Saunders, after seven years of sticking with it, is making money as a writer. His latest note summarizes the situation: "I still have a long way to go before I become the filmmaker that I'd like to be; however, I do believe I'm through the worst of it. I no longer have doubts whether or not I can be a writer. I am a writer. Now I struggle with the question of whether or not I'll be a good one. It's always something. Thanks and best wishes, George Saunders"

## WITH A SCRIPT IN HAND

What if you already have a completed script in hand and you have no idea what to do with it? Are agents or personal contacts the only options? The answer is a qualified "no": there are other ways to get material read, but be prepared to invest a substantial amount of time tracking them down — which means that your first dilemma is deciding whether this script is worth the trouble. It may well be that you didn't know enough when you started to write a screenplay that would be competitive. If this is the case, the script is not wasted, it's just a step in your learning process. All of us have file drawers full of early material that mercifully never saw the light of day. Oliver Stone wrote eleven unsold features before he got an agent. Asked in an interview if he planned to resurrect any of them, his answer: "Absolutely not." Oliver is smarter than most of us. Somewhere in the back of every writer's mind is the fleeting notion that those projects can be dusted off when we're wildly successful and produced to great acclaim. But the truth is that most of mine will never get further than the file cabinet. And the world is a better place for that.

Before you invest any more time, find out how good the script really is. Give it to other writers for feedback. Is it great? If it's not great, is it salvageable? If it is, read scripts from the genre, study the form, re-outline, rewrite, polish, and rewrite some more.

When you and your critics are confident this script is really the one that Hollywood is waiting to see, do some market research. For a feature, find out which production companies, producers and directors make this kind of movie. Don't mail them the script. Instead, call and find out if anyone would be interested. If you're telephone shy, write an endearing fan letter. Lists of studios and independent producers are available from a variety of directories including *The Feature Directory, The Writer's Market,* and *The Hollywood Bluebook* published by *Hollywood Reporter.* Assume, however, that thousands of other writers are making the same call, so the competition for reading time will be tough. I do not recommend listing a summary of your script in any of the flourishing number of so-called producers directories out there. I have not met the legitimate producer who reads these listings. A survey in *Screenwriters' Forum* confirmed this impression: most respondents said that the only results they had from their $100-plus listings were solicitations from other directories.

If your script is for television, decide which shows are of a similar style and structure. Call and find out if anyone would be interested in reading your script. Lists of addresses and phone numbers of television shows in production in Hollywood are published regularly in the *WGA Journal, Variety,* and *Hollywood Reporter.* Look especially for new shows that haven't aired yet or are early in the production process. These shows tend to be more open to the work of new writers.

If any studio or story editor is interested in reading your work, assume that unless you have an agent, you will be asked to sign a release form freeing the show or producer of liability if some part of your ideas turn up in the next episode or major hit. Sign it or your script won't — *can't* — be read. Submissions without agents are almost non-existent in television, partly because of a flood of lawsuits over allegedly stolen ideas, nicknamed the "*Quantum Leap* phenomenon."

If initial efforts prove fruitless, now is the time to put some of that clever writing skill into a clever selling mode. How can you get this script to other people who should read it? Start with your friends and play a game of "Who Knows Who?" Who do they know in a studio? At a network? Or a television show? In an agency? Who do they know who knows someone in a studio, a network, etc.? There's an old saying that each of us is only five people away from anyone else in the world.

At American Film Institute seminars we've played this game with participants to great results. Regardless of whether the seminar is in Houston, Minneapolis, or Boston, participants find that through a route of friends of friends they could get a script to any producer, studio or television show. Sometimes the route is complicated and takes time, but it exists. Cultivate a network of writer friends who help each other and you'll find you have many more contacts than you realized.

## SCREENWRITING CONTESTS

Another option is screenwriting competitions, such as those sponsored by universities, state film boards, or film festivals. The number of submissions is high, but the readers in the best of these competitions are established professionals in the industry who will sometimes recommend promising work to other producers and writers. It isn't always the winning script that gets recommended: promising also-rans may show more commercial potential. Contests are popular with state film boards as a way to encourage scripts set in their states.

Be wary, however, of screenwriting competitions that cost money to enter, such as those sponsored by agencies. A legitimate university that charges a modest entry fee for processing is fine, but stay away from unknown organizations that charge hefty entry fees. It is also considered unethical for agents or production companies to charge a reading fee. This practice is specifically barred by the WGA for signatory companies, but the Guild has no control over non-signatories. And don't assume that winning a contest will change your life.

If you decide to hire a script consultant, ask for credits and references before you send the check. Since most consultants charge big fees, be sure the script is in the best possible condition before contacting them. That way, you won't be paying for a basic lesson in screenwriting, you will be taking advantage of their knowledge of nuances and subtleties that can make a script better. Finally, remember most professional script consultants are not in the mainstream of the entertainment industry. As a result, they are comparing your material to other scripts by new writers. The script they deem ready may only be brilliant in the context of the huge number of bad scripts they've read.

A controversial spin-off of the script consultant is reading services that will read, critique and, ostensibly, send your script to producers for a fee. Some of these services are performed by established story analysts and readers from studios, people who would be in a position to recommend the work of promising writers. There is no guarantee that the well-known reader is doing the actual reading and critiquing. Reports of scripts that went on to studios or sold are sketchy. For now, follow the editorials in the *WGA Journal* on this topic and before you use any reading service or consultant, find writers who have had good experiences that produced tangible results.

There also are ads in the trades by production companies soliciting material. The ad reads "Low Budget Feature Screenplays Wanted." Some are "Read For A Fee" services in disguise and others are non-union companies looking for writers they can convince to do a lot of work for free. One such ad was placed by a student I know who wanted to find a script he could direct. Dozens of scripts arrived. But the student had no contacts, and with no production credits, he would be a liability to any writer. How did he have the nerve to raise the false hopes of so many writers as well as cost them the money of xeroxing and postage?

I'm told a few of the companies or producers are legitimately looking for good scripts. Since they are not Guild signatories, they cannot find writers through the agent system, hence the ads. Again, be careful. Find out about the company before you start sharing ideas, sending in scripts, or doing free work. And ask for a contract or letter of agreement.

# CHAPTER FOURTEEN

# FOUR ESSENTIAL SCREENWRITING SKILLS

Screenwriters have a number of tools at their disposal that are not integral to the writing process itself, but are important in a writer's life.

## PITCHING

Few screenwriters in their right mind would call pitching a resource or a tool to help writing. But that's exactly what it is. It's how projects are sold without having to write the script first. So, yes, writers have to talk, too. More specifically, they have to pitch, which means to explain an idea in the least possible time with the most possible excitement for the express purpose of selling it. In that moment, a writer becomes a television evangelist.

Pitching is an important process in every market in film and television. Freelancers pitch episodic ideas to television series in order to get an assignment. Story editors pitch producers to gain approval for their own scripts. Producers pitch ideas to the network, both to get clearance for stories they'd like to do and to sell the pilot idea in the first place. Both producers and writers pitch ideas to networks for television movies, to studios for features, and to pay cable companies for specials. For a profession based on the written word, there is a certain irony in that so many projects are initially sold by talking about them.

There are two reasons for the pitch: time and simplicity. Network executives and producers don't have the time or inclination to read voluminous numbers of scripts in order to make a single buy decision. The pitching process gives the powers that be a chance to hear dozens of story ideas a day without reading dozens of scripts. Similarly, pitching can be to the writer's advantage — work can be rejected before the writer has gone to the trouble of writing a hundred pages. Secondly, relying on pitching forces writers and producers to keep ideas *simple*. This makes the process of saying yes or no easy. Conventional wisdom says that a complicated pitch will translate into a complicated film or television show that will strain the attention span of its audience. Studies have found that even with the emphasis on simplicity, television audiences do not understand sixty percent of the plots they see.

There has been, over the last few years, a major change in the pitch. In feature films we've witnessed the rise of spec script madness. Suddenly spec scripts were going to auction, bringing upwards of $3 million for *Basic Instinct*. Scripts by new writers were regularly fetching prices in the $200,000 to $500,000 range. Studio executives proclaimed the pitch is dead; spec scripts (even by established writers) quickly became the way to go. The reasoning went that good pitches weren't producing good movies; by buying completed scripts, the percentages would improve. They didn't.

Spec scripts, even good ones, proved almost as hard to turn into good movies as good pitches. By all accounts, spec script frenzy has already subsided, a short-lived trend even by Hollywood standards. According to Judy Cech of Triad Artists, "Scripts that would have sold in a weekend a year ago are now going untouched."

Is the pitch back in features? Well, no, not entirely. Most studios and production companies are still open to pitches and spec scripts, especially those from writers with produced films, but the trend is now studio-generated ideas. The studio comes up with a concept, a magazine article, a book, and then looks for a writer to do the screenplay. This practice has created an audition atmosphere in which writers come in and present their approach to the project; the studio hires "the winner." On some projects as many as twenty writers have presented ideas. The advantage to a studio is that it gets to hear twenty versions of the story and can hire the one it likes. The disadvantage to the other nineteen writers is that they've done an enormous amount of work — on an idea that's not their own — for no pay.

Does this mean from now on all feature films will be studio-generated concepts? No. Sooner or later executives will realize their ideas aren't any better at getting movies made than were the pitches or expensive spec scripts. The assumption is that the feature business will strike a balance among all three approaches.

Which brings us back to pitching. No one keeps records, but pitching still remains the single most common activity in Hollywood. Every studio hears twenty to thirty pitches a week. The networks hear roughly five thousand pitches a year for pilots; each freelance writer on an episodic show pitches five to ten ideas per meeting; a hundred thousand projects are registered at the WGA annually (and those ideas are being pitched somewhere). Conservatively, that adds up to a million or so pitches a year. And those are just the formal ones. Projects are also pitched at dinner parties, charity events, tennis matches, casual telephone conversations, and table-hopping at studio commissaries. The opportunity to pitch may be as easy as ''What are you working on now?'' or as sneaky as ''That reminds me of a story idea.''

The sad truth is that most pitches, formal and informal, don't work. Either the story idea is not interesting enough, there is no story, or the listener doesn't understand the talker. A good pitch is a reduction of a thirty-minute, sixty-minute, or two-hour story into a few precious minutes. Most story editors will observe that the first two minutes of a pitch are the most important; by then, the listeners will have decided two things:

1. If they like the project.
2. If they like the person pitching.

The importance of the latter cannot be overemphasized. Many a project has sold because the producer liked the writer, even though he or she may not have been overwhelmed by the particular idea.

Structuring a successful pitch is a difficult process because good pitching is not simply a matter of telling the story. The pitch is a sales meeting. It should capture the overall energy and interest of a project — the concept. The process is comparable to commercials where the essence of a product is reduced to thirty or sixty seconds. Advertisers work hard to find the one detail that will induce viewers to buy product. Cheer does not detail the step-by-step process by which its detergent cleans clothes; instead Cheer is "all temperature." Soft drink commercials don't detail the ingredients or describe the taste (except that it's better). Pitching requires the same philosophy. The worst approach is to laboriously explain the characters and move step-by-step through the outline. Instead, find the hook, the heat of a project, and sell the hell out of it.

The structure for pitching varies according to the market. Writers pitching television episodes are encouraged to bring in a variety of ideas. Some may only be notions rather than fully developed stories. The process is fast: short, clean summaries of the ideas. Producers reject quickly: "not our show," "too similar to one we're doing." The acceptance process is slower — lots of questions, suggestions for changing the story, etc. Decisions are usually made in the meeting.

Pitch meetings in features, television movies, and the alternative markets are about one specific idea or project. The pitch should be short and clear, but there is an opportunity to provide more color and detail. One goal never changes — as quickly as possible, get the producers or network or studio talking. It's boring to listen to ideas; it's interesting to discuss them. It's another irony of this business that as soon as producers start changing your idea and making it — at least a little bit — theirs, you've probably sold it. So shut up at the earliest possible opportunity and let them talk.

Some writers and producers have mastered the art of pitching. One producer renowned for his skill is Stephen Cannell. Network executives actually look forward to a meeting with the creator of *The A-Team* and *Hunter*. The reason? He's entertaining. Cannell defies traditional pitching philosophy. When selling a pilot, he doesn't summarize the concept — he acts out the entire pilot episode in the most minute detail, down to car chases and explosions. Bouncing around the room like a man possessed, Cannell lays out the proposed show so clearly the executives see it. This gift for salesmanship has sustained a major independent company.

The Cannell approach works for Cannell. Taking an hour to pitch a story will strain the attention span of most story editors and studio types. Every writer has to find a system and tone for pitching that works for his or her individual personality and style.

The most widely-accepted approach is to distill the story idea into its shortest and sexiest version. Capture the heat or bigness if it's a movie; emphasize the impact on regular characters if it's an episode of a television show; the promotable *TV Guide* hook if it's a television movie. To convey the tone, provide more detail about a particular scene or character, give examples of the humor if it's a comedy. Tell the two major twists. In short, find whatever it is about a particular project that captures the concept of that project and makes it saleable.

Arnold Margolin (*Love American Style*) has developed a formula that works for him: "One minute to give them the most interesting part." If they respond, he goes to the second layer of a story for a minute, then a third layer for another minute. The longest he's ever pitched: seven minutes. He's sold over twenty comedy pilots with this approach.

Other writers find it's a good idea to describe the opening sequence in detail to set the mood and tone of a project, especially if that sequence is exciting or intriguing, then briefly summarize the major beats of the story. Avoid introducing the characters first; instead, work them into the story in the way the audience will meet them. Long character descriptions up front are boring — they separate the characters from the story, and the listener won't remember them anyway.

Most agents advise writers not to bring written treatments to a pitch meeting. The reasoning is: the listeners will help to shape the story they buy and a good pitch adjusts to that enthusiasm. As a result, any treatment or summary the writer prepares in advance will not match the story the producers may now be considering. Far better to provide the treatment a day or two later with a charming cover letter or in an in-person visit so there's follow-up contact.

Remember, the project a writer is selling is not necessarily the project he or she will actually be writing. Stories change and develop from pitch to outline to script. Many of the elements that seemed important in the first meeting will not reach the final script.

Visual aids are entirely appropriate, especially in feature films and pilots. Stephen Cannell is his own visual aid producer. Thom Mount (*Bull Durham*) uses pictures of well-known actors — Debra Winger, Kathleen Turner, Stephen Collins. As he tells the story of intricate relationships between characters, he moves the pictures around so the studio executives can see how the story develops as they hear it. In order to sell *Wild Women*, producer Susan Lecock showed a home video of her women friends with the explanation she wanted to capture *this* in a film. "*This*" being the humor and patterns of interaction among the group. *Karate Kid* was sold with a VCR tape of the California magazine show *Two on the Town*. And on a pilot for CBS, the producers and I shamelessly brought in five pregnant women to sing a musical number. But glitz doesn't always work. The pilot didn't sell.

The changing form of the pitch in features has created a new problem for writers. Although the initial pitch should be brief and clean, smart producers know the studios ask far more questions these days. No longer is selling movies an "I can summarize that film in three words" game. That may be a great opening, but from then on the writer needs to provide detail.Here are some general rules and suggestions for preparing a pitch:

1. The best pitch is always **short**.
2. **Never lapse into rambling narrative.** Keep the pitch high energy. Show lots of enthusiasm for the project.
3. **Research** the people and the studio to which you'll be pitching. Know their credits, their meeting style. This research will tell you what kinds of projects a studio likes.
4. **Match your pitch to the genre.** If you are pitching to an episodic show, emphasize the impact of the stories on the main characters. If you are pitching a feature movie, emphasize the visuals. Make it clear why this story is different than similar versions.
5. **Move around.** If bounding around the room isn't comfortable, use body language and gestures to enliven the presentation.
6. **Use visual aids** when appropriate.
7. **Lead the meeting.** Former agent David Dworski has produced some valuable tapes on pitching. One of his primary points:

"Keep the focus on you." When meeting a producer for example, don't gush over his previous projects. That makes him the star of the meeting, not you. If possible, initiate the pitch before the listeners ask for it.

8. To keep from getting sidetracked, **work from notes.** Don't read your pitch.

9. **Don't repeat** information.

10. **Try to control where you sit** in the room to avoid looking back and forth from one executive to the next as if you were at a tennis match.

11. **Be prepared for interruptions** and questions. Although these may disrupt the practiced pitch, they are a good sign, evidence that the listeners are listening. After answering questions, go back to the planned pitch as appropriate. Don't be rigid. Go with the tone of the room. Take notes if that's appropriate; people know you're listening to them.

12. **Adjust the pitch** according to the reactions of the listeners. If they are particularly enthusiastic about a point in the story, emphasize that point. If they suggest a change in the story or characters, incorporate that into the rest of the pitch. If the pitch is dying — executives shift uncomfortably, eyes glaze over — stop. Find a clever way to stop mid-story on a cliffhanger and end the misery. This story may be dead, but if you show the good sense not to drag them to their death, maybe you'll get invited back.

13. If more than one person is pitching (i.e., two writers or a writer and a producer) **you both have to talk.** One should pitch the basics of the story and the other do color, as in sports announcing. Interrupt each other, help each other out, but *never* contradict your partner's pitch. In one infamous *Moonlighting* meeting a writer leaned back while his partner was talking and announced, "I never liked this part." That ended their chance of a sale. Producers have enough problems — they're looking for writing *teams*, not *War of the Roses*.

14. When you're done, **never say "what do you think?"** The executives know it's their turn to talk. Don't ask "what did I do wrong?" Trust that the executive will give a blow-by-blow critique to the producer or your agent later.

15. **Practice.** Practice. Practice. Test versions of the pitch on friends and fellow writers. Refine and develop the pitch so carefully that eventually it seems unrehearsed and spontaneous. Don't memorize it. You'll only get rattled with the interruptions.

## TREATMENTS

Treatments are a misunderstood tool of the screenwriting business. Stories are bought and sold from pitching or spec scripts, not treatments. A written treatment is merely a tool of the pitching process — either as an introduction to get in to pitch or, more likely, as a follow-up to summarize the story so that executives can, in turn, pass the story idea along up their hierarchy with some accuracy.

The form for treatments has changed radically. As recently as a decade ago, freelance writers were advised to submit ideas in treatment form to episodic shows in order to get an assignment. That practice is now unheard of. Today's freelancer submits full scripts as writing samples and is subsequently invited in to pitch other ideas.

The treatment of ten years ago was ten to twenty pages; now, the treatment has split into two distinct forms: the short treatment (a few pages) that is used to sell a concept and the long treatment (referred to here as a scene outline) that details the project.

Treatments are still used in various screenwriting markets, but the functions are specific to each market.

In episodic television, a treatment is prepared by either the staff of the show or by the freelancer as a way to clear a story area with the network. An episodic treatment is short — never much more than two or three pages. It may even be just a paragraph on the concept.

In television movies and pilots, a treatment is prepared by the writer, most often after the first pitch meeting. It is then passed up the hierarchy for consideration by studio executives and networks. Usually, the treatment is a prelude to further pitch meetings. Lower-level executives who heard the first pitch use the treatment as notes for their pitch to higher-ups. Later, the writer will more than likely be invited in to repeat the pitch to the next level in the decision-making process. The treatment is also short — three pages or fewer.

In features, a treatment might be used to generate the initial meeting. More likely, the treatment also comes after the meeting. Short treatments are used less in features than in television; the long-form scene outline is a payment step in the WGA contract. Since studio types have traditionally been more interested in finished scripts than lots of pre-script meetings, most feature writers have not been asked to do scene outlines. Instead, the main beats of the story were pitched and the writer was sent off to write. Now at many studios, a scene outline is required.

I dislike the narrative form of an outline. So I've tried to find an alternative: I've gone visual. As the plots and subplots of a movie are necessarily complicated, I use a corkboard and post-its that lay out the beats and scenes, so that the producers or studio executives can see the story unfold step-by-step. Color code the plot and subplots, and you may dazzle your way past the outline stage.

The alternative markets use treatments sparingly, although they sometimes function as a summary for a game show, documentaries, an industrial or as part of a grant application for PBS.

Whatever the market, the rules for treatments are constant:

1. **Keep them short** — two to five pages, unless it's a scene outline. There is no such thing as a hybrid treatment/outline. Do one or the other. The only exception is when you're submitting a project to a foreign company. Most European and Asian production companies are not used to the American-style pitch, and instead take ideas only in writing. Ten- to twenty-page treatments are still the norm.
2. **Deal with the concept,** not the details of the story.
3. **Use treatments** as a supplemental sales tool, not as a substitute for pitching.
4. **Keep the writing lively,** clear, funny.
5. **Don't put in too much detail.** This only gives an executive more to say no to.

Here are treatments from different markets. Both have been used as samples to hand out to other writers. Most notable is that each treatment demonstrates how the story is matched to the particular genre. The business of marriage brokers is enough story for a sixty-minute show; unless it were a true story, however, it couldn't sustain two hours. "Rent-a-Kid" is a lighthearted story for a television movie but it wouldn't be big enough for a feature.

## EPISODIC TREATMENT

TRAPPER JOHN, M.D.
"Go For Broker"
*by Carl Sautter*

Harry Davis, a doctor at SFM, is finally getting married at age forty-eight. It's not that he hasn't tried before, but Harry's a victim of his own outdated ideas — he wants a wife without a career or opinions . . . a woman whose life will be totally devoted to his. And now he's found her. No one at the hospital has met Harry's fiance yet. And, as it turns out, neither has Harry. Harry Davis is part of a wave of lonely men who cannot cope with the changes in American women, and who are fueling a booming new business — international marriage brokers. For a substantial fee, brokers match American men with young Asian wives. Asian women are preferred because of the traditional roles they are taught to play.

Maritza Agaya, age 24, arrives in San Francisco from the Philippines to meet her husband-to-be. But Harry and the pending marriage quickly become the subject of ridicule at the hospital. Harry's less sensitive colleagues tease him about having a mail order bride; the nurses are outraged at his attitudes of what a wife should be.

But Maritza is, above all, practical. Trained as a teacher, she could not find work in a country that educates women but won't hire them. She's corresponded with Harry for four months before this meeting; she believes him to be a good and decent man. For her the arrangement is fair. She can live in the country she's idolized since childhood and send money home to help support her family. She is hurt and confused by the outcry; she never expected such cruelty in this country. And then, to compound her problems, it is discovered that she is seriously ill.

Embarrassed by the controversy, Harry uses Maritza's illness as an excuse to call off the deal. She is, in effect, damaged goods. The wedding is scrapped; Maritza is to go back. Gonzo sees the red flag of injustice — Harry Davis can't drag the woman here and then send her back like the Book of the Month Club! What's more, Maritza needs surgery — and she needs it now!

Trapper and Gonzo perform the critical operation — but Maritza, humiliated by the uproar and the dishonor of Harry's rejection, is a poor candidate for recovery. Her condition deteriorates quickly. Determined to save his patient, Gonzo rallies the nurses to Maritza's cause — urging them to remake her subservient attitudes and rebuild her sense of self-esteem. Meanwhile, Gonzo and Trapper work on Harry, helping him to realize that his selfishness is actually jeopardizing the girl's life.

Confronted by his guilt, Harry remembers that his months of correspondence with Maritza — and their first days together — were the sweetest, happiest times of his life. Despite everything else, he has fallen in love with her strength, her newfound sense of herself . . . the very qualities he thought he didn't want in a wife. But by now Maritza knows she does not belong in this country — she must go back home. If Harry cares as much as he claims, it's up to *him* to follow *her*. The question is will he or won't he?

The subplot centers on a vacant seat on the hospital's advisory board to be elected by SFM employees . . . a position with too many meetings and no power: so, no one wants the job. At the last minute, two staff members file, thinking they'll run unopposed: Brancusi, irate about the staff apathy, who thinks she'll make the board a forum for change; and Stanley, who sees the uncontested election as a chance to break a string of election losses dating back to his defeat for homeroom chairman in the first grade. Each confident of easy victory, Brancusi and Stanley plunge into the serious business of campaigning.

Stanley has money, a campaign manager (Jackpot), and a baby to kiss (his own). Brancusi has organization (the nurses) and issues — including the antiquated attitudes of doctors at SFM as exemplified by Dr. Harry Davis.

## TELEVISION MOVIE TREATMENT

### CHILD'S PLAY
#### by Michael Sarafin

BILL and JAYNE WARNER are bright, attractive, ambitious, trendy. They occupy a huge high-tech San Francisco loft, love to travel, know all the right places to dine, and exactly what to eat when they get there. And being rather typical Yuppies, they've decided not to have children. But then again, there's little ALYSON . . . who really doesn't exist.

It all started when Bill promised his dying grandfather that he would produce an heir. This was seven years ago. But it happened that the old man (who lives in England) didn't expire. For fear that the truth would be fatal to an already weak heart, Bill and Jayne were forced to continue the charade.

No one ever expected Bill's grandparents to make the difficult trip from London to San Francisco. Until now.

Thrown into a panic, Bill and Jayne must now produce a daughter or destroy an elderly man's cherished dreams. In a frantic search, the two Yuppies turn to an adoption agency, only to be rejected by the director who thinks they're nuts. No one rents kids for a couple of weeks.

They also visit a talent agent, which doesn't work out, and then actually consider borrowing one of the building superintendent's kids, but change their mind. Getting rather desperate, Bill and Jayne turn to a friend who's only too happy to lend them her daughter. But the kid turns out to be a brat and a snob and is quickly sent home.

Then it happens that Bill and Jayne come across THERESA, a streetwise, tough little seven-year-old who usually fends for herself. In fact, they "meet" Theresa while she's trying to pick Bill's pocket in a crowded elevator.

It turns out that Theresa is living with an AUNT who has little use for her and is willing (for a price) to let the couple borrow her niece. Theresa also negotiates her own financial reward for pretending to be sweet little Alyson.

Racing against the clock, Bill and Jayne try to mold this street urchin into their own child. Even as she's given lessons in everything, Theresa can't help but poke fun at some of Bill and Jayne's ideas and pretensions.

In the end, no one knows if the plan is going to work. As scheduled, the grandparents arrive and take a fancy to Theresa/ Alyson, though, of course, a lot of things don't jibe with all the letters and pictures Bill and Jayne have sent over the years. With Theresa and her "parents" acting up a storm, things often get very confused.

The grandparents are mystified, but can't help falling in love with this child, who gives them a new lease on life. There are any number of complications (the surprise arrival of Jayne's parents from Springfield, Illinois; the appearance of Theresa's aunt who wants more money), but somehow things seem to work out. And sometimes in unexpected ways.

Not only are Bill and Jayne getting used to Theresa, but this little girl is beginning to believe that she is part of the family. In fact, she secretly hopes they won't send her back to her Aunt after Bill's grandparents leave. Unfortunately, Theresa's bubble eventually bursts. After being wrongly accused of taking something (remember, this whole thing started when the kid was a pickpocket), Theresa accidentally blurts out the truth about "Alyson" to the confused grandparents.

These two elderly people feel betrayed, naturally, and Theresa, who is deeply hurt, runs away. Now, for the first time, Bill and Jayne realize how much this little girl means to them. She has made a difference in their lives. It takes some doing, but Bill and Jayne eventually find Theresa and ask her to come back . . . home.

Of course, Bill and his grandparents have to settle a few

things first, which they finally do (and in the process establish a new, wonderful relationship).

But what's most important is the child's welfare. In the end, Bill and Jayne come to understand what it's like to be parents. Maybe now (if an adoption can be arranged), they can also be a real family.

After all, three Yups can live as happily as two.

The tone of choice for a good treatment is breezy — short, lively sentences that make the narrative easy to read. The story should be told clearly, its strongest selling points emphasized but not over-sold. Stay away from dialogue, complicated explanations of the characters, or step-by-step explanations of the plot. Think concept. Don't get cute. No happy faces, clever stick drawings, or poems. Don't put anything in a treatment that distracts from the sales pitch. You run the risk that the stick drawing will be all they remember.

Above all, a treatment should be a good read. The best treatments have a casual air about them (which is hard to accomplish since the writer labored over every word). The goal of a treatment is to make the reader want to hear more.

## WRITING WITH A PARTNER

Writing teams have some distinct advantages in screenwriting. Ideally, a two-person team has the ability to generate twice as many story ideas, cultivate twice as many contacts, and, most important, has a built-in process for critiquing. There is immediate feedback if a story begins to go off-track or if a joke doesn't work. This makes partnerships a valuable learning experience for new writers. Additionally, some writers can't abide the isolation of writing. For them, a partner provides companionship and motivation. There is someone there to help with the difficult scenes or to force work on the days when you're blocked. There is also feedback about meetings — evaluating how a pitch session went or why a producer is an idiot.

Writing with a partner requires a common sensibility and a willingness to compromise. Debra Frank, who was my partner on *Moonlighting*, describes a writing partnership as being just like a marriage ''without the good part.'' To make matters worse, partners have to agree on everything. A husband and wife can agree to disagree, but a writing team has to come to terms with every plot point, joke, and scene. And that's tough because even the most compatible teams don't agree on everything. If they did, they probably wouldn't be a very good team. The differences that each partner brings to a script are as important as the elements they have in common. The best teams join writers with different sets of skills.

Most writers look for partners with whom they have a lot in common, so teams are homogenous — usually two men or two women about the same age, from the same background, and with similar educations. Less prevalent but still common are husband and wife writing teams. Least common are unmarried male/female teams, black and white writing teams, or old and young writers working together. If the personalities of the writers are compatible, teams with built-in diversity will have an advantage because they stand out from the other teams in town and because the distinct backgrounds will add a unique texture to their writing.

There is no correct way to write with a partner; every team has to find its own patterns. Frank Cardea and George Schenk, creators of *Crazy Like a Fox*, write every word together. One sits at a typewriter, the other paces, and they haggle over each line of dialogue and stage direction as it is created. They never write separately. Deborah Dawson and Victoria Johns, producers of *Trapper John*, divide up scenes, write first drafts separately (while in the same room). Then they jointly rewrite and polish. Caroline Thompson and Larry Wilson (*The Addams Family*) divide up scenes, go off on their own to write drafts, then trade. They rewrite these separately and then work together on a final polish.

In addition to finding their own styles of writing, teams develop their own tricks to deal with the problems of disagreements and getting on each other's nerves. Writing teams have to learn that a partner is not the enemy. After all, both partners have the same goal — to write the best script in the least painful manner.

If the partners have different skills, there may be a tacit understanding that the writer with the better dialogue abilities makes the call about a line of dialogue. Debra and I traded jokes and plot points. If one of us loved a joke that the other was not wild about, it became a credit for something in the future. The system helped us past the minor conflicts and infused humor into the potentially tense process of rewriting each other. Some teams have an agreement not to change each other's words unless absolutely necessary; so the scenes each team member writes go into the final script basically intact.

A writing team is treated as one person, and WGA minimums are the same whether one writer or two did the script. This means that a team has to generate twice as much work to earn the same amount of money as a single writer. And just because there are two writers doesn't mean that the work goes twice as fast. Depending on the system the team has developed, the work may take just as much time as a single writer if not more.

One of the frustrations for teams is that they tend to be valuable only as a team and not as individual writers. Another example of the "you are what you write" syndrome, a team may be hot, but one partner by himself or herself is viewed as half a team. When teams break up or decide to write projects separately, they often find they have to revert to spec scripts in order to prove they can write by themselves. But not in all cases — Tom Patchett and Jay Tarses created *Buffalo Bill* together and were one of Hollywood's premiere comedy writing teams for years. Eventually they parted and were able to establish major careers separately. Patchett went on to write and produce *ALF* and Tarses went on to *Days and Nights of Molly Dodd*.

## HOW TO FIND A PARTNER

If you're interested in writing as part of a team, don't first go to your best friend or spouse. There can be an advantage in working with someone with whom there is personal distance. Partners don't have to be best friends to work together. They do have to have professional respect for each other and an ability to get along.

Some criteria to use in evaluating a potential partner are:

1. **A common sensibility** about what's important, how a story should develop, what's funny, what's touching.
2. A writer who can **complement your strengths;** from whom you can learn and who can learn from you.

3. A writer you can **get along with** on the bad days. Don't kid yourself, every team has them.
4. A writer whose **opinions you respect** and who can accept criticism from you.
5. A writer who **wants to write the same genres** as you do. A sitcom writer will be miserable with a feature writer unless the agreement at the beginning is to find projects that take advantage of both skills.

Don't flatter yourself about finding a major writer with lots of screen credits. You'll probably end up with a partner at roughly the same level of achievement as you. A good source for potential partners is references from other writers. Also, the Writers Guild sponsors regular social events to introduce writers to each other. In Los Angeles it's call The Hitching Post. Non-WGA members can come with WGA members. Other groups such as theatre companies bring writers together in playwrights workshops or writer support groups. And an ad in the local paper is always a good way to find out who else is out there.

Make sure you read each other's work and are comfortable with criticisms the other offers. This is no time to be gentle. If you're going to be a team, find out how you will work together once the honeymoon is over. Don't make a lifetime commitment.Take the process one step at a time. Come up with story ideas together, do scene exercises, practice polishing each other's work. Find out what style of work the two of you do best. Above all, treat the whole process of developing a writing team much like any other relationship: let it evolve.

## CRITICISM: HOW TO TAKE IT

Probably the most underestimated skill required for any kind of writing is the ability to take criticism and suggestions about your work and to give useful criticism to others about their work. This is especially important in screenwriting, where the whole process is called "giving notes." It is inescapable: story editors, producers, other writers, actors, networks — everybody gives notes. Learning how to listen, what to listen for, who to listen to, and what to say, can teach a writer more than any other screenwriting skill. Script consultant Linda Seger advises writers: "It's not the writing, it's the rewriting that counts."

It's important, therefore, to keep in mind that screenwriting is no place to be word proud. Every screenplay is re-written, edited, polished, and re-written again; scenes are restructured by directors; dialogue is changed by actors; whole sections of a script are eliminated in editing. Many scripts are given to other writers to be completely redone. If a writer can't take criticism or learn from this process, screenwriting will be a frustrating endeavor.

The proof is in who has the power. In television the combination of short deadlines, tight budgets, ongoing series with existing characters, overworked actors, and network meddling combine to give power to whoever can get a show on the air. That's the producer, and so TV is known as a producer's medium. Actors and writers quickly learn this.

Almost every successful TV writer is a writer/producer, and actors Larry Hagman, Rosanne Arnold and Bill Cosby all get "producer" credit on their respective shows.

Feature films, on the other hand, are considered a director's medium. Because shooting schedules are longer, much of the decision making happens on the set. The look and style of a film are for the most part the director's responsibility. In most cases the film is a "go" for filming only after a director is attached. From that point on, he or she is actively involved in making decisions about rewrites, casting, and production. Writers are expendable by comparison; the pattern for feature scripts often is to use more than one writer, some receive screen credit, some do not for various stages of the rewriting of a screenplay. This is why so many theatrical writers want to direct.

If the most important goal for you is to have your words presented exactly as written, consider playwriting. Plays are considered the true writer's medium. And, unlike screenwriting, the playwright owns the product and leases it for production: The screenwriter sells the product and has no further rights.

## WHEN YOU ARE RECEIVING NOTES

Don't give your script to anyone (even your mother) expecting that all you are going to get is praise. Never in the history of film or television has someone read a script and said "it's absolutely perfect . . . don't change a word." When it comes to writing, everyone has a better idea. If you're not willing to listen to their opinions, don't ask for them. The best philosophy is always to assume that you overrate your own work and that you have a lot to learn.

1. **Pick readers carefully.** Remember both your ego and theirs is on the line. Other writers are a good choice — they'll probably take the task seriously. And in the future they may ask you to critique their work.

2. Make it clear to your readers that what you want from them is specifics and **an honest opinion.** Then mean it.

3. **Assist the note-givers** by being open to ideas and helping them structure comments in a useful order. The best approach is to begin with the script overall (tone, impact, purpose), the characters, then plot lines and structure, the scenes and finally the dialogue and any details. If the note-giver mixes these elements together, the notes will be too confusing to be useful.

4. **Don't take every suggestion** or criticism you're given as fact. This is as foolish as taking no suggestions. Evaluate each comment carefully and objectively to see if it fulfills your purposes in improving the script.

5. **Write down what you are told.** It is difficult to listen objectively if you are feeling at all that your writing is under attack. You'll find that when you reread the notes later, the suggestions make far more sense and you will be able to evaluate them more objectively. More and more people are taping note sessions. Particularly if you are resistant to criticism, you may not hear important notes otherwise. And a tape can settle a disagreement between partners about what was really said.

6. A valuable approach is to **ask the critiquer to write notes on the script** — suggested line changes, questions about the plot,

sequences to cut. The discussion phase can then focus on the script overall rather than going through line by line. A notated script also means you won't have to rewrite from memory. For the second draft of this book I sat down with twenty different marked-up versions of the manuscript from different writers and compared them to see the pattern of points to clarify, questions, suggested changes.

7. **Bear in mind the biases of the person** who is giving notes. This does not negate what they say, but is a reminder to evaluate their suggestions with a view to how they might be slanted.

8. If you counter each note with an explanation, the note-giver will quickly give up on the whole process. **Don't respond to notes except:** 1) To ask questions; 2) To say "that's a good point" (this encourages the notegiver to relax and be more specific); and 3) To clarify a suggestion you don't understand.

The worst possible approach is to start arguing. Take all those notes, look for patterns, and rewrite, rewrite, rewrite. The best career investment a writer can make is to do draft after draft of a spec script.

## WHEN YOU ARE GIVING NOTES

Giving notes to other writers on their work will do as much, if not more, for your writing skills than getting notes on your own script. The process teaches objectivity, thereby honing your skills to identify problems in your own writing.

When you have an opportunity to critique work, take advantage of it. If you agree to read another writer's script, take the process as seriously as you want someone reading your work to do.

1. Before reading a script, **make certain the writer wants notes** and not just praise. It is sometimes helpful to ask in advance which parts of the script they are most worried about; then you can concentrate your suggestions on problems they already perceive if the atmosphere gets tense.

2. When giving notes, **be sensitive about feelings.** Offer observations about both what is good and what is problematical

in the script. Avoid blunt comments. "How could you put in that dumb scene?" It is also not appropriate to use this opportunity to get even because they didn't like your last movie idea.

3. If a writer becomes glassy-eyed or overly sensitive about your comments, **back off.** At that point, your suggestions are serving no purpose.

4. Offer notes in **an organized fashion** — the script overall, plot lines and structure, characters, scenes, dialogue, and other details. Giving clear notes is instructive to you as well as the writer. Encourage questions about your comments or parts of the script you might not have mentioned. Leave behind a written summary of the notes or a marked-up manuscript for future reference.

5. Wherever you can, **be constructive.** It is not helpful to say "this character is boring" — offer specific instances where you see the problem. And heed Linda Seger's advise (*Making a Good Script Great*): concentrate on problems, not solutions. Typically readers offer suggestions — "add a car chase," "cut that scene," "wouldn't it be funny if . . . ," "have him try to kill the critic" (exactly what the writer is thinking) — before they've identified the problem they are trying to fix. And their solution may or may not fix it. Far more useful to identify the problem first — i.e., the main character isn't moving the story, there's a jump in plot logic, or this scene repeats an earlier one — then talk about options the writer has to fix the problem. Suggest alternatives so that the writer realizes the decision-making process is still his or her own.

6. **Be aware of your own biases** as a writer and announce these before you begin any critique. If you can't stand a particular sitcom and you've been asked to read a spec episode, the writer should know in advance.

If you are in a working situation with a producer, it is appropriate to ask for notes in writing. Suggest the producer have an assistant in the room who can take notes, then type them up. The advantage is that the producer will review these notes before sending them on, and will usually change some of the dippier suggestions himself. The disadvantage is the notes are now committed to print and are harder for the writer to ignore.

CHAPTER FIFTEEN

# SURVIVAL AND OTHER CONSIDERATIONS

## IS THERE LIFE FOR A SCREENWRITER OUTSIDE OF LOS ANGELES?

The primary buyers of product for film and television, major studios, and networks, continue to be based in Los Angeles and New York. However, there are more and more markets opening in other parts of the country. Atlanta, Boston, Chicago, Dallas, Denver, and Orlando, among others, are increasingly important media centers, particularly for alternative markets such as cable, documentaries, home video, commercials, and industrials.

Until recently, agents and producers advised would-be screenwriters that they had to move to L.A. Now that's simply not true any more. Most writers could fly into L.A. in less time than it takes me to drive across it. With the advent of the fax, expanded airline schedules, and overnight delivery services, it is increasingly possible to be a successful screenwriter outside L.A. The exact degree of flexibility depends on the market.

### EPISODIC TELEVISION

The primary markets for television writers are in Los Angeles, and to a much lesser extent, New York. It has traditionally been impossible to build a career in episodic television without living in Los

Angeles at some point or commuting there on a regular basis for meetings and pitch sessions. Even though several series shoot in other parts of the country, most are still produced on the West Coast, which means they are also written there. As much as *Dallas* shot in Dallas, for example, there were no Dallas-based writers on the show. Over the years, the producers were approached with a number of scripts that made their way onto the set, but there was a standing policy not to read them.

There is no reason for episodic writers to move to L.A. to be unemployed. With patience and persistence a number of writers have sold or gotten work from their spec TV scripts, and then moved to L.A. Robert John Guttke in Minneapolis submitted nine drafts of a spec *Beauty and the Beast* to the show. A producer began reading them at draft three — after Robert discovered they had a mutual friend. Ann Collins (*Matlock*) lived in Denver when she sat at a luncheon with one of the producers of *Hawaii Five-O*; she eventually did two scripts for that series before moving west. On the *Lucky Luke* series we hired three writers from Minneapolis and two from Atlanta because they had the best writing samples.

Collins challenges the notion that staff writers have to live in L.A. She is a producer on *Matlock* and lives in Seattle. From there she does original episodes, takes notes, and rewrites scripts via telephone, Federal Express and FAX. She is the first to admit it's an unusual arrangement. Sneakier, but not so unusual, is Madeline DiMaggio (*Writing for Television*) who, unwilling to give up her home in Santa Cruz, maintains a Los Angeles phone number and an answering machine as if she lived there.

## OTHER PRIMETIME TELEVISION

Television movies have led the migration of production out of Los Angeles. Lower production costs, new locales and aggressive recruiting efforts by other states have resulted in filming in every state of the union. It's easier to have a career in TV movies (as opposed to other forms of television) away from the two coasts because deadlines are more relaxed and there aren't the same number of story meetings. Also, since cable companies such as HBO and Turner appreciate completed spec scripts, it doesn't matter to them where they're written.

One of the biggest beneficiaries of the flight of production from California has been Canada. Toronto is the world's third largest production center for film and television. Lower production costs and tax incentives have attracted TV movies, features, and some episodic series. Currently, twenty-five percent of U.S. TV movies are filmed in Canada. This has been a boon for Canadian writers because production companies get points for hiring Canadian citizens. As a result, writers, directors, actors, and others who are Canadian citizens are much in demand. There is an irony in this, according to Canadian Darryl Vickers (*Tonight Show*) because Canadians aren't being hired in Canada. Instead, "We all moved to Los Angeles so we can be sent back to Canada to work!"

## FEATURE FILMS

Features involve longer deadlines and, during the writing stages, writers are ignored by everyone — so a writer can live anywhere. Los Angeles and New York provide the advantage of social contacts and gossip, but the writing process itself is not bound by geography. For new writers hoping to sell a spec feature script, there is no reason to relocate. Studios don't buy geographic proximity; they buy good scripts. Richard Graglia has sold five features from his home base in Denver, and commutes periodically to Los Angeles or New York for meetings. He prefers writing full scripts and trying to sell them to taking assignments.

Tom Pope (*Lords of Discipline, FX*) lives in Minnesota and says he's never lost a job because of it. "If anything, because I'm flying into L.A. from out of town, they schedule fewer meetings and take my time more seriously." Sam Hamm (*Batman*) feels the same. He lives in San Francisco "so as not to get sucked too far into Hollywood's weird social network."

Clever writers and producers are discovering that they don't need Hollywood for contacts. Regional film centers and festivals can be just as valuable — Sundance Institute in Utah and filmmakers' groups in media centers such as San Francisco, Minneapolis, and

237

Seattle, for example. Entrepreneurs in states such as Texas, Illinois, and Florida raise money locally to produce films. At various times groups such as Film Dallas (*The Trip to Bountiful* and *Kiss of the Spider Woman*), have been very influential.

## ALTERNATIVE MARKETS

The producers of product for alternative markets are decentralized, far more than the major network and feature suppliers. These companies can't afford the overhead in L.A. or New York. There are regional opportunities for new writers, particularly in news, home video, industrials, and commercials in areas as diverse as Atlanta (now a mega-broadcast center, thanks to Turner), Miami, Nashville, New Jersey, Oregon, Washington, D.C., and Maine. And it is an advantage to live in these areas. Charles Hyatt suggests that "you don't have to be a superstar to make a nice living at what you love to do. Start by targeting a smaller regional market."

Often writers who gain their first break in a regional market get noticed and move on to larger projects in the key markets. Those writers make strong arguments for not moving to Los Angeles and New York and offer the following advice:

1. **Don't move until you're good enough.** It's harder to be unemployed in Los Angeles writing your fifth spec script than it is to be employed in Des Moines doing the same thing.
2. **Don't move until you have a reason to.** A good reason is that you've sold a feature, found a "knock 'em dead" agent, or married a producer.
3. **Take advantage of local opportunities.** While the feature shooting in town is already written, the one that production company will do next is not.

Colorado writer Kate Phillips had been trying to get her feature script to Richard Roundtree. She found out he would be in the state for a charity benefit and through his agent made arrangements to meet him at a bowling alley. That access wouldn't have been offered to her in Los Angeles or New York. Roundtree probably doesn't hang out at bowling alleys in L.A. Producers, directors and actors are at their most relaxed and accessible when not on their home turf.

Don't become a cliche. Nothing kills enthusiasm faster than hanging out with bitter writers on either coast who have lost their willingness to learn to write better. "The temptation to be bitter is great," offers Nancy Nigrosh. "And the temptation to believe you're the only one who knows what they're doing is even greater." One way to avoid that is to have a normal life. Jeff Arch moved to a small town in Virginia to help regain his perspective. He has subsequently sold a spec feature to Tri-Star, did *Exit the Rainmaker* as a TV movie for CBS and has projects pending with Imagine. "When I left, everyone said how unwise it was. But I felt if I had a good script, no one would care where I lived. Now those same people say how lucky I am not to have to live in Hollywood."

Some writers have actually been hired *because* they live out of town. Jenny Wingfield (*The Man in the Moon*), who lives in Gladewater, Texas, was the first choice to script a Sally Field project because she lives in the South. Larry Brothers (*An Innocent Man*) has had much the same experience writing from Cloud Croft, New Mexico, surrounded by national forest.

Tom Wright believes that screenwriting of all types can be done anywhere and should be. While working on *New Jack City*, he spent three months living in the East Village of New York and rode with drug enforcement agents on their street beats. On a project for Fox about the uprisings in Tiananmen Square, he spent time in Beijing interviewing students. Writing for him is not sitting in an apartment exploring your inner terrain — "it is of and in the world around you — in touch with politics or sociological aspects of what's happening. Where you live is secondary to where your writing is living."

Additionally, every state has a film board that promotes production in that state. These boards or commissions are an excellent source of information on upcoming productions. Some even have programs to encourage local screenwriters. Contact your state government for information. In Florida, for example, the Florida Screenwriters Competition is designed to create "Florida films, made in Florida, by Florida producers, hopefully written by Florida writers" says Bob Allen of Disney/MGM Studios. Entrants must be residents of Florida, and the scripts set 75% in Florida locales.

## WHAT ABOUT AFFIRMATIVE ACTION?

All new writers have tough times getting started. According to statistics, if you are not young, white, and male, the road is even tougher. In a series of reports described as "scathing" by the trades, the Writers Guild analyzed patterns of employment among its membership. The result caused a furor.

Women — fifty-two percent of the U.S. population and forty-four percent of all employed authors, are only twenty percent of employed film and television writers. Ethnic minorities, eighteen percent of the overall population and six percent of employed authors, are less than three percent of screenwriters. The report concluded that in addition to these patterns of sexism and racism, there is ageism in the writing business. Writers over forty earn only 83¢ to every dollar earned by the average writer under forty. The Guild report did not accuse production companies or networks of deliberate discrimination, but rather of discrimination by omission. "It is a common belief that white male writers can write anything, while women and minorities can only write about women and minorities," the report stated.

The Guild has instituted programs in response to the report in an effort to provide affirmative action opportunities. The most visible of these is the script submissions program under which women, ethnic minorities, people over forty, and writers with physical disabilities can submit spec scripts to production companies. Reading is guaranteed and the writer receives critical feedback, although not necessarily a job offer. These programs are extended only to writers who are affiliated with the Guild. Some studios have also implemented special training or recruitment programs. Disney has a program for ethnic minority writers. Other studios such as Twentieth-Century Fox, Warner Brothers, and Universal have sponsored programs to cultivate new writers. AFI has special programs for both women and ethnic minorities.

In addition, shows with major women or ethnic minority stars have actively recruited writers from these groups. *The Cosby Show* and *In Living Color* continue to seek submissions from black comedy writers; shows such as *Golden Girls* look favorably on submissions of women writers. Therein lies the trap discussed in the WGA report — the perception that women and minority writers can only write for women and minority-oriented shows.

The outlook is not all bleak. By acknowledging that there is a problem in employment patterns, the Guild is putting much-needed pressure on companies to consider new writers from these groups. There are also active coalitions and support groups both inside and outside the Guild that provide networks of contacts and information. The WGA sponsors the following committees as described in the WGA Manual:

- Age Discrimination: Investigates and lobbies against discrimination based upon age in the entertainment industry; works to sensitize potential employers to the issue of age discrimination.
- Black Writers: represents the interests of black writers.
- Disabilities: represents the interests of disabled writers.
- Latino Writers: represents the interests of Latino writers.
- Women: Promotes means of ending discrimination against women writers in the industry; works to improve the image of women on film, television, and radio; and sponsors events designed to increase knowledge of the craft and the marketplace.

In addition, there are cooperative councils among the various Hollywood unions, including actors, writers, directors, and musicians in the following fields:

- InterGuild Minorities Council: representatives of AFTRA, SAG, Actors Equity, Writers Guild, Directors Guild
- InterGuild Women's Council: representatives of AFTRA, SAG, Actors Equity, Writers Guild, Directors Guild, and the musicians' union

All the unions and guilds have affirmative action programs. A variety of independent organizations also serve the needs of women and ethnic minorities in the entertainment industry.

- Association of Asian Pacific American Artists (AAPAA): Monitors portrayal of Asian/Pacific peoples in the entertainment industry and the portrayal of Asian/Pacific life; an annual awards show.

- GLAAD: promotes the responsible portrayal of gay issues and characters; an annual awards show. Hailed by the *Los Angeles Times* as "the best" of the awards shows.
- IMAGEN: monitors portrayal of Hispanics in the entertainment industry; an annual awards show.
- Media Office on Disability: promotes employment of persons with disabilities in the entertainment industry; the accurate portrayal of disability issues; an annual awards show.
- NAACP Image Awards: monitors racial portrayals in the entertainment industry; lobbies for employment opportunities; an annual awards show.
- Women in Film: a membership organization of women in the entertainment industry designed to encourage "networking" of women professionals, and yes, they have an awards show — the prestigious Crystal Awards. There are also regional chapters in Chicago, New York, and San Francisco.

Contact local civil rights and women's organizations that represent these constituencies for information on support groups or activities in your local area.

## HOW DO YOU OVERCOME WRITER'S BLOCK?

Every writer has them — those days when no matter how hard he or she tries, there's no inspiration. In marathon running it's called "hitting the wall." This condition in writers may not be as physically painful as it is for runners, but the result is the same — the mind is saying, "Enough punishment, can we stop now?"

The coining of the term "writer's block" is a disservice to writers because it gives a name to their biggest bugaboo: the fear that when they're supposed to write, they can't. The obsessive fear of writer's block is probably as much the cause of it as anything else.

Not knowing what to write isn't a block as much as a slowing down of the process — a delay. Delays happen constantly for writers — stopping to rethink a character, agonizing over a line of dialogue, or questioning whether the whole plot makes any sense at all. Delays and blocks, starting and stopping, *are* the writing process.

When faced with monumental delay, each writer handles the crisis differently. Some figure if they sit long enough and stare at the typewriter intently enough, the creative juices will flow. Other writers take the opposite tack. Instead of beating themselves up, they do something else — perhaps an easier scene in the script or proofing what's been typed so far, or — if they're like me — they walk away. I decided early on I didn't want to be miserable when I was writing, so if I'm not reasonably enjoying it, I stop. This rule requires a somewhat unrealistic level of confidence: that I *will* enjoy the script at some point, enough to finish anyway. And that's not always been the case. But for the most part, leaving the computer to do something unrelated allows me to return relaxed with new perspective.

One of the keys to handling these delays is to head them off. Every writer has his or her own rhythms — some write best in the morning, others late at night. Some write in bursts — fourteen-hour marathons, then nothing for a day or two. These writers are the opposite of writers who enjoy a rigid structure — at the typewriter every day at 8:00 A.M. with a cup of coffee . . . break at 10:30, lunch at 12:15 . . . etc. Find what works for you.

One ploy that works is to create a writing zone that triggers the impulse to write. It may be a yellow legal pad in your favorite chair in the den or a computer surrounded by diet soda cans in a smoke-filled room. Experiment and find out what triggers the "it's time to write" response. Don't worry if what you discover is a little eccentric. Fred Rappaport (*Cagney and Lacey*) rewards himself with Twinkies when he finishes a tough scene. Debra Frank writes only with a sharp #2 pencil on yellow pads, careful never to tear the pages off, writing the entire scene in the margins, never in the center of the page. In moments of truth, all writers will admit to their own peculiarities, rituals, and tricks.

## WILL THEY LET ME WRITE THAT?

It is not possible to talk about the real rules of screenwriting without mentioning censorship. Review of scripts and finished product to monitor violence, sexual situations and language is a constant in all screenwriting markets. The standards for acceptability are established by the major producers, associations, and distributors, such as networks in each market. In feature films, the primary review mechanism is the MPAA (Motion Picture Association of America) ratings system under which every film is screened before its release and assigned a rating based on suitability for audiences. These ratings range from:

G — General Audience.

PG — Parental Guidance suggested.

PG-13 — Not recommended for children under 13.

R — Restricted. Attendee has to be 17 or over or accompanied by an adult.

NC-17 — No one under 17 admitted.

X — No one under 21 admitted.

Studios are careful not to produce films that receive an "X" rating since many theatres won't show them and many newspapers won't advertise them. Pictures are frequently edited to earn a less restrictive rating.

In television, there is a line-by-line review of scripts by studio officials and by each network by their Standards and Practices divisions. Memos are issued to the producers of a show to make modifications on each script. It is an established ritual that producers will then argue against some of the notes and "trade" one change for another. A "bitch" may be worth two "hells" or an off-color joke can be saved by toning down the "damns" and "bastards" in other parts of a script. Certain shows are notorious for the feistiness of the producers in such matters and are given more leeway. *L.A. Law, Moonlighting,* and *Golden Girls* all earned reputations for bucking network censors. But unquestionably the show that pioneered that movement was *Soap.*

Here is an excerpt from a censor memo to the producers of that series that is among the most widely duplicated and circulated documents in the industry. It can be found on the bulletin board at almost every television show.

"Soap" represents a further innovation in the comedy/dramatic form presenting a larger-than-life frank treatment of a wide variety of controversial and adult themes such as: pre-marital sex, adultery, impotence, homosexuality, transvestitism, transsexualism, religion, politics, ethnic stereotyping (and other aspects of race relations), etc.

Accordingly, great caution will have to be exercised to carefully balance controversial issues; provide positive characterizations to balance ethnic stereotyping; delicate matters of taste will need to be handled with sensitivity and discretion; and the gratuitous, sensational or exploitative will need to be avoided.

"SOAP"

PART I

| | |
|---|---|
| Page 5 | Please delete ". . . the slut." |
| Page 6 | Please delete "Some Polish slut." |
| Page 7 | Avoid visual I.D. of Penthouse cover and photos. |
| Page 16 | Please insure that Benson's self-effacing portrayal is always played tongue-in-cheek and that he continues to stay "one-up" vis-a-vis his antagonists. |
| Page 23 | Delete "fruitcake . . ." |
| Page 28 | In order to be able to treat the Mafia storyline here and throughout, it will be necessary to introduce a principal continuing character of Italian descent who is very positive and who will, through the dialogue and action, balance and counter any negative stereotypes. |
| Page 32 | In order to treat Jodie as a gay character, his portrayal must at all times be handled without "limp-wristed" actions or other negative stereotyping. |
| Page 29 | Please insure that Peter and Jessica are adequately covered in this bedroom sequence. Here and throughout, there will need to be a deemphasis of "illicit" sexual encounters. It is preferable to handle such matters in dialogue rather than treating the viewer to bedroom scenes such as this. |

| Pages 38-40 | Please substitute for Jessica's "Oh God's" and "Oh my God." |
| Pages 43-44 | Please insure that Peter's dressing scene is suitable for TV viewing. Please revise the colloquy between Jessica and Peter — delete all references to getting "boffed." |
| Page 45 | Delete Jessica's "Oh God," |
| Page 46 | The colloquy between Peter and Jessica here, which relates to cunnilingus/fellatio, is obviously unacceptable. |
| Pages 48-49 | Please substitute something less graphic than "get your clothes off." The direction that Peter "starts to disrobe" should go no further than his commencing to unbutton his shirt. |
| PART II | |
| Page 3 | "Oh my God." |
| Page 6 | Please delete "did it hurt?" |
| Page 12 | "Oh my God." |
| Page 26 | Please delete "It doesn't grow back." |
| Page 28 | Substitute for "Good God," "what the hell." |
| Page 31 | Please direct Claire to dump the hot coffee in some part of Chester's anatomy other than his crotch. |
| Page 43 | Substitute for "tinkerbell." Substitute for "fruit." Substitute for "slut." |

As a matter of further guidance, the following subjects/plots, etc. outlined in the bible *must* be avoided or modified as indicated:

1. Please change Burt Campbell's last name to avoid the association with Campbell Soup Co.

2. Corrine's affair with a Jesuit priest, her subsequent pregnancy as a result, and later exorcism are all unacceptable.

3. The CIA or any other governmental organization is not to be involved in Gen. Nu's smuggling operation.

4. The matter of Burt's impotence will have to be dealt with in a non-explicit, tasteful manner.

5. Father Flotosky's stand on liberalizing the Mass will have to be treated in a balanced, inoffensive manner. By way of example, the substitution of Oreos for the traditional wafer is unacceptable.

6. The relationship between Jodie and the football player should be handled in such a manner that explicit or intimate aspects of homosexuality are avoided entirely.

Many of the "problems" cited in this memo would now be overlooked by standards and practices. Even censorship is affected by changing times and values. Although Oreo cookies are probably still a "problem."

# HOW TO SURVIVE
# WHILE WAITING FOR THAT FIRST BREAK

The slogan of a current string of commercials for deodorant is "never let 'em see you sweat." It's appropriate that one of the segments focuses on an actor. The rule in Hollywood is "never let 'em see you desperate." Nothing makes an agent more leery than the anxious writer who keeps calling because he has to pay the rent. Nothing irritates and embarrasses a story editor more than the spec writer checking in two or three times a week to see if you've read it yet. If a writer has to sell a script in order to eat, he or she is adding additional stress to an activity that is already inherently stressful. It's much better to organize your life from the beginning so that every script rejection does not take on life and death proportions.

For example, *don't* do what I did — leave a stable income in government and declare yourself a writer. I gave myself six months to make my mark. Of course, it didn't happen and I ran through my savings account in no time. Worst of all was the devastating moment of realization that I had become a Hollywood cliche — the starving writer living from one possibility to the next. I heard myself pressing friends to read scripts faster or blurting out story ideas at every opportunity, whether appropriate or not, in the hope someone would buy something. My desperation was hurting any chance to get lucky.

Not every writer agrees with this advice. The notion of the struggling artist in a garret is a romantic image — the "true art means suffering" school. Not in Hollywood. A secure writer who doesn't write from desperation will always win out.

As for me, I eventually came to my senses, resumed government work part-time, and became a full-time writer gradually. Pursing two careers during the transition period was difficult, but preferable to feeling suicidal each time a script meeting didn't work out. By not depending on a script sale to make ends meet, a writer has the luxury of patience. And patience is rewarded by a more relaxed style of writing and confidence. Indeed, if a writer is willing to get better with each script and learn from mistakes and criticism, the odds are that it will get better. If not, a smart writer has already set in motion a back-up plan.

That back-up plan can take any number of forms. I re-established myself in government so I could continue that career and pursue writing as a hobby if need be. Many writers take this two-career path. Scott Gordon (*Moonlighting*) kept his job as a high school teacher until he landed a staff writing opportunity. Doug Molitor (*Sledge Hammer, You Can't Take It with You*) continued writing prize descriptions for game shows while building a career in sitcoms, one assignment at a time.

These back-up plans are important even for writers who do sell a script or two. Contrary to popular belief, successful screenwriting is not instant fortune. The money paid per script only seems generous if you don't analyze the realities. An hour episodic writer, for example, earns about $20,000 (WGA minimum) per script for a story outline and two drafts of the teleplay (assuming sole credit — shared credit with a partner or story editor reduces the total proportionately). This also assumes the writer didn't get "cut off" during the process. A writer cut off at story will receive 30% of the minimum; 70% if cut off after the first draft.

But the writer doesn't take home $20,000. Taxes and pension and welfare take about 40% off the top. Some may come back later in the form of tax refunds, but at this point, the writer ends up with around $12,000. Ten percent of the gross goes to an agent, leaving the writer with $10,800, which, by the way, is paid in installments. A typical assignment from pitch to final draft will take three months. This does not include the time involved in preparing pitch ideas or waiting for the staff to read that first writing sample. All of which translates to annual take-home pay of $32,300 if a writer lands three hour episodic assignments per year, which is optimistic. The only real options are to find supplemental sources of income, and work on more than one project at a time. A typical freelancer is writing one project, pitching to another show, submitting writing samples to others, and earning a predictable income (full or part-time) doing something else.

The situation can improve quickly. A writer who goes on staff at a network hour show is guaranteed a weekly income of at least $3,000 and script assignments (for which he or she is paid the $20,000 per). Additionally, residuals from reruns or syndication can bring in payments up to two-thirds of the original figure. These residuals are not commissioned by agents. But residuals only exist if a show gets on the air and lasts long enough to get into reruns.

The situation is similar for feature writers. A freelancer working at minimum on a union/low budget movie ($2.5 million or less) will receive about $30,000 gross for a treatment (scene outline) and two drafts of the script. The slow pace of features can drag this process out for six months. After agents, taxes, etc., the writer who does two low-budget features a year is left with $35,000. Extra money may show up in the form of tax refunds, supplemental payments for an extra polish or rewrite, and, eventually, production bonuses and residuals if the film is made and released. That extra income can't be counted on and certainly not in the same year the scripts are written.

Smart writers plan ahead to be able to survive until they get established. One plan is to finish school. Earn a degree in something that might be useful: computers, accounting, management, law. That preparation will be valuable to a successful writer and invaluable to an unsuccessful one. Second, don't live from one dead-end job to the next. Los Angeles is already filled with writers and actors who've spent twenty years doing day labor, waiting for that big break. Third, don't move to Los Angeles or New York or any other media center the minute you're old enough to leave home. There's no reason to join the competition until you're able to compete. Develop your craft first. And develop secondary skills and job experience so that you can earn a decent living once you get there. Remember, writing as a second career can be an advantage. Dalene Young (*Cross Creek, Lil' Darlings*) says "Writers who've had life experiences before they succeed will have something to write about."

Should you be a secretary? "Yes and no." says Emmy winner Courtney Flavin (*Bill Cosby, A Matter of Sex*). "I typed for everybody. When we were on strike, every time I turned around on the picket line there was somebody I'd typed for, including the president of the Guild. It comes in handy when I need a recommendation. Because I was lucky enough to work for enlightened people, they take me seriously in spite of my former lowly status. Make no mistake about it: it is lowly — although I've noticed secretaries with word processing abilities are prized."

If you should choose the secretarial route, try to be a writer's assistant on a show in production. For one thing, it's fun. For another, it's educational. You can learn a lot about writing by watching scripts get written and rewritten and rewritten. Working on a television show provides you an excellent perspective. A new writer will see that scripts are often changed, not because of the quality of the work, but because an actor is sick that day or a script has been moved up in the shooting order and pertinent information has to be squeezed in. And finally, there are those ever-important contacts. The story editors you type for today will most likely be producers in a couple of seasons.

Another possibility is to assist a writer/producer in development. It is far less exciting than working on an in-production television show, but if the person you're working for looks upon you kindly, you may be rewarded with a script or even a staff writing job if the project goes forward. However, it may take a long time for a project to be developed, especially a movie. One the plus side, there will be plenty of free time on the job you can use to write your own scripts.

Other good industry-related activities: researcher, reader, production assistant for a film company on location, public relations. And Jurgen Wolff (author of *Successful Sitcom Writing*) urges writers to supplement their lives with other activities that get them away from the word processor: "Write film reviews or a television column; do audiovisual presentations for charitable groups, take acting improvisations or a speech class — in short, do anything that will develop new skills and make writing fun." And don't give up.

Is happiness just a thing called "sold?" Not according to Rick Hawkins, (*Mama's Family, Major Dad*) who advises prospective writers not to abandon the other parts of their lives in the headlong pursuit of screenwriting. "Take the opportunity *now* to get your personal life straightened out. Because once you start working regularly, you won't have the time. And if your personal priorities aren't worked out by that point, they never will be." Good advice. But now I'm really depressed.

CHAPTER SIXTEEN

# HOW TO SELL YOUR SCREENPLAY

1. Get good — learn to write as well as you possibly can.
2. Work smart — write projects that have a chance of selling or generating other work.
3. Be nice — the lowly folks you treat well may be in a position to help you later.
4. Be happy — there are enough miserable people in this industry; we don't need any more. Besides, you'll write better.
5. Be patient — there are few real overnight sensations in this business.
6. Be realistic — don't quit your day job (just yet!).

# APPENDIX A

# SPECIAL

# FORMATS

FADE IN (weeks later) to that moment when you've written the last word of the last scene and typed "The End." How does your script look? Probably it's a mess — a jumble of typed scenes, handwritten editing, odd-sized pages with arrows and question marks, and notes everywhere. It's time to transform this collection into a neat, tidy script. Because according to producer-writer Frank Cardea (*Crazy Like a Fox*), "How well your script is presented is nearly as important as how well it's written. If you're lucky enough to get someone to read your script, don't give them any excuse not to like it."

This part is like an English class. Spelling counts, punctuation counts, neatness *really* counts. It might be worth your while to spring for a professional typist for the final draft. If that's beyond your means as an aspiring writer, buy the recommended format books (Appendix D) as a guide.

Be sure to use the right-sized type. Pica is large, elite is small. *Use pica*. Courier 10 type face is the standard at the moment. Don't use script. Leave a generous left-hand margin — there will eventually be three holes in it.

For sitcom scripts, you should know by now if the show is on film or tape. You cannot necessarily tell by the blurb at the end of the show. Even taped shows announce that they were "filmed before a live studio audience." If you are in any doubt, call the production office and ask. This is not confidential information, and someone will probably tell you. At the same time you might ask for a sample script. If you get one, it may be a shooting script with assorted colored pages and a number of schedules and charts. *Don't duplicate these schedules and charts in your script.* A cast list and set list in the front of a spec script indicates you are an amateur.

The following formats are provided as a general guide and for easy reference. They do not deal with all the nuances such as ''voice-overs'' (VO) or complicated chase sequences. Consult a full-fledged format book for these. The samples provided do contain offbeat hints that other books might not.

SAMPLE FORMAT FOR ONE-HALF HOUR
THREE CAMERA TAPE SHOW
(AS IN TAPE SITCOMS)

ACT ONE

Scene One

INT. PLACE — TIME OF DAY

(DESCRIPTION OF ACTION GOES HERE. SINGLE SPACED AND ALL IN CAPS. THE TEXT IS FORTY TO FORTY-FIVE SPACES WIDE, INDENTED IN TEN TO TWELVE FROM THE LEFT SIDE OF THE PAGE. SOUND EFFECTS OR LIGHTING EFFECTS GO ON A SEPARATE LINE AND ARE UNDER-LINED.)

(YOU CAN OCCASIONALLY START A NEW PARAGRAPH IF THE BLOCK OF TEXT IS GETTING TOO LARGE.)

(THEN WHEN PEOPLE START TALKING, IT GOES LIKE THIS:)

CHARACTER NAME

All dialogue is double-spaced, thirty to thirty-five spaces wide, indented five to ten spaces from the left margin. If you want to describe how a line is to be given or to indicate a brief description of action you capitalize and put it in parentheses and put in the left margin. Then you go on with the dialogue adding (Cont'd) after the character name.

(FRANK UNFOLDS THE MAP.)

FRANK

So where is this place anyway?

(SFX: DOORBELL)

In a sitcom script, if a character's speech won't fit on one page, put it in its entirety on the next page. If it's an exceptionally long speech — and watch out for those — it can be broken up between pages like this:

STAN

I don't know what to say, Frank. Now I know The Kid's a friend of yours, but he stole the toaster, and that's all there is to it.
(MORE)

_____ (end of page)

STAN (Cont'd)

I know it wasn't a valuable toaster, but it's the principle of the thing. A man's toaster is sacred.

Never make the reader turn the page in the middle of a joke.

SAMPLE FORMAT FOR ONE-HALF HOUR
MULTI CAMERA FILM SHOW
(AS IN FILMED SITCOMS)

ACT ONE

Scene One

INT. PLACE — TIME OF DAY

DESCRIPTION OF ACTION GOES HERE, SINGLE SPACED AND ALL IN CAPS. THE TEXT SHOULD BE SIXTY TO SIXTY-FIVE SPACES WIDE, INDENTED TEN TO TWELVE SPACES FROM THE LEFT SIDE OF THE PAPER. KEEP IT BRIEF —

ONE'S EYE NATURALLY GOES PAST GREAT BLOCKS OF TEXT. YOU CAN UNDERLINE IMPORTANT INFORMATION, AND SOMETIMES THE ENTRANCES AND EXITS OF CHARACTERS ARE UNDERLINED. DON'T BE AFRAID TO BE HUMOROUS IN YOUR DESCRIPTION, BUT DON'T GET CARRIED AWAY EITHER.

SOUND EFFECTS OR LIGHTING EFFECTS GO ON A SEPARATE LINE AND ARE UNDERLINED.

THEN WHEN PEOPLE START TALKING, IT GOES LIKE THIS:

CHARACTER NAME

All dialogue is double-spaced. The text is thirty to thirty-five spaces wide and is indented twelve to fifteen spaces from the left margin. If you want to describe how a line is to be given (SARCASTICALLY) or if you want to indicate a brief description of action (OPENING THE BOOK) you put it in capitals and in parentheses and then go on with the dialogue. However, if it's a long description or if the character speaking is not doing the action, go back out to the left margin.

FRANK UNFOLDS THE MAP.

FRANK

So where is this place anyway?

ED

You've got the map. How am I supposed to know? (STARTS FILLING THE THERMOS WITH ICE CUBES)

FRANK SPREADS THE MAP OUT ON THE COFFEE TABLE. IT DOESN'T FIT.

ED (Cont'd)

Who drank all the cream soda?

<u>SFX: DOORBELL</u>

FRANK CROSSES TO ANSWER IT.

FRANK

Ask The Kid.

THE KID ENTERS, CARRYING A TOASTER, AND STARTS SINGING TO THE TUNE OF ''THE HALLELUJAH CHORUS.''

THE KID (SINGING)

English muffins, English muffins, A bagel, a bagel,
a ba-a-a-gel.

FRANK AND ED GROAN SIMULTANEOUSLY AS WE:
CUT TO:

Begin the next act on a new page. If this is the last scene in the act, write:

FADE OUT.

END OF ACT ONE

or, if it's the last act:

THE END

SAMPLE FORMAT FOR ONE-HALF HOUR OR HOUR
ONE-CAMERA FILM TELEVISION SHOW
(AS IN HOUR DRAMATIC OR TELEVISION MOVIE)

ACT ONE

INT. PLACE — TIME OF DAY

Description of action goes here, single spaced. The text is sixty to sixty-five spaces wide, indented ten to twelve spaces from

259

the left side of the page. Keep it brief -- one's eye naturally goes past great blocks of text, and be sparing with exclamation points. You can underline or capitalize important information and generally the character names are capitalized all the way through, although some people prefer to capitalize the character name when it first appears and then go to upper/lower case for the rest of the script, except when the character speaks:

CHARACTER NAME

All dialogue is single-spaced, thirty to thirty-five spaces wide, indented ten to fifteen spaces from the left margin. Again, be sparing with exclamation points. If you want to describe how a line is to be given or if you want to indicate a brief description of action, it goes on a separate line, indented five spaces.

(opening the book)

However, if it's a long description or if the character speaking is not doing the action, go back out to the left margin.

Frank unfolds the map.

FRANK

So where is this place anyway?

ED

(reasonably)
You've got the map. How am I supposed to know?

He starts filling the thermos with ice cubes.

ED

It's going to be a great trip.

Frank spreads the map out on the coffee table. It doesn't fit.

ED

Who drank all the cream soda?

The doorbell rings. Frank goes to the door to answer it.

                    FRANK

    Ask The Kid.

THE KID enters, carrying a toaster, and starts singing to the
tune of ''The Hallelujah Chorus.''

                    THE KID
       (singing)
    English muffins, English muffins,
    A bagel, a bagel, a ba-a-a-gel.

Frank and Ed groan simultaneously as we . . .
                                        CUT TO:


    Sound effects can also be written: The DOORBELL RINGS or:
The doorbell RINGS.

    A new act starts on a new page.

    A character's speech can be broken up if it is long. Just be sure
that you have more than one line of text on either page. Thus:


                    STAN

    I don't know what to say, Frank. I know The Kid's
    a friend of yours, but he stole the toaster, and that's
    all there is to it.
                    (MORE)
_____ (end of page)


                STAN (Cont'd)

    Now I know it wasn't a valuable toaster, but it's
    the principle of the thing. A man's toaster is sacred.


and not:


                    STAN

    I don't know what to say, Frank.

(MORE)

_____ (end of page)

STAN (Cont'd)

I know The Kid's a friend of yours, but he stole the toaster, and that's all there is to it. Now I know it wasn't a valuable toaster, but it's the principle of the thing. A man's toaster is sacred.

Nor should it be:

STAN

I don't know what to say, Frank. I know the kid's a friend of yours, but he stole the toaster, and that's all there is to it. Now I know it wasn't a valuable toaster, but it's the principle of the thing. A man's toaster is

(MORE)

_____ (end of page)

STAN (Cont'd)

sacred.

The same is true, incidentally of scene description. Don't put the slug line (INT. LIVING ROOM — NIGHT) at the bottom of the page with only a line of text (or no text at all) and the rest on the top of next page. Thus is isn't:

INT. LIVING ROOM — NIGHT

The Kid is taking the upside down toaster apart with a

_____ (end of page)

screwdriver. Crumbs from the previous decade fall out from the toaster as he works. But suddenly his efforts pay off.

It is:

INT. LIVING ROOM — NIGHT

The Kid is taking the upside down toaster apart with a screwdriver. Crumbs from the previous decade fall out from the toaster as he works. But suddenly his efforts pay off.

## FEATURE FILM FORMAT

The only difference between a feature script format and the television movie format is that a feature script has no act breaks. So use the one-camera television format, but keep in mind the following.

The text should be as reader-friendly as possible. This means avoiding the temptation to put in classy-sounding technical directions. (Those come later, with a director.) The inclusion of technical directions in an early draft (i.e., MEDIUM CLOSE-UP, CAMERA PANS RIGHT) is a turn-off to readers and smacks of amateurism. ANGLE ON is about as technical as you should get.

EXT. STREET — DAY

Carrying the toaster in a paper bag, The Kid crosses the street, smiling nervously at the POLICEMEN on the corner.

ANGLE ON

The Policeman. The Kid does not see him signal to an UNDER-COVER COP in the doorway of the hardware store.

ANGLE ON

The Undercover Cop looks down at a poor photocopy of a line drawing. Although it's a sketch, there's no mistaking The Kid.

CUT TO:

INT. SUPERMARKET — DAY

Frank is trying to decide between English muffins and bagels. A better way to show a new angle without using ANGLE ON is simply to begin a new paragraph.

EXT. STREET — DAY

Carrying the toaster in a paper bag, The Kid crosses the street, smiling nervously at the POLICEMAN on the corner.

The Policeman watches The Kid go by. The Kid does not see him signal to an UNDERCOVER COP in the doorway of the hardware store.

The Undercover Cop looks down at a poor photocopy of a line drawing. Although it's a sketch, there's no mistaking The Kid.

CUT TO:

INT. SUPERMARKET — DAY

Frank is trying to decide between English muffins and bagels.

A word about TRANSITIONS. Transitions are editorial instructions: CUT TO, DISSOLVE TO, FADE OUT, FADE IN. In feature scripts, some writers leave out "CUT TO" altogether — since one automatically cuts between scenes — and indicate dissolves and fades when appropriate, usually to show time passing. But, other writers feel that "CUT TO" is like a period on a sentence and should always be used to give the reader a feeling of finality: this scene is over and the next scene is beginning. Some writers use "CUT TO" *within* scenes, especially action scenes, to emphasize a particular moment, or special transitions that emphasize a point or help build a joke, e.g. SMASH CUT TO:, SHOCK CUT TO:, SLOW DISSOLVE TO:, ETC.

On some feature scripts the work "CONTINUED" may be found in the bottom right hand corner if a scene indeed continues to the next page (and on the top left hand of the page onto which it continues). This is to help in the "budget breakdown" of a script, and it is not necessary to include them in a first draft script. It is also a mistake to number the scenes; this is done in later drafts.

## SOME POINTS FOR BOTH FEATURE AND TELEVISION FORMATS

Be careful about using slang in dialogue — it doesn't read as well as it sounds — and never use it in stage directions. Avoid dialects — they never read well. Instead, hint at them with word choices and sentence structure, but write in recognizable English.

Parenthetical directions which give character attitude are sometimes necessary to explain the meaning of a line. The parenthetical directions in the following give profoundly different meanings to the same line of dialogue:

SAM

(irate)
Who the hell do you think you are?

or

SAM

(with a wink)
Who the hell do you think you are?

Too many parenthetical directions disrupt the flow of the dialogue. Use them only when absolutely necessary. In the best scenes the attitude of the character should be apparent from the dialogue and the build of the scene without having to point it out too often.

Stage directions should be clear, economical and grammatically correct. You may get extra credit for humor in the stage directions, as long as you don't get carried away, but don't let them overwhelm the dialogue. So, for example, the stage directions in an episode of *Moonlighting* when Maddie and David kiss, reads: "The longest, hungriest kiss in the history of television." It *is* the act break, after all. Shane Black's widely-read spec script *The Last Boy Scout* launched a wave of what's known as "too hip" stage directions. So now it's common to find lines like "Hey, it's television, after all" in spec script narratives. The smirky tone breaks the rhythm of the script and is not recommended.

In general, when writing dialogue, don't underline or capitalize for emphasis unless absolutely necessary. And be careful of exclamation points — the effusive perkiness they add gets very(!) irritating(!) very(!) quickly(!): Book, movie and magazine titles (contrary to current punctuation standards) should be put in quotation marks.

Remember that the key to a good read is the momentum of the story and the writing. Each scene, each line of dialogue, should propel the reader on so that before they realize it they've finished the script. Anything that stops this flow, whether parentheticals, bad grammar, misspelled words, exclamation points, underlining, overwritten speeches or stage directions, work against the momentum.

Your friendly neighborhood readers might be grateful to find a list of the principal characters and brief description (especially the relationships such as husband, lover, brother) between the title page and the first page of the script. This is only allowable in a feature with lots of characters, in case the reader gets confused. But confusion is never a good sign. If the reader can't keep the characters clear, they're probably not sufficiently distinct or there are too many of them. Before adding a character list, try re-editing your script to simplify. Professional readers at studios and producers will regard a character list as the sign of an amateur.

*Do not* put in a treatment, a summary, or a scene outline. The danger is the reader will read these instead of the script and the writer will get no points for dialogue, stage direction, or scene structure. The all or nothing rule is in effect here. Either give the reader a whole script or pitch the story instead.

*Before* you give the script to friends for criticism, put it into correct format, perfectly typed, the right length. If readers have to follow arrows, squint to read line changes, or decipher misspelled words, you are not getting the full benefit of their critiquing abilities. Similarly, it's valuable for a writer to do his or her own rewrite from a clean, newly typed manuscript. That way the whole project may seem new and the author can be more objective in reading it.

### THE FINAL TOUCHES

When the notes are in and the rewrites are done, it's time to put on the final touches.

**Photocopying:** A perfectly typed script may be undone by poor photocopying. If the copy is too light or too dark, or pages have come out at an angle, return to the copy shop and demand a reprint. *Always* check each copy to make sure all the pages are there and in the right order.

**Covers:** Scripts get tossed around from desk to desk, and a cover lengthens the shelf life. But it shouldn't be anything fancy. A heavy paper cover is sufficient and, if it starts looking worn, can be easily replaced. (You are in luck if your agent has preprinted covers.) You don't need to pay extra to have the title of your script printed on the cover and don't put an illustration on it either.

**Binding:** Do not put a fancy binding on your script. It should be three-hole-punched and fastened with brass fasteners (also known as brads). Make sure the brads are the right size. If they're too small, the script falls apart, and if they're too large, they poke the reader. You don't want to poke the reader. You don't want to do anything to alienate the reader.

# APPENDIX B

# THE
# WRITERS GUILD

Throughout this book, references to WGA jobs versus non-WGA indicate the importance to screenwriters of Guild contracts and services. But, let's lay one myth to rest: being a member of the Writers Guild does not make any difference in a writer's employability. The 75% unemployment rate within the Guild is testimony that membership does not equal employment. The Guild does not hand out jobs or find work for its members. Producers do not ask if you're WGA before they'll meet with you. A non-Guild writer with a great script still has the advantage over a Guild member with a bad one.

What Guild membership does do is provide a certain stamp of legitimacy to what you do — an indication that you're a contender.

The Writers Guild is important in creating rules and contracts that protect writers in providing residuals, and in arbitrating disputes over credits and payment schedules. There are two Writers Guild offices: Los Angeles (WGA West) and New York (WGA East).

Anyone can join the Writers Guild after selling a script or a story idea to a Guild signatory company. Full membership in the Guild is based on a credit system. If a writer co-writes a project, the credits are reduced proportionately. When a writer earns twelve credits within a two-year period, he or she is eligible for full membership and full benefits including voting rights, pension funds, and health insurance.

**The following information was prepared by WGA West:**

The Guild represents writers primarily for the purpose of collective bargaining in the motion picture, television and radio industries.

We do not obtain employment for writers, refer or recommend members for writing assignments, offer writing instruction or analysis, nor do we accept or handle material for submission to production companies.

Literary material should be submitted directly to the production company or through a literary agent. To obtain the current list of our franchised agencies by mail, send your request with $1 to the Guild office. Guild office hours are 9:30–5:30, Monday through Friday.

For writing instruction or advice, we suggest that you communicate with film schools, the state colleges, universities, or with your local board of education.

Guild policy prevents us from disclosing the address or phone number of any Guild member. First class correspondence may be addressed to a member in care of the Guild and will be promptly forwarded to members without a referral address such as an agent. Please contact the agency department for further information.

## WHEN YOUR SCRIPT IS READY TO GO

Register a copy with the Writers Guild. The Guild's registration service has been set up to assist members and non-members in establishing the completion date and the identity of their literary property written for the fields of theatrical motion pictures, television and radio.

*The Guild does not accept book manuscripts, stage plays, music, lyrics, photos, drawings (story boards) or articles of public record for filing.*

Registration does not confer any statutory protection. It merely provides a record of the writer's claim to authorship of the literary material involved and of the date of its completion. The registration office does not make comparisons of registration deposits to determine similarity between works, nor does it give legal opinions or advice. Questions regarding copyright protection should be directed to the United States Copyright Office in Washington, D.C. or an attorney specializing in that area of the law.

*Registration does not take the place of registering the copyright on your materials with the U.S. Copyright Office.*

**Coverage.** Registration with the Guild does not protect titles (neither does registration with the United States Copyright Office).
**Procedure for Deposit.** One 8½″ × 11″, unbound (no brads, staples, fan-fold, etc.), copy is required for deposit in the Guild files. When it is received the property is sealed in a Guild Registration

envelope, timed and dated. A receipt is returned. Notice of registration shall consist of the following wording: REGISTERED WGA W NO. _____ and be applied upon the title page or the page immediately following. Scripts specifically intended for radio, television, and theatrical motion pictures are registrable as are television series formats, step outlines, and storylines. The specific field of writing and the proper writing credits should be noted on the title page. Each property must be registered separately (exception: three episodes, skits or sketches for an existing series may be deposited as a single registration). Be sure that the name under which you register is your full legal name. The use of pseudonyms, pen names, initials or familiar forms of a proper name may require proof of identity if you want to recover the material left on deposit.

**Fees.** $10 for members of WGA W and WGA E, $20 for non-members.

The fee must accompany the material that is to be registered.

**Copyright.** The Guild does not have a copyright service. For forms and instructions call: (202)707-9100.

**Duration.** Material deposited for registration after September 1, 1982 is valid for a term of five years; material deposited for registration prior to September 1, 1982 is valid for a term of ten years. You may renew the registration for an additional ten-year or five-year term, whichever is applicable, at the then-current registration fee. You authorize the Guild to destroy the material without notice to you on the expiration of the term of registration if renewal is not made. The fee should accompany the request for renewal.

**Procedure for withdrawal.** The registration copy left on deposit cannot be returned to the writer without defeating the purpose of registration, the point being that evidence should be available, if necessary, that the material has been in the Guild's charge since the date of deposit.

However, if the writer finds it necessary to have the copy returned, at least forty-eight hours notice of intended withdrawal must be given to the Guild. A manuscript will be given up only on the signature(s) of the writer(s). If the registration is in the names of more than one person, the written consent of all is required to authorize withdrawal. In case a registrant is deceased, proof of death and the consent of his representative or heirs must be presented.

In no event, except under these provisions, shall any of the material be allowed to be taken from the Guild office unless a court order has been acquired.

If any person other than the writer named in the registration shall request confirmation of registration, the registration number and/or date of deposit, to see either the material deposited, the registration envelope or any other material, such request shall be denied unless authorization from the writer(s) or a court order is presented in connection therewith.

> Writers Guild Registrations
> 9009 Beverly Boulevard
> West Hollywood, CA 90048-2456

**Hours.** 10:00 A.M.–12 NOON, 2:00 P.M.–5:00 P.M., Monday through Friday. All mail must be sent to:

> 8955 Beverly Boulevard
> West Hollywood, CA 90048-23456.

Writers residing west of the Mississippi River may apply for membership in the WGA, West, Inc. Writers residing east of the Mississippi River are advised to contact:

> WGA, East, Inc.
> 555 West 57th Street
> New York, NY 10019

**Requirements for admission to the WGA, West, Inc.** An aggregate of twelve units of credit as set forth on the schedule of units of credit, which units are based upon work completed under contract of employment or upon the sale or licensing of previously unpublished and unproduced literary or dramatic material is required. Said employment, sale or licensing must be with a company or other entity that is signatory to the applicable WGA collective bargaining agreement and must be within the jurisdiction of the Guild as provided in its collective bargaining contracts. The twelve units must be accumulated within the preceding two years of application.

**Schedule of units of credit.**

- Two units:
  For each complete week of employment within the Guild's jurisdiction on a week-to-week or term basis.
- Three units:
  Story for radio play or television program of less than thirty minutes in duration shall be pro-rated in five-minute increments.
- Four units:
  Story for a short subject theatrical motion picture or for a radio play or television program of not less than thirty minutes nor more than sixty minutes in duration.
- Six units:
  Teleplay or radio play of less than thirty minutes in duration which shall be pro-rated in five-minute increments; Television format or presentation for a new series; "Created By" credit given pursuant to the separation of rights provisions of the WGA Theatrical and Television Basic Agreement.
- Eight units:
  Story for radio play or television program of more than one hour but not more than two hours in duration; Screenplay for a short subject theatrical motion picture or for a radio play or teleplay of not less than thirty minutes but not more than sixty minutes in duration.

**The following shall constitute twelve units:**

- Story for a feature-length theatrical motion picture or for a television program or radio play of more than two-hour duration; Screenplay for a feature-length theatrical motion picture or for a teleplay or a television program or a radio play for a radio program for more than one-hour duration.
- Bible
  Long-term projection as used herein shall be defined as a bible, for a specified term, on an existing, five-times-per-week non-prime serial.
- A rewrite is entitled to one-half the number of units allotted to its particular category as set forth in the schedule of units.

- A polish is entitled to one-quarter the number of units allotted to its particular category as set forth in the schedule of units.

- Sale of an option earns one-half the number of units allotted to its particular category as set forth in the schedule of units, subject to the maximum entitlement of four such units *per project* in any one year.

- Where writers collaborate on the same project each shall be accorded the appropriate number of units designated in the schedule of units.

In all cases, to qualify for membership, if the writer's employment agreement or purchase agreement is with a company owned in whole or in part by the writer or writer's family, there must be an agreement for financing, production and/or distribution with a third party signatory producing company or, failing such agreement, the script must be produced and the writer must receive writing credit on screen in the form of "Written By," "Teleplay By," or "Radio Play By."

The applicant writer is required to apply for membership no later than the thirty-first day of employment.

In exceptional cases, the board of directors, acting upon a recommendation from the membership and finance committee shall have the power and authority to grant membership based upon work done prior to two years before the applicant has filed an application for membership.

For purposes of the credit requirements in the foregoing provisions, audio credit for a writer employed to write radio or a writer who sells literary material for radio programming will suffice.

The initiation fee of $1500 is payable only by cashier's check or by money order. No personal or corporate checks will be accepted. All membership applications are to be supported by a copy of executed employment or sales contracts or other acceptable evidence of employment or sales.

# GLOSSARY

To save time by communicating difficult concepts in a word or two, Hollywood has invented its own language. As with all professional jargon, usage serves as a litmus test for who's really in the industry and who isn't.

**Act breaks.** The final plot point in each act. Should propel the viewer or reader into the next act, either by surprise or by tension.

**Acts.** 1) Classic dramatic structure: three acts, beginning, middle, end.

2) Commercial acts on television.

**Approved.** As in "approved list." Writers have to be approved by networks and studios for high-prestige projects such as television movies and pilots.

**Arc.** The changes that occur in a character (character's arc) from the beginning of a story to the end.

**Area.** Also called "arena." The setting for a story, not to be confused with the story itself.

**Assignment.** If a writer sells an idea to a television series, he has an assignment.

**Backdoor pilot.** A television movie or segment of an existing series to determine whether the concept can sustain its own show.

**Back nine.** Following an initial order of thirteen episodes, networks pick up the show for nine more episodes to complete a full season of twenty-two.

**Back-up scripts.** Scripts ordered that may or may not be filmed, either because the series is not on the air yet or its future is not yet determined. Writers get fifteen percent above scale to offset the insecurity.

**Back-up series.** A show planned as a replacement for mid-season.

**Bankable.** Take it to the bank, guaranteed box office, as in a bankable star.

**Beat.** 1) A pause.

2) An important point or moment in a story or plot.

**Beat sheet.** A listing of the major plot and character moments in the story.

**Bible.** The master plan for the storylines of a show for the full season, used mostly on serials.

**Big guns.** Established writers, producers, or directors.

**Big moment.** A major plot point, action sequence or a great joke that grabs an audience or reader. Sometimes called an inciting incident. Conventional wisdom is that a big moment should happen within the first ten pages of a feature script and within the first two to five in a teleplay.

**Bits.** Sequences of jokes or physical comedy.

**Breakdown.** 1) Analysis of a script for costs, shooting schedules, etc., done by the producer.

2) A "to be cast" list of actors' parts circulated to agents on a daily basis.

**Bumper.** A teaser or tag.

**The business.** The entertainment industry.

**Button.** A last line or physical bit that ends the scene, most often with a laugh.

**Clear.** As in "clear a story." Get approval from a studio or network.

**Cliffhanger.** Episode-ending or season-ending jeopardy, especially in serials. The audience is left hanging for a week or even the summer. The most successful was *Dallas*'s "Who Shot J.R.?" In recent years, cliffhangers have also been used by studios as leverage against actors who want big pay raises for the next season.

**Commercial.** A project or idea that shows potential for big audience or box office. One of the gentlest (and least truthful) forms of rejection for a script is to say "It's not commercial enough."

**Commissary.** The eatery at each studio where the real menu is who's eating with whom.

**Conflict.** The source of drama in a scene or story; jeopardy, tension, or characters operating at cross purposes.

**Cute.** "I hate it."

**Cut off.** A writer is removed from script mid-assignment. He or she is paid only for the steps completed.

**Deal-breaker.** An item in the studio/agent negotiations that will break the deal unless it's settled.

**Dramadys.** A hybrid of comedy and drama such at *The Days and Nights of Molly Dodd* or *Wonder Years*.

**Exposure.** How much money a company is liable for through contracts and deficit financing of a show; for example, a company with a series that it deficits $100,000 per episode has an exposure over a thirteen-show order of $1,300,000.

**Failing up.** The Peter Principle is that everyone works at one level above their competence. In film and television, some people "fail up" until they become executive producers or studio executives.

**Filmspeak.** The language of the entertainment industry.

**First look deal.** A studio or network buys the rights to the first option on any project a writer, director, producer, or actor develops.

**Fish out of water.** A frequent theme in movies, television and literature: the stranger dropped into an unfamiliar environment.

**Franchise.** The elements in a show which are the same each week: how the leads get into stories, the kinds of stories they do. Networks believe that a certain sameness week to week builds audience loyalty.

**Freelancer.** A writer who is not on staff at a show or studio and who moves from one project to the next.

**Funny.** In the eyes of the beholder or producer.

**Galleys.** Also called "sides" — the typeset proofs of a book before it is published.

**Genre.** A style of show within a particular market.

**Gentlemen's agreements.** Unwritten contracts by which many Hollywood deals are made. Often considered more inviolate than any document.

**Giving notes.** Critiquing a script.

**A go.** The project will be made. Also known as greenlighting.

**Grip.** Crew member on a show; holds and moves equipment, hence the term grip.

**Heat.** 1) The bigness in a film that will generate box office.

2) Writers also have heat if their last project was a big success.

**Hook.** A story concept, idea, or plot twist that intrigues a reader or viewer and compels them to keep reading or watching.

**Hyphenate.** A writer who does more than one job; i.e., writer/producer, writer/director.

**If/come.** An if/come deal is like an option. "*If* we can sell the idea to a studio, then *come* work for us." Dollars are set as part of the initial contract.

**Indie-prod.** Indie is industry as in "the industry" and prod is production as in "going into" usually means a deal between an independent producer and a studio.

**Jeopardy.** A threat to the characters, either physical or emotional.

**Logline.** The one sentence summary of a story or project that would appear in *TV Guide*.

**Longforms.** Television movies and miniseries.

**Low budget feature.** Studios define this as $6,000,000 or less; WGA as $2,500,000 or less.

**Made for.** Aimed toward a specific alternative market, such as "made for home video" or "made for cable."

**Minimum.** Also called "scale" — the lowest amount a writer can receive for a particular project under Guild contract. The WGA has negotiated an MBA (Minimum Basic Agreement) for each screenwriting market over which it has jurisdiction. A writer working at scale is being paid the minimum for that genre.

**Movie block.** Segments of a television station's schedule set aside for made-for-television movies and features.

**Movie of the week.** MOW. Television movies, telefilms.

**Multiparters.** Also called "miniseries." Longforms that play for two nights or more on television.

**Multi-pic pact.** A deal with a writer, producer, director, or actor to do a series of pictures that will probably never be made. The writer/producer/director/actor gets paid anyway.

**Multiples.** A guarantee of script assignments (most often three) on a series to a particular freelance writer or team.

**Narrowcasting.** Aiming for a specific audience. A word play on broadcasting, which implies trying to reach the broadest possible audience.

**Non-pro.** A grating label used by the trades in wedding and birth announcements to describe someone who is not in show business; i.e., "Bride is a vice-president for Paramount; groom is a non-pro." It doesn't matter if the groom's a *Fortune* 500 CEO, in the eyes of the industry he's a non-pro.

**Notes.** Criticism and suggestions regarding a script. Notes are given and taken.

**Notion.** Half of a story, usually the first half.

**Ooh response.** A good idea.

**On the nose.** A too-obvious choice. Applied to plotpoints, characters, scenes, dialogue, and most pilots.

**Option.** As in "my script's been optioned." A fee paid by a producer to the writer for the rights to try to sell a script or idea to a studio or network.

**Order.** The networks give studios a commitment for a certain number of episodes.

**Pay or play.** A contract guaranteeing pay to an actor/director/ producer/writer, even if the project doesn't happen.

**Pilot.** The first episode of a new television show. Used by networks and television stations to determine whether or not to buy the full series.

**Points.** 1) Percentages of the usually non-existent profits of a picture.
       2) As in story points, the major plot points in a script.
       3) In Canada, each member of the creative team is worth points.

**Producers.** Humorist Max Steiner defines them as "people who know everything, if only they could think of it."

**Producer's rewrite.** A freebie rewrite in features requested by the producer before submitting a script to the studio. Banned by the WGA, but a widespread practice anyway.

**Punching up a script.** Making it funnier or livelier.

**Quote.** The price for an established writer based on his or her previous payment in that market. If the writer received $70,000 for his or her last unmade feature, the quote for the next one might well be $80,000. If the last movie was a box-office hit, the quote will be much higher.

**Reverses.** Also called "twists, surprises." Major plot turns at the first and second dramatic acts.

**Rights.** As in "buy the rights." Payment for a true story, a book, or a script. Similar to optioning a project.

**Rolling out.** Playing a film in a limited number of theatres so that it gradually reaches various markets and builds good word of mouth.

**Season.** The television season for first-run programs is September through April/May.

**Second season.** Television shows that debut January through April.

**Short order.** Less than the traditional thirteen episodes for the television series. A short order is usually for six episodes for a mid-season show.

**Signatory companies.** Production companies that have agreed to the Writers Guild Minimum Basic.

**Sitcom.** Situation comedy.

**Sketches.** Short, self-contained comedy routines on a variety show.

**Spec script.** A script written on speculation with no guarantee it will be sold or even read.

**Staff writer.** Works full time on a particular television show and receives a weekly salary; the writer is exclusive to that show.

**Strip show.** A television series that airs in the same time period five days a week.

**Sweetening.** Adding recorded laughs to a sitcom to make it seem funnier that it is. Also called a laugh track.

**Tag.** A short vignette, two minutes or less, at the end of a television show, before the closing credits. Comments on the stories just completed. Also known as a bumper.

**Take/do a lunch, do/take a meeting.** Interchangeable for let's get together.

**Taking notes.** Receiving criticism on a script.

**Teaser.** A short vignette, two minutes or less, before the opening credits of a television show. May or may not have anything to do with the story to follow. Also known as a bumper.

**Telefilm.** A television movie.

**Teleplay.** The script for a television show.

**Ticking clock.** Deadline in the plot that lends urgency. The term comes from the ticking clock of a bomb that will explode unless the hero defuses it.

**Trades.** Short for the trade papers. *Hollywood Reporter* and *Daily Variety*.

**Trauma dramas.** Television movies that are based on true stories taken from sensational newspaper headlines.

**Turnaround.** In features or television movies, a script that has been paid for, but the studio has decided not to make. Other studios can then buy it.

**Warmadys.** Hour shows that are a blend of light comedy and drama such as *The Waltons* or *Life Goes On*.

**Word of mouth.** Also called "buzz, advance." What audiences, critics, and the industry are saying about a film. Good word of mouth is important to sustain box office.

**Writing zone.** The environment and circumstances that trigger the impulse to write.

# RESOURCES AND BIBLIOGRAPHY

A screenwriter should build and maintain a library of reference materials. At the top of the priority list are film and television scripts that can be traded with other writers. Second is an array of professional books and publications to consider.

The best books are the straight-ahead, how-to, this-is-the-way-it's-done books, and the more specific the writer describes markets and offers suggestions, the better. Least useful are the books that are compendiums of essays of different writers or so-called workbooks: the former may be interesting reading, but they don't provide much practical information; the latter give practical exercises, but are often second-rate sequels to an author's previous book. Keep in mind that in the entertainment industry, screenwriting books over five years old offer advice that is now ancient history.

There has been an explosion in the screenwriting teaching business in recent years with a corresponding increase in the number of books available. Most are not very good. Among the worst: books discussing the business of screenwriting by writers who once sold a story idea or television episode; books about how to write by successful writers who have sold scripts but do not know how to teach. Also be cautious of seminars or books that proclaim the One True Path. If there was such a Path, the author would have a career writing million-dollar screenplays instead of how-to books. Also, most format books offer dated advice or tell the reader far more than any screenwriter needs to know. There is no need to spend twenty dollars on a tome about camera angles.

Those caveats aside, there are several very helpful books and publications. Below are the ones I recommend. Another good source for recommendations is the newsletters from screenwriter's groups.

## BASIC GRAMMAR AND REFERENCE

1. A dictionary. Spelling counts.
2. A thesaurus. A useful tool to find synonyms for the word you've overused. A disaster if you start using replacement words whose meaning and subtext you don't entirely understand.
3. An encyclopedia — any good one. Important for story ideas, fact finding and historical details to add texture to a script. Computer programs such as Prodigy serve the same purpose.
4. *Bartlett's Familiar Quotations* by John Bartlett. Great for quotes to make a character sound literate or for finding titles for a finished product.
5. *The Elements of Style* by E.B. White and William Strunk, Jr. Required reading for all writers. No exceptions.

## FORMATS

*The Complete Guide to Standard Script Formats* by Judith H. Haag and Hillis R. Cole, Jr. (CMC Publishing, 7516 Sunset Boulevard, Hollywood, California 90046). One of those books that tell you far more than you need to know, but this is the industry standard.

## DRAMATIC STRUCTURE AND WRITING

The following two books are considered the classics of screenwriting:

*Screenplay* by Syd Field. Criticized as gimmicky because of the emphasis on structure, but a standard; very readable. A good introduction to feature film writing. Nowhere near as impressive are Field's follow-up books *The Scriptwriter's Workbook* (1984) and *Selling a Screenplay: The Screenwriter's Guide to Hollywood* (1989). The former is a rehash of *Screenplay* with exercises. The latter is a series of interviews with screenwriters that provides virtually no advice on the selling described in the title.

*The Art of Dramatic Writing* by Lajos Egri (1946). Esoteric and sometimes difficult to understand, but considered the pioneering treatise on developing characters, creating conflict, and the basic elements of dramatic storytelling.

Two other how-to-write books consistently surface on the recommended list of screenwriting groups, universities and specialty bookstores. Both are well-written, to the point, and avoid giving advice on subjects with which the authors are not familiar. Both authors are on the seminar circuit, so it's relatively easy to follow-up their books with face-to-fact contacts.

*Writing Screenplays That Sell* by Michael Hague (McGraw-Hill, 1988). The Samuel French catalog summarizes the book as follows: "A guide to writing saleable screenplays. Covers story concept, character development, character growth, theme and structure, and contains detailed analyses of successful scenes and screenplays, plus advice on the business of screenwriting — how to market and sell work." Highly recommended for new writers; to my mind, *Writing Screenplays* is far and away the best and most contemporary how-to-write book.

*Making a Good Script Great* by Linda Seger (Dodd Mead & Co., 1987). The Samuel French summary: "The focus of this book is on rewriting — on how to get a script back on track. Hollywood script consultant Seger shares her techniques for solving script problems: momentum, insufficiently developed ideas, creating dimensional characters, defining character functions; and creating conflict; and making subplots work, while still preserving the writer's creativity."

*Making a Good Script Great* is unique in its emphasis on rewriting. Many writers report they use it as a step-by-step guide in reshaping the various drafts of a script. Valuable especially because it addresses the needs of intermediate and advanced screenwriters. From the same author comes . . .

*Creating Unforgettable Characters* by Linda Seger (Henry Holt & Co., 1990). The first contemporary book to focus exclusively on the development of characters, not only in film and television, but also novels. As with *Making a Good Script Great*, Seger has focused on a neglected part of the screenwriting process. Particularly valuable for more advanced writers.

## FINDING THE MUSE

Just as important as mastering the craft of writing is finding the energy to keep at it and the personal voice that makes the effort worthwhile. Three books are consistently mentioned by screenwriters' groups as the most inspirational in this regard.

*A Writer's Time*, Kenneth Atchity (W. W. Norton & Co., 1986). A practical, step-by-step guide for developing a writing *process* that is satisfying, do-able and meets deadlines. Perfect for the writer who can never get started or never get finished.

*Writing Down the Bones*, Natalie Goldberg (Shambhala Press, 1986). Considered by many the classic "free yourself to write" book. Looks at how to find your particular, unique view of the world and how to translate it to the page. An uplifting reminder about why we bother to write at all.

*How to Write a Movie in 21 Days*, Viki King (Harper & Row, 1988). The "21 days" part always causes skepticism about this book. But who cares? It's a breezy, readable, upbeat discussion of how to get the story in the writer's heart onto the page. As a result, the "Inner Movie Method" is a refreshingly simple counterpoint to the over-analytical, self-important nature of most screenwriting books. While others paralyze writers with rules about structure and paradigms, *21 Days* says relax and enjoy the writing; you'll fix it later.

## MARKETS

Industry Directories: There are a number of books and publications about markets for writers that list producers, readers at studios, etc. It's difficult to know which ones provide good leads, but if it's in a directory, assume that thousands of other writers have mailed letters ahead of yours to every listing.

There are also vast numbers of specialty books that address specific markets such as soap operas, sitcoms, home video, industrials, animation, etc. For advice on which is the best for your needs, ask fellow writers. Track down a local bookstore that specializes in this field and ask their advice. There are specialty stores in cities like New York, San Francisco, Washington, D.C., Seattle, Boston, Atlanta, etc. Many of these also stock scripts. Failing that, you can call the two largest specialty bookstores in Los Angeles:

> Larry Edmunds
> 6658 Hollywood Boulevard
> Los Angeles, CA 90028
> (213) 463-3273

> Samuel French
> 7623 Sunset Boulevard
> Los Angeles, CA 90028
> (213) 876-0570

Both mail orders from their Los Angeles offices. Write or call for catalogue information. Both stores can provide good suggestions as to which books are best.

If you can't find sample scripts through other writers, writers' groups, film boards or your local bookstore, here are the three largest Los Angeles sources:

> Script City
> 1765 N. Highland Avenue
> Suite 760
> Hollywood, CA 90028
> (213) 971-0707

> The Script Source
> 10521 National Boulevard
> Suite 573
> Los Angeles, CA 90034
> (310) 204-5691

> Script Warehouse
> 2265 Westwood Boulevard
> Suite 590
> Los Angeles, CA 90064
> (818) 843-5715

## CURRENT INFORMATION AND NEWS

In order to get into the information flow of the entertainment business, a writer needs to subscribe to the news publications of the industry. There are a number to choose from, but the *Daily Variety* and *Hollywood Reporter* are the leaders, known collectively as the trades. These daily publications provide the ratings of television shows, the box office of movies, new trends and markets, and general gossip about who's doing what in the entertainment industry. Both publications also contain regular listings of shows and movies in production. They tend to duplicate information, so a writer may not need to subscribe to both. The cost runs approximately $140 a year.

> *Daily Variety*
> 700 Wilshire Blvd. #120
> Los Angeles, CA 90036
> (213) 857-6600
>
> *Hollywood Reporter*
> 6715 Sunset Boulevard
> Hollywood, CA 90028
> (213) 464-7411

In addition, *Variety* also publishes a weekly version in New York: 154 W. 46th Street, New York, NY 10036. The weekly publication has been substantially upgraded to eliminate duplication with *Daily Variety*. Much of the focus these days is on regional film/television activities and international markets.

*TV Guide*. A must for television writers. Valuable for log lines, gossip, and industry issues.

## OTHER PUBLICATIONS TO CONSIDER

*Electronic Media*. A useful weekly publication for information especially on the alternative markets: syndication, cable, and regional television. 740 Rush St., Chicago, Illinois 60611.

*Emmy Magazine*. Available through the Academy of Television Arts and Science. Good interviews and features. $18 a year to non-members. 3500 West Olive, Suite 700, Burbank, CA 91505. (818) 953-7575.

*Premiere Magazine* (formerly *American Film Magazine*). Provocative interviews and articles about feature film.

*The Journal* (Writers Guild). Any writer can subscribe to this magazine without being a member. The alternative is to locate a WGA member who will share his or her copy each month. Contains exceptionally valuable interviews with writers, story editors and producers on the requirements of specific shows and genres, alternative markets, a monthly listing of television shows in production and who to contact, and a monthly list of free research sources from AIDS to veterinarians. 8955 Beverly Blvd., Los Angeles, CA 90068. Free to members, $40 to non-members.

*Hollywood Scriptwriter*. Newsletter format with information on the industry, agents, workshops and gossip. Good interviews. 1226 N. Wilcox, #385, Hollywood, CA 90028. $44 a year. (818) 931-3096.

*Freelance Screenwriters Forum*. A national newsletter which particularly emphasizes services to writers outside the Los Angeles area. Regular columns, detailed interviews. Reviews books, computer software and seminars. Post Office Box 7, Baldwin, MD 21013, $28 a year.

Finally, it's important that any writer stay informed about current events. Since film and television deal with issues and trends, writers should read their local newspaper, national news magazines, and special interest publications. These will prove to be sources of story ideas, characters, and that most elusive element of all, contemporary jokes.

And, by all means, at least watch *Entertainment Tonight*. It has terrific features and the best gossip of anybody.

## SEMINAR PROGRAMS

As indicated, there are literally hundreds of seminars, conferences, and adult extension classes offered each year that deal with screenwriting and its various markets. As a rule, the least useful for me have been panels of renowned and not-so-renowed writers. The primary problem is focus: they don't have a group point to make so presentations quickly degenerate into personal anecdotes. Although amusing, these are not substitutes for specific how-to information. Invariably, there is one person whose advice is down-to-earth, and I find myself frustrated that other panelists feel obliged to talk. The best sessions are those with one or two speakers or a strong moderator who can make panelists stick to the subject.

## AMERICAN FILM INSTITUTE

AFI's educational division offers fall, winter, and spring workshops and seminars with topics varying from acting to screenwriting to production. Workshops are taught by professionals within the various fields co-sponsored with regional arts and film groups. Sites include Los Angeles, New York, Washington, D.C., New Orleans, Minneapolis, Boston, etc. AFI members receive quarterly catalogues.

## WRITERS GUILD EAST AND WEST

Both branches of the Guild offer seminar programs such as "Getting an Agent," "Alternative Markets," and "Word Processing" for members. Non-members may sometimes attend as guests of a member. Sessions tend to be low-cost, candid. See Appendix B.

## WRITERS CONNECTION

Sponsors a well-regarded annual "Selling to Hollywood" conference. Also provides seminars on all types of writing, including script writing, one-day and weekend conferences, and special events. For the $40 membership fee, writers receive discounts on seminars and books. Membership also includes a subscription to Writers Connection's sixteen-page monthly newsletter. 1601 Saratoga-Sunnyvale Road, Suite 180, Cupertino, CA 90514. (408) 973-0227.

## STATE FILM BOARDS

Since every state and most larger cities have their own film boards, these are logical places to find out what's going on. They will be

aware of screenwriters' groups in their state and the workshops offered. Many boards sponsor their own competitions, film festivals,
and seminars. A good source for regional activities and a listing of
film boards is the magazine *Location Update*. Write to P.O. Box 17106,
North Hollywood, CA 91615 to request a sample copy.

# INDEX